Birmingham University Field Archaeology Unit
Monograph Series 5

I0096060

A Prehistoric and Romano-British Landscape

Excavations at Whitemoor Haye Quarry, Staffordshire, 1997-1999

Gary Coates

with contributions by

Alistair Barclay, Lynne Bevan, Marina Ciaraldi, Rowena Gale, James Greig, Annette Hancocks, Kay Hartley, John Hovey, Gwilym Hughes, Rob Ixer, Erica Macey, Elaine L. Morris, David Smith, Steven Willis and Ann Woodward

LAFARGE AGGREGATES

BAR British Series 340
2002

Published in 2016 by
BAR Publishing, Oxford

BAR British Series 340

Birmingham University Field Archaeology Unit Monograph Series 5
A Prehistoric and Romano-British Landscape

ISBN 978 1 84171 447 9

BAR Publishing is the trading name of British Archaeological Reports (Oxford) Ltd.
British Archaeological Reports was first incorporated in 1974 to publish the BAR
Series, International and British. In 1992 Hadrian Books Ltd became part of the BAR
group. This volume was originally published by Archaeopress in conjunction with
British Archaeological Reports (Oxford) Ltd / Hadrian Books Ltd, the Series principal
publisher, in 2002. This present volume is published by BAR Publishing, 2016.

Printed in England

BAR
PUBLISHING

BAR titles are available from:

BAR Publishing
122 Banbury Rd, Oxford, OX2 7BP, UK
EMAIL info@barpublishing.com
PHONE +44 (0)1865 310431
FAX +44 (0)1865 316916
www.barpublishing.com

A Prehistoric and Romano-British Landscape:
Excavations at Whitemoor Haye Quarry, Staffordshire, 1997-1999

CONTENTS

List of Figures

List of Tables

List of Plates

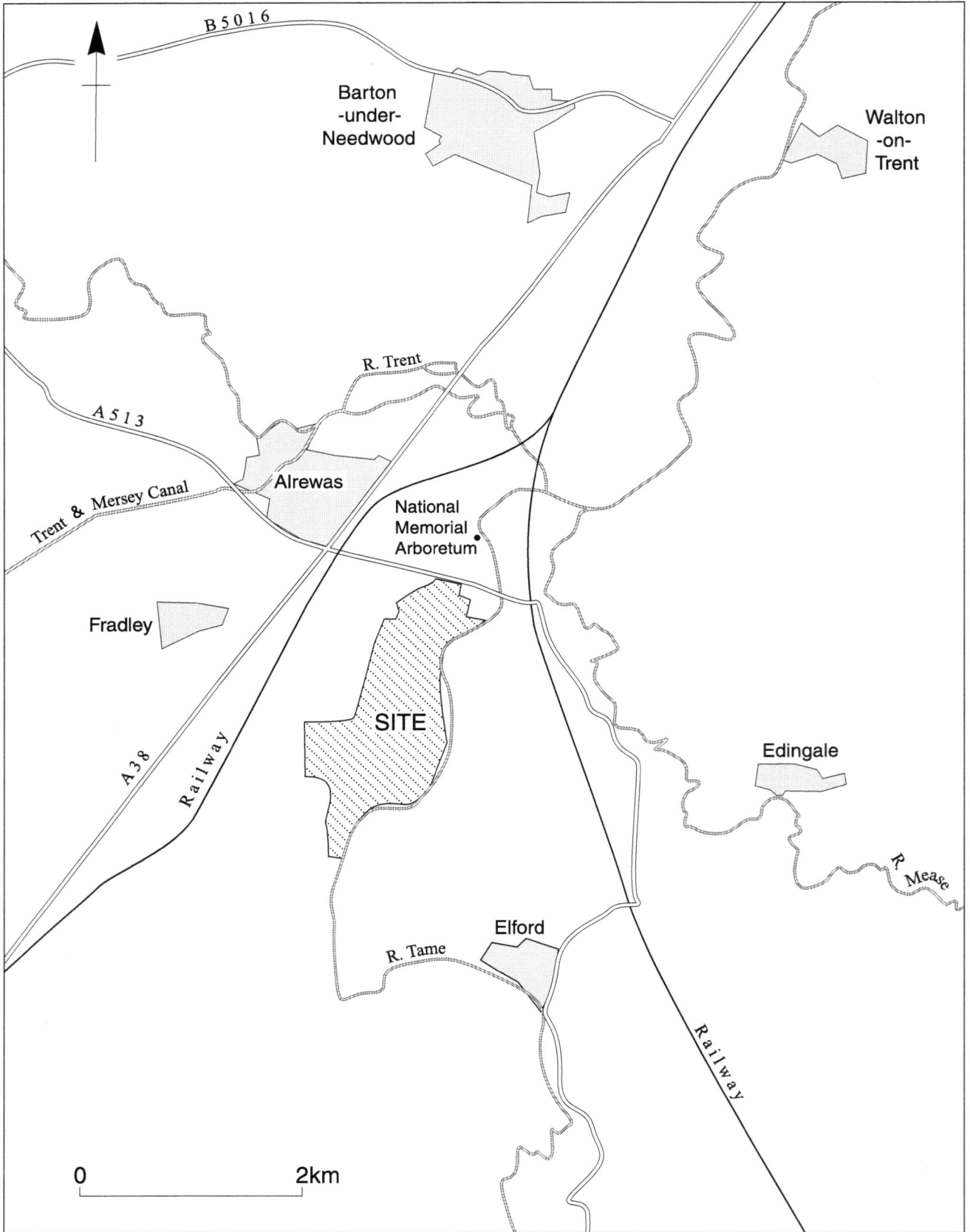

Fig. 1: Whitemoor Haye Quarry: Location map

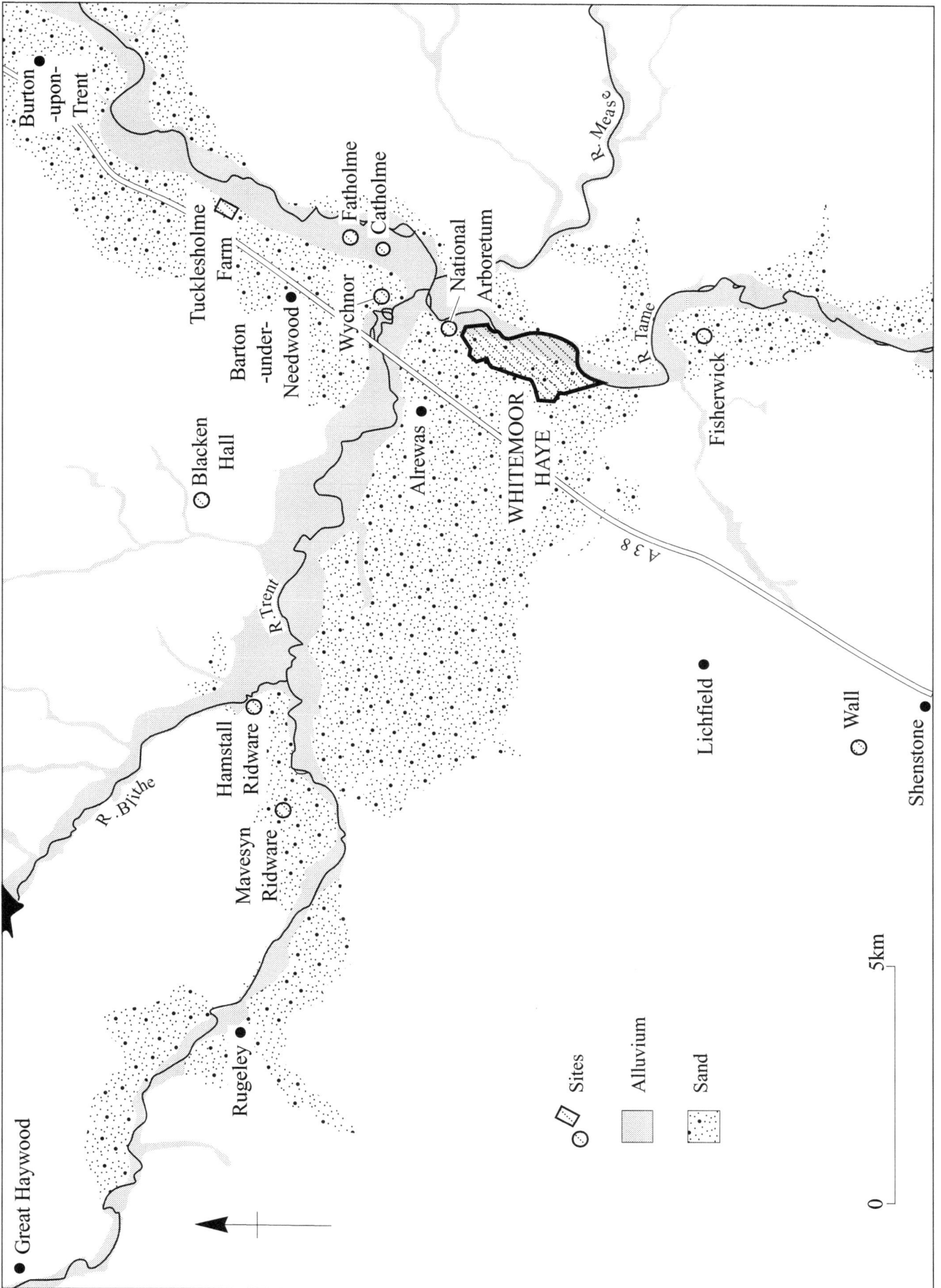

Fig. 2: Local geology and associated sites

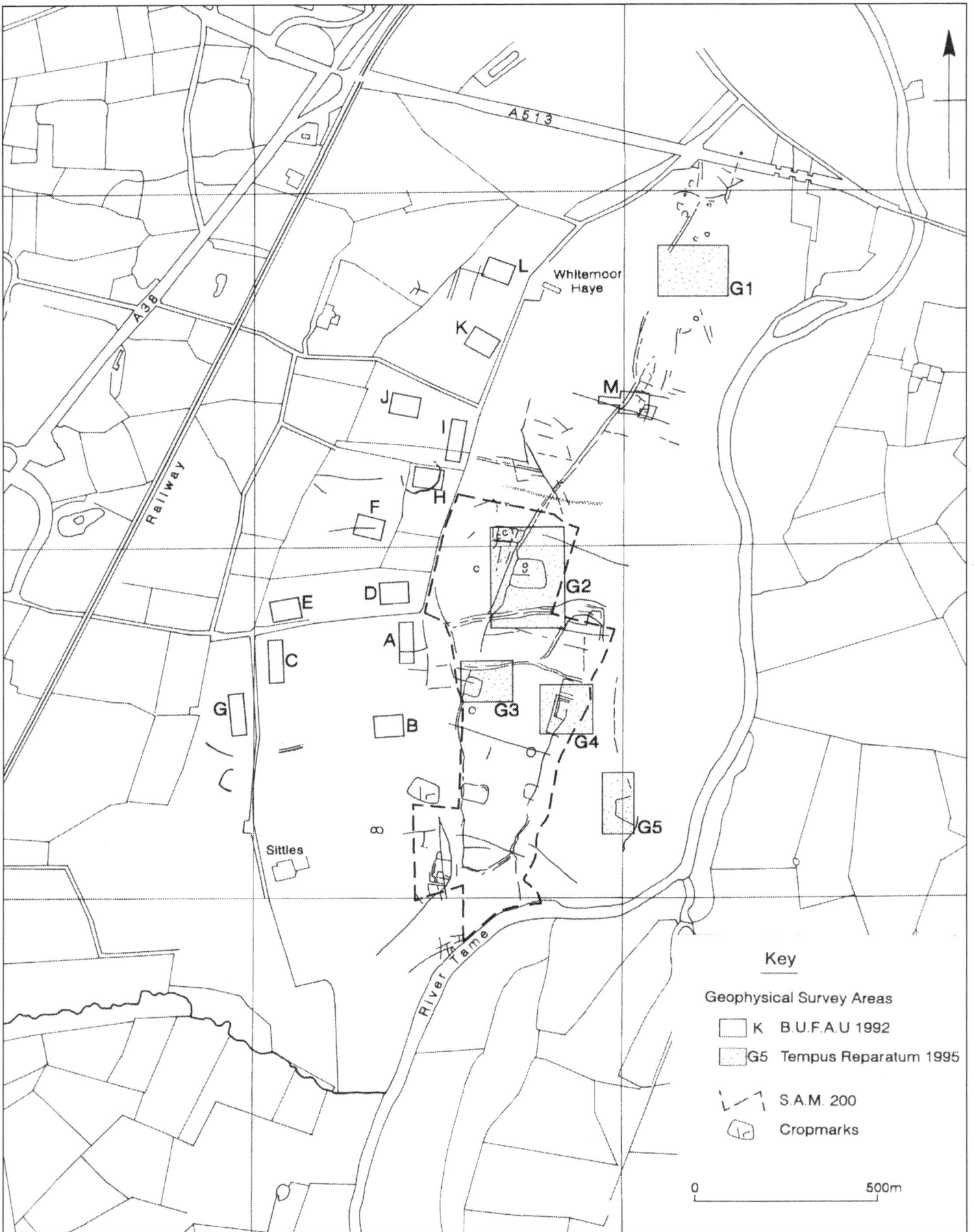

Fig. 3: Location of geophysical surveys

Key

Geophysical Survey Areas

☐ K B.U.F.A.U 1992

▨ G5 Tempus Reparatum 1995

⌐⌐ S.A.M. 200

⬠ Cropmarks

0 _____ 500m

A Prehistoric and Romano-British Landscape:
Excavations at Whitemoor Haye Quarry, Staffordshire, 1997-1999

By Gary Coates
with contributions by Alistair Barclay, Lynne Bevan, Marina Ciaraldi,
Rowena Gale, James Greig, Annette Hancocks, Kay Hartley, John Hovey,
Gwilym Hughes, Rob Ixer, Erica Macey, Elaine L. Morris, David Smith,
Steven Willis and Ann Woodward

Summary

Over several seasons of archaeological excavation and watching brief, the historic landscape of Whitemoor Haye quarry has been vividly brought to life. A late Neolithic and Early Bronze Age ritual area in the north of the site, characterised by evidence of barrows and possible Beaker burials, contrasted with a later agricultural Iron Age and Romano-British area in the south. Land divisions appeared from the Early Iron Age onwards in the form of two double pit alignments, followed by rectangular and curved enclosures containing hut circles, possibly occupied in pairs. The environmental evidence suggested the presence of crop processing and grazing land for stock, with little corroborating evidence for widescale human occupation. These largely pastoral agricultural activities continued in the Romano-British period, with a defined north-south droveway and associated enclosures. Artefactual evidence pointed to a wider distribution network associated with the general growth of trade routes in Roman Britain. The archaeological record is sparse for the following centuries, but what evidence exists suggests a continued, predominately pastoral landscape right up until the modern quarrying programme.

INTRODUCTION

This report describes the results of the excavation of seven areas at Whitemoor Haye Quarry, Alrewas, Staffordshire (NGR SK180130, centre), undertaken by Birmingham University Field Archaeology Unit (BUFAU) between September 1997 and July 1998. It also includes a description of the results of a watching brief carried out on topsoil stripping in the quarry concession during this period and up to the end of October 1999. The work was commissioned by Lafarge Aggregates Limited in advance of gravel extraction, and was carried out in accordance with specifications prepared by Phoenix Consulting Archaeology Limited (Richmond 1997).

Whitemoor Haye lies in the valley of the River Tame and, along with many other parts of the Tame and Trent valleys, its archaeological significance was first brought to attention through aerial photography, mainly carried out in the 1960s and '70s. The aerial photographs, principally by Jim Pickering, revealed on the gravel terraces a palimpsest of cropmarked enclosures, trackways and boundaries, the greatest concentration of which was subsequently designated as a scheduled ancient monument.

The excavation and watching brief followed on from a programme of aerial photographic assessment and rectification, extensive geophysical survey and trial trenching on the site. The first geophysical survey was carried out by Geophysical Surveys of Bradford in 1992, prior to trial trenching undertaken by BUFAU in 1992. A further gradiometer survey was undertaken in 1995 by the Bartlett-Clarke Consultancy, prior to the trial trenching carried out by Tempus Reparatum Archaeological and Historical Associates in the same year.

The report also includes discussion of the results of salvage recording undertaken by BUFAU in October 1997 on the site of a multiple ring ditch at the nearby National Memorial Arboretum (SK 1854 1460).

Archaeological Background

Location and Geology (see Figs. 1 - 4)

The site is located in southeast Staffordshire, c.3.0km northeast of Lichfield and c.1.5 km southeast of the village of Alrewas. Its borders are defined by the River Tame in the east and south, the A513 in the north, and in the west by the road running south from the A513, past Whitemoor Haye farm and up to Sittles Farm. The topography of the landscape within the site is undulating, varying in height from 51.0m to 53.5m AOD and, prior to extraction, was an area of arable farming. A large area (c.40m) of the southern extent of the site is a Scheduled Ancient Monument (Staffordshire S.A.M. 200; Fig. 3).

Recent alluvial deposits, up to 7.5 m in thickness, overlie Pleistocene gravels. There are two river terraces, with fossil evidence suggesting a pre-Devensian date for the upper terrace. These gravels generally overlie Triassic Mercian Mudstone, sandstones and Bunter Beds. Beyond the extent of the alluvium, the soils tend to be slightly stony, sandy loams and are classified as gleyic brown earths (Jones 1979). Most soils in the study area are well suited to modern arable farming, although areas adjacent to the river are susceptible to seasonal flooding.

Archaeology of the Region *by Gwilym Hughes*

The ancient landscape at Whitemoor Haye forms part of a broader pattern of ancient settlement in the major river valleys of southeast Staffordshire. A useful regional 'study area', with Whitemoor Haye at its heart, may be defined to comprise the valley of the Tame, from Tamworth north to its confluence with the Trent, the Upper Trent valley from Great Haywood to Burton, and the Blithe valley from the Blithfield reservoir to the confluence with the Trent (Fig. 2). The gravel and alluvial deposits within this area cover approximately 105 square kilometres; at about 180 hectares the area designated for quarrying at Whitemoor Haye represents a significant sample of this landscape, approaching 2%.

Information on past settlement and land use in the study area has been mainly obtained from aerial photographic surveys (Plate 1). This work, largely carried out by independent researchers, most notably Jim Pickering, has produced a considerable amount of information regarding the distribution of complex cropmark sites. However, following a recent survey of similar sites in the middle Trent valley, Whimster (1989, 6) concluded that 'to this day the date and significance of the vast majority of newly discovered cropmark sites remains unknown' and acknowledged that further elucidation of the cropmark data could only be achieved through complementary structured survey and excavation. It has been suggested by English Heritage that in the West Midlands overall 'there is little knowledge of settlement patterns, social structure and economic relations before the medieval period outside the towns' (1991, 16), a comment which is very apposite for southeast Staffordshire. However, it is possible to provide an outline settlement sequence for the study area on the basis of the limited work that has been carried out to date.

The earliest archaeological finds recorded in the area are a Lower Palaeolithic cleaver from the lower terrace of the Tame and an Acheulian quartzite handaxe from Shenstone (Shotton 1973; Cane and Cane 1986). Evidence of Mesolithic settlement in the area is largely restricted to chance finds, of which the most significant is a pebble 'macehead' which has been tentatively dated to this period (Hodder 1982). However, excavation of a cave/rock shelter at Bower Farm produced evidence of a lithic scatter, which has been interpreted as indicative of a seasonal hunting camp (Hilton 1979, Cane and Cane 1986).

Material dated to the Neolithic period is also rare and is largely represented by occasional finds of polished flint and stone axes (Gunstone 1964; Vine 1982). Several cropmarks in the Trent valley have been interpreted as possible causewayed enclosures, including sites at Alrewas and Mavesyn Ridware, and two cursus monuments have been identified at Catholme, just to the north of Whitemoor Haye (Hodder 1982; Palmer 1976; Jones 1992). The latter features are particularly interesting as they are in close association with a series of cropmarks which together constitute a 'monument complex', significantly located at the confluence of the Trent and Tame (Jones 1992). These cropmarks include a large post-built henge and a circular enclosure with radiating lines of pits. Excavated evidence of activity in this period is very rare. At present it is impossible to determine whether the gulley in the northern part of the Whitemoor Haye quarry area (Tempus Reparatum, Trench B; Fig. 4) which contained Late Neolithic Peterborough Ware, or the enclosure (SMR 1374; next to Tempus Reparatum Trench AC, Fig. 4) on a gravel 'island' in the alluvial floodplain in the south of the area, which likewise produced a small amount of Peterborough Ware, represent 'domestic' or 'ritual' activity. However, excavation in advance of quarrying at a Roman site at Fisherwick, just to the south of Whitemoor Haye, uncovered a series of features which may have formed part of a house, and which was in association with Late Neolithic pottery and a small number of flints (Miles 1969).

Bronze Age domestic occupation is equally elusive. Until recently, this had largely been represented by groups of post-holes revealed during the excavation of ring ditches, and assumed to represent the remains of structures pre-dating the barrows, e.g. Willowbrook Farm and Fatholme (S.C.C. 1991, Losco-Bradley 1984). A more substantial discovery resulted from the excavation of a series of cropmarks in advance of quarrying at Fisherwick (Smith 1976). Here, most of the features identified from aerial photographic survey were proven to be of geological origin. However, a number of smaller features were interpreted as part of a house and were associated with radiocarbon determinations ranging between 1170 ± 140 and 850 ± 140 uncal BC.

Cropmarks of ring ditches are frequently presumed to be of Bronze Age date, representing the ploughed-out remains of round barrows (Gunstone 1965, Vine 1982). They are distributed across the study area and are particularly frequent in the Tame valley where they attain a density of 1:0.87 sq. km (Hodder 1982). However, there is a clear tendency for these features to cluster around the confluence of the Tame and Trent where densities may exceed 4:1 sq. km (Vine 1982). Although there is excavated evidence to support the Bronze Age date generally assigned to these features, caution is necessary. An important new dimension has been added by the excavation of two circular burial mounds surrounded by ring ditches at Tucklesholme Farm, Barton-under-Needwood, in the Trent valley to the northeast of Whitemoor Haye (Gifford and Partners Ltd. 1995). One barrow produced no evidence of burial while the other contained an unurned central cremation and was associated with an adjacent flat cremation cemetery comprising 14 burials, five in urns of the Middle to Late Bronze Age Deverel Rimbury tradition. The demonstrated variation within the ring-ditch class of site suggests that they may have had a variety of forms and functions, and that we should be wary of interpreting them simply as funerary monuments by analogy with other areas (Bradley 1992; Ferris 1992; Hughes 1991).

There are no hillforts within the study area. Consequently Iron Age settlement in the area is generally assumed to be represented by the extensive cropmark complexes revealed through aerial photography. However, as already stressed, the majority of these complexes are in fact undated (Whimster 1989, 6). Where modern excavation has taken place these sites frequently turn out to be palimpsests. The most extensive excavation to date was carried out by Christopher Smith (1979) in advance of quarrying at

Fisherwick, to the south of Whitemoor Haye. This site is particularly important. Smith excavated a series of settlement features, including enclosures containing roundhouses, in association with a field system covering 10 hectares. The site was inhabited between the 3rd century BC and the 1st century AD. Although bone was poorly preserved, pollen, seeds, insects and wood were preserved, allowing a reasonably detailed reconstruction of the local environment. This suggests that the area had been cleared by the time of the occupation, and that both pastoral and arable activities were being carried out. The preserved wooden artefacts from Fisherwick, which included oak planks, hazelwood pegs and an ash 'toggle', are particularly evocative. As Fulford (1992, 26) has pointed out, it is on such waterlogged sites that 'we are as near as we are ever likely to be to the peasantry of late Iron Age and early Roman Britain'.

The area probably came under Roman rule at an early stage of the occupation. The nearest Roman urban centre, *Letocetum* (Wall), was occupied during the Claudian period, possibly by the XIVth Legion prior to their move to Wroxeter (Webster 1975). The later settlement's defences, which cover 2.4 hectares, are not well dated, although Webster (1975, 78) has suggested that the settlement was a late 'burgus' under Constantius Chlorus. Although there has been a suggestion that Wall may have been a late Roman civitas capital, there is no evidence that the civilian settlement served as a major market or service centre following its early military occupation (Crickmore 1984, 47). On present evidence the study area would appear to fall between the Cornovii and the Corieltauvi, with the border possibly following the line of Ryknield Street (Webster 1975; Todd 1991). There is little evidence that Roman occupation created a major impact on the lifestyles of the native population. Villas are not numerous within the region of the Corieltauvi or Cornovii, and only one possible unpublished villa site is recorded within the study area near Blacken Hall (SMR04094). However, some caution should be urged, as Fulford (1992, 36) has noted that the apparent lack of villas is a general gravel phenomenon and that this may result from 'vernacular building styles' and the use of different types of building material.

Excavated data, including the Romano-British settlement excavated by Miles (1969) at Fisherwick and the enclosure excavated in 1996 by Gifford and Partners at Tucklesholme Farm, suggest that habitation sites of the period were not very different to those of the late Iron Age. Smith (1980) has suggested a settlement density of 1:2.3 sq. km. for the Tame valley, but we should be cautious about such figures given the paucity of detailed data. Likewise, Smith's (1980, 11) suggestion that there was a decline in settlement density during the late Roman period remains unproven.

The archaeology of the area in the post-Roman period is far from clear, despite the fact that Tamworth develops into the recorded capital of Mercia during the 7th century. Lichfield, the successor of *Letocetum* (Wall), may have been the centre for the early Bishopric of Diuma, and written records suggest that the Trent valley was densely settled by the 8th century (Gelling 1992, 148; Losco-Bradley and Wheeler 1984, 101).

A number of 6th-century cemeteries and individual burials have been located, including those at Wychnor, Stapenhill (Burton-on-Trent) and Tucklesholme (Gelling 1992, 28; Losco-Bradley and Wheeler 1984, 105; Hughes 1991). At Tucklesholme a possible cremation burial has recently been dated to AD 409-440.

The discovery and excavation of an extensive early 6th-century Anglo-Saxon settlement at Catholme, containing 15 structures in its earliest phase, provides an invaluable insight into settlement in the area and its relationship to the earlier Roman period (Losco-Bradley and Wheeler 1984, 104). However, Gelling (1992, 28) has commented that 'it is only by virtue of lying adjacent to Derbyshire that Staffordshire scrapes into the category of counties which have pagan Anglo-Saxon remains'. Yet it should be noted that the large settlement at Catholme was located on the basis of three hut-shaped cropmarks, only one of which actually proved to be an archaeological feature. This suggests that further discoveries of this nature may be possible.

During the later Medieval period it is likely that Tamworth declined because of its lack of a strategic position, although Lichfield, a centre for pilgrimages to the tomb of St Chad, was established as a new town during the mid-12th century (Gelling 1992). Within the study area, Smith's (1980) analysis of the landscape around Fisherwick indicates the progress of enclosure in the creation of the modern landscape. Excavation of rural medieval sites within the area has been very rare. The only record within the survey area is the limited evaluation of a possible deserted medieval village at Hamstall Ridware (Meeson 1991).

Geophysical Survey (Fig. 3)

There were two principal periods of geophysical survey at Whitemoor Haye: one in 1992, prior to the BUFAU evaluations, and one in 1995, in advance of the 1995 Tempus Reparatum trenching.

The 1992 geophysical survey followed on from an aerial photographic assessment carried out by Air Photo Services (Palmer 1992). This gradiometer survey was carried out by Geophysical Surveys of Bradford and 13 areas were investigated (A to M), in which very 'few anomalies of definite archaeological interest were identified' (BUFAU 1992, 3) and the cropmarks were not located, which at that point suggested that they no longer existed as archaeological features or had a low magnetic susceptibility. Those anomalies that did show up were tested with trial trenches.

The 1995 gradiometer survey, carried out by the Bartlett-Clarke Consultancy, investigated five areas (G1 to G5), and produced results suggesting a degree of correspondence with the cropmark plot. The lack of response from some cropmark features was possibly due to different fills, and there was little suggestion of areas of concentrated settlement (Tempus Reparatum 1995, Appendix 6, 1-6). There was also an electromagnetic and resistivity survey conducted by British Geological Survey, primarily designed to identify the topography of the underlying gravel, but it did provide information relating to at least two north-south aligned palaeochannels (*ibid.*, 4.42).

The results, in general, guided the evaluative trial trenching subsequently carried out, but excavation indicated that the low level of results from the surveys was not a true reflection of the level of archaeology present.

A further geophysical survey was carried out in 1998 by the Barlett-Clarke Consultancy in advance of area excavations not discussed in this volume.

1992 BUFAU Evaluation (Fig. 4)

The 1992 evaluation took the form of the excavation of 29 trial trenches (Fig. 4, numbered 1-8 and 10-30) aimed to target potential archaeological features identified by the aerial photographic assessment and geophysical survey (BUFAU 1992, 2). The trenches within the scheduled area highlighted a circular feature, with associated Bronze Age pottery (Tr. 31), a V-shaped profile enclosure ditch (Tr. 32), and the north-south droveway ditch (Tr. 33). There were also trenches (Trs. 4, 18 and 20) that identified an east-west, triple-ditch system at the southern terminus of the north-south droveway. Further south, a double-ditched east-west feature (Tr. 23) was identified together with a rectangular enclosure (Tr. 22), although nothing to correspond with the circular cropmark (Tr. 26). To the east of these features was a straight-sided enclosure of Romano-British date (Tr. 27). At the southernmost point of the concession area were three rectilinear enclosures, of which Trench 28 identified a ditch containing sherds from a possible Early Bronze Age urn, while Trench 30 failed to identify the enclosure there.

Those trenches located to the west of the scheduled area failed to identify the features plotted from the aerial photographic assessment, while Trenches 2 and 17, in the north of the evaluation area, identified the double-ditched droveway and the presence of a rectilinear enclosure to the east of the droveway (Tr. 1), but there was no sign of the ring ditch in Trench 3.

This evaluation provided an initial interpretation of the settlement enclosures spread out along the north-south droveway, and some limited dating evidence for three of the enclosures. In Trench 27, the recovery of hobnails and some bone fragments from a feature of Romano-British date pointed to the possibility of the presence of burials within this enclosure.

1995 Tempus Reparatum Evaluation (Fig. 4)

Tempus Reparatum excavated 17 trial trenches in 1995, of which 11 were random trenches designed to examine the character of archaeological deposits within the floodplain, and the remainder were designed to examine the northern area of the gravel terrace not included in the 1992 evaluations. Only 10 of these trenches yielded features of an archaeological nature.

On the northern gravel terrace, Trench A found evidence for the double-ditched droveway, which also appeared in Trench 17 of the BUFAU evaluation, and Trench B identified one of two ring ditches. This trench produced Middle Neolithic pottery sherds, which may have been associated with the ring ditch. Those trenches in the floodplain identified a few archaeological features that may have been connected with the prehistoric field system, but generally established a lower level of past activity in this area than identified on the gravel terrace.

Aims and Objectives

The aims and objectives of the current programme of excavations are detailed in the *Specifications* document (Richmond 1997, pp. 11-15). The following is a re-iteration of the relevant areas of national priority, as defined by English Heritage, where the excavations were thought to offer some contribution (*ibid.*, 15, *Sec.* 3.4.1):

1. The clarification of the typology and date of ritual monuments and their possible relation with other contemporary sites.
2. The date and possible function of enclosure sites and their relationship with field features (field boundaries and trackways).
3. The origin and evolution of field systems over time.
4. The determination of water-management structures.
5. The relationship between the natural landscape and its human transformation over time.

Methodology

All excavated areas were surveyed using a total station EDM and the initial overburden was excavated by a machine fitted with a 1.6m-wide toothless ditching bucket. The 0.30m depth of topsoil was machined off separately from any underlying subsoil, which was also removed to identify archaeological features, and stored separately from the topsoil. After the removal of overburden, initial plans of the excavated areas were established with the use of the EDM total station, with hand cleaning of specific areas to clarify the presence and nature of identified features, particularly within the confines of any apparent structures. Sample excavation of these features adhered to the sampling strategy laid down in Appendix 1 of the *Specifications* (Richmond 1997), although it was often difficult to establish dates for the features both prior to, and after, excavation.

The hand excavation of these features was carried out by professional staff. Recording was undertaken using *pro-forma* record cards supplemented by scale section and plan drawings, photographs and levels where appropriate. Soil, radiocarbon and thermoluminescence samples were also taken where appropriate. All artefacts were kept and processed at the Field Unit prior to examination by appropriate specialists.

A final post-excavation plan of all features was drawn for all areas and overall post-excavation photographs were taken, with the use of a hydraulic tower where access and safety allowed.

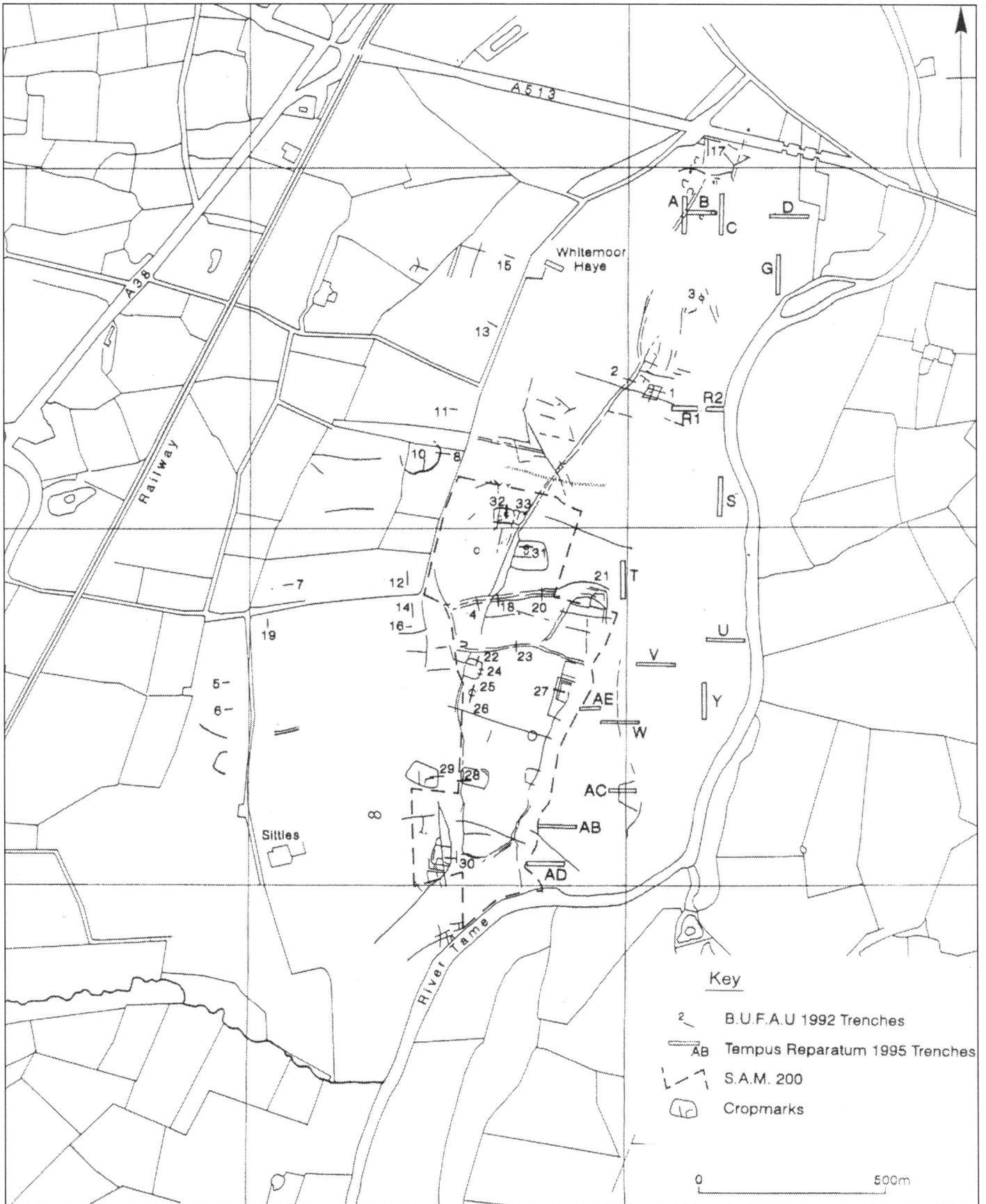

Fig. 4: Location of evaluation trenches

Outside the areas of formal archaeological excavation, the watching brief was carried out on a frequent basis during the stripping of the topsoil and subsoil prior to sand and gravel extraction; this monitoring was intensified in the area of the scheduled monument. Features were selected for sampling on the basis of their apparent uniqueness in comparison to features already excavated within the designated areas. Previously sampled features received minimal further sampling in order to identify any changes in form or to supplement the available dating evidence. A plan was generated using a total station FastMap surveying system to locate the features and their position in relation to those already excavated. All feature and context recording was undertaken according the format outlined above, and the archive was collated along with the main excavation archive for deposition with the City Museum and Art Gallery, Stoke-on-Trent.

At the time of writing, all excavation areas have been released into the aggregate extraction programme.

Acknowledgements

The project has been managed at various times by Simon Buteux, Gwilym Hughes and Alex Jones. The excavations were directed by Gary Coates, assisted by John Hovey, John La Niece and Richard Cuttler, and were carried out by Gino Bellavia, Graham Brown, Bob Burrows, Martin Campbell, Julie Candy, Matt Colburn, Lucie Dingwall, Mary Duncan, Sally Finter, Georgina Holt, Chris Hewitson, Christian Kaye, Roy Krakowicz, Cath Kidd, Simona Losi, Derek Moscrop, Chris Patrick, Ellie Ramsey, Eilidh Ross, Dan Slater, Christine Winter and Josh Williams. Technical support was provided by Ed Newton and Jon Sterenberg. The illustrations were prepared and drawn by Mark Breedon and Nigel Dodds. Annette Hancocks was the Finds Manager for the project. All specialists are thanked for their contributions to this report and James Greig would like to thank English Heritage for their support in doing this work. In 'The Site' the pottery summaries were contributed by Annette Hancocks and Ann Woodward. The volume was edited by Simon Buteux and Ann Woodward. Ann Humphries compiled the camera-ready text for publication.

Dr Andrew Richmond and Dr Chris Howlett of Phoenix Consulting monitored the project on behalf of the sponsors, LaFarge Archaeology Limited, who were represented by Jonathon Craig and Ross Halley. The quarry manager, Len Mudd, was always happy to resolve any day-to-day problems. Jimmy Docherty, the owner of the plant contractors on the quarry, was always helpful and obliging, as were his staff.

The excavations were monitored by Sue Cole and Dr. Paul Stamper for English Heritage and Chris Welch and Chris Wardle for Staffordshire County Council.

Fieldwork at the National Arboretum Memorial was carried out by John Hovey and Chris Patrick. This project was managed by Gwilym Hughes, who thanks Anthony Darbyshire of Environmental Design Associates and Chris Wardle of Staffordshire County Council for their role in the project.

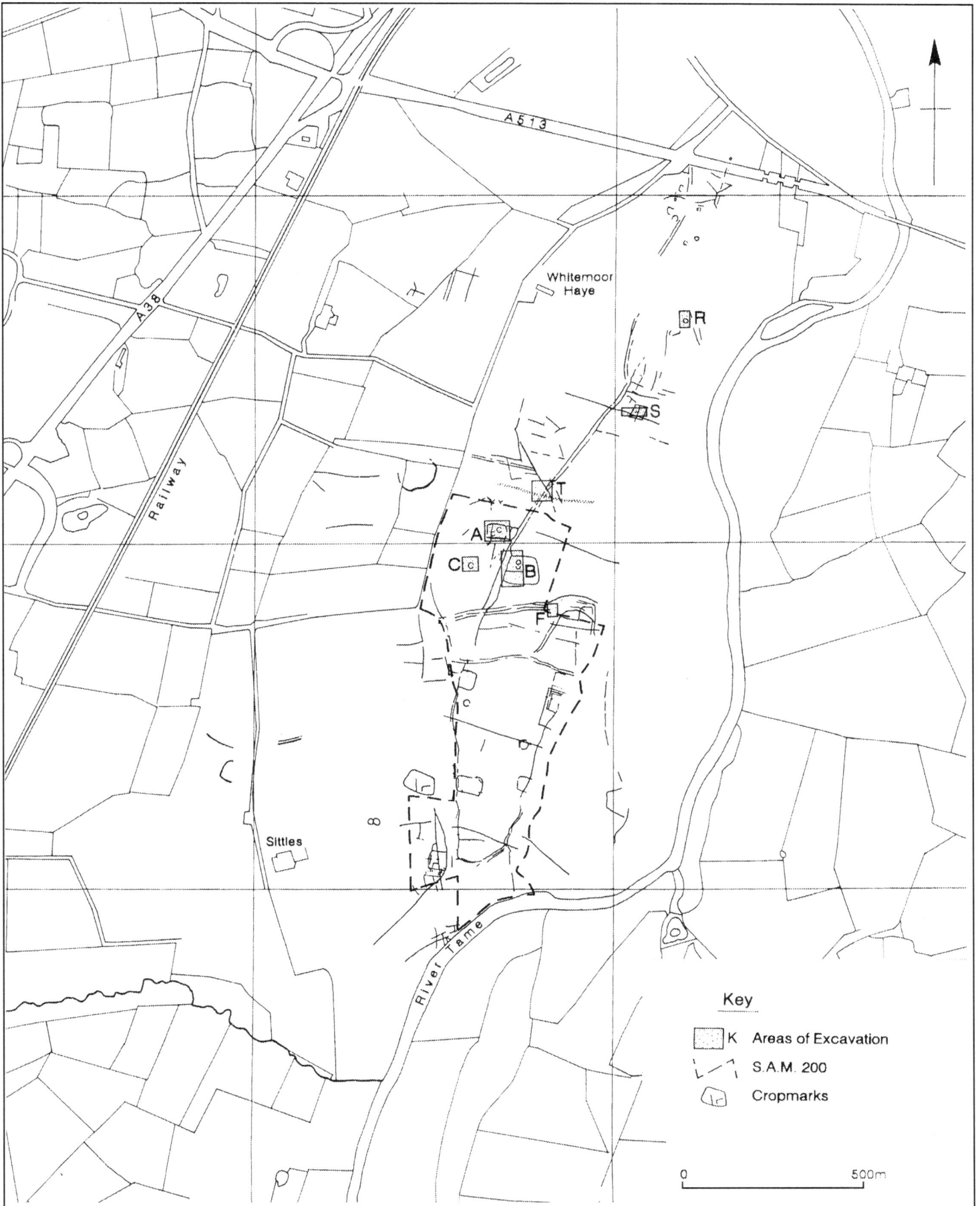

Fig. 5: Location of excavation areas

Area R

0   10m

F622

F616/617

F623

F630

F628   (S2)

F626

(S1)

F612

F629

F615

(S3)

F625

Evaluation Trench No. 3

Projected
Barrow

F610

F621

F614

F627

F613

F601

F600

F602

F624

F605

F603

F611

F604

F608

Plough
Furrows

Land
Drains

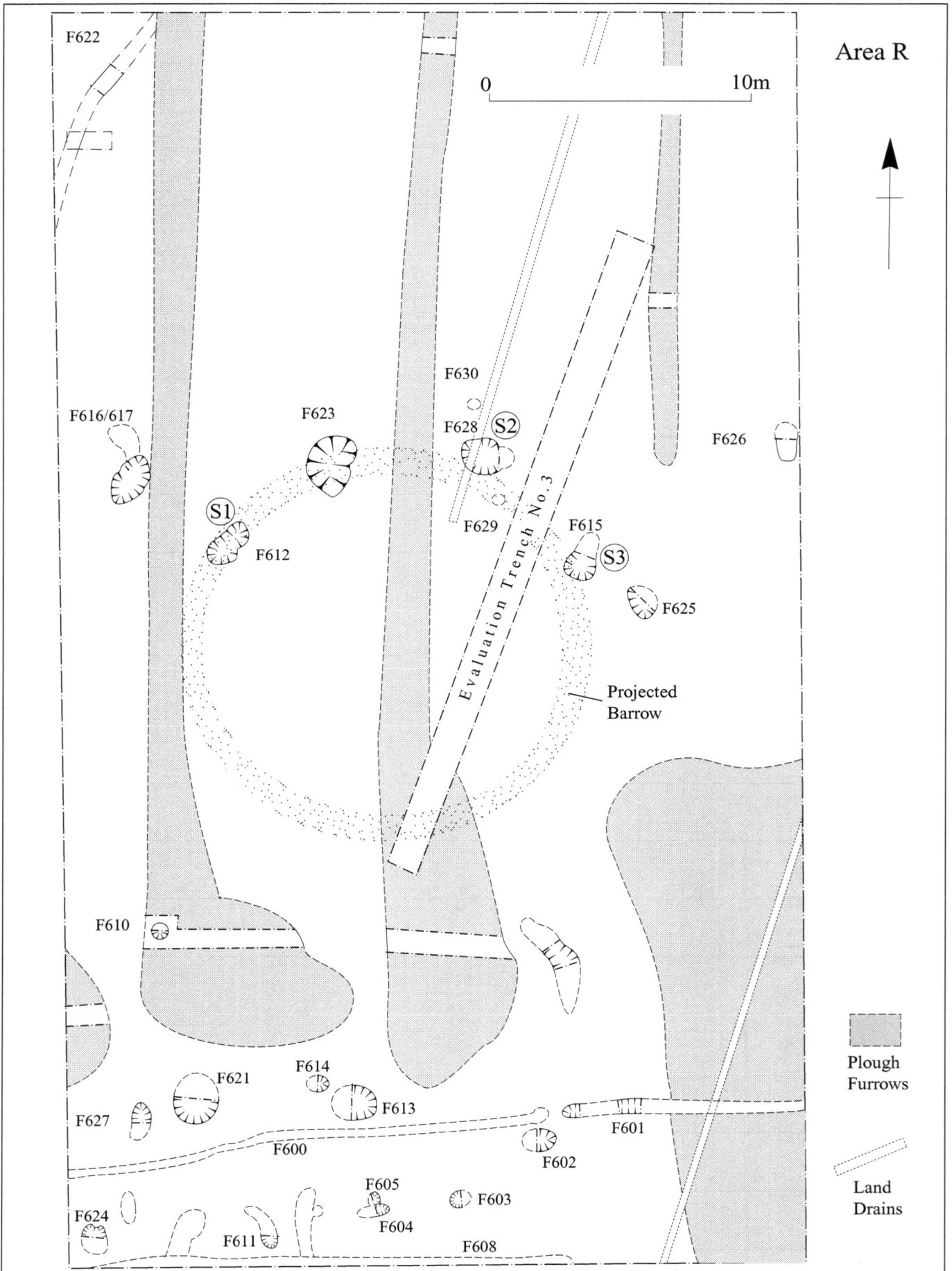

Fig. 6: Area R: Plan of all excavated features

THE SITE (Fig. 5; Plate 2)

Phasing

Four main phases of activity were identified during excavation and post-excavation analysis. There were also a number of features which were difficult to assign to any period due to absence of dating evidence or stratigraphic relationships. These were allocated as 'Undated'. The four periods are as follows:

Period 1   Late Neolithic/ Early Bronze Age
Period 2   Iron Age
Period 3   Romano-British
Period 4   Post-Medieval

Period 1 Late Neolithic/ Early Bronze Age

Area R (Fig. 6)

The cropmark plot had shown a circular feature in this area, but this was not identified in either Trench 3 of the 1992 evaluation or the subsequent excavations and it remains possible that the feature originally photographed has been ploughed out. Figure 6 illustrates the most likely location of the cropmark, if it had survived, based on scaled measurements from the rectified cropmark plot (BUFAU 1992, 9ff.). This would suggest that any central burial or feature may have been truncated by a Post-Medieval plough furrow. The cropmark plot also suggests a possible size for this circular ditch somewhere in the region of 16m in diameter and 1-2m in width.

Pit F612 was oval in shape, 2.0m long by 0.9m wide, and had concave sides, gently sloping to a flat bottom, 0.26m deep. Filled with a brown silt-sand (6019) and charcoal-flecked sand (6023) (Fig. 7, S1), there was part of a Beaker vessel in the northwestern sector of this pit (Plate 3). However, there was no evidence of staining to indicate the former presence of a body, although the shape of this feature and the position of the pottery may indicate that it had held a Beaker inhumation. A further possible pit (F628) was located in this group of features (Fig. 7, S2). It had a rectangular shape and vertical sides with possible post-holes (F629 and F630) either side of it. If the plot of the ring ditch is accurate, then both these pits may have been cut into the base of the ditch, or through its filling.

Dating evidence

Context 6019, from F612, produced a radiocarbon date range of Cal BC 3615 to 3595 and 3525 to 3100 at the 2 sigma range (Beta-135228; see Appendix 1) along with numerous sherds of a single Beaker vessel datable to the Early Bronze Age. The discrepancy between the radiocarbon date and the pottery from this feature may be explained by the presence of residual material in the fill. This material may be associated with earlier Neolithic clearance activity in the vicinity.

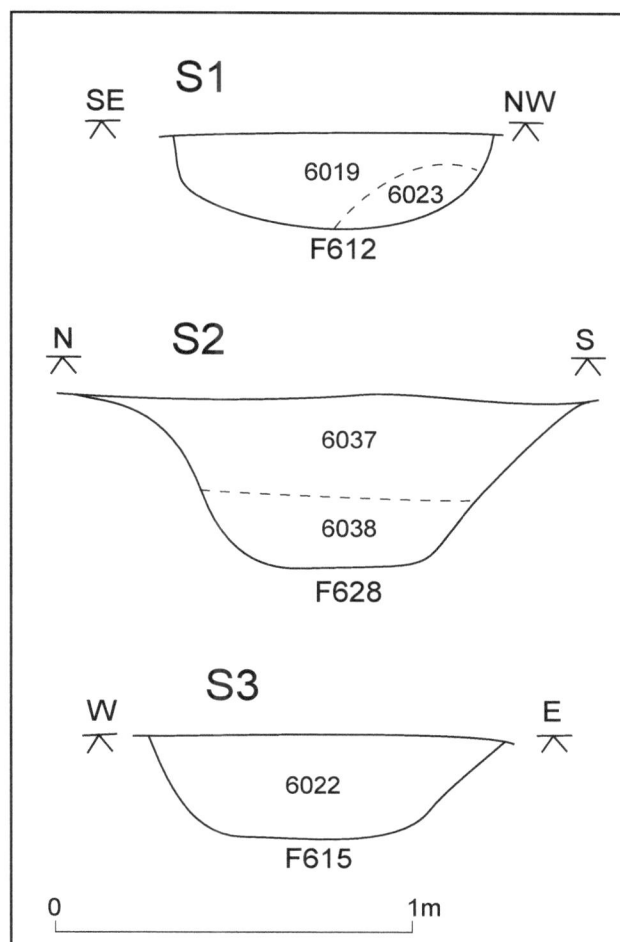

Fig. 7: Area R: Period 1 sections

National Memorial Arboretum site, Alrewas *by Gwilym Hughes and John Hovey* (Fig. 8)

This section describes the results of archaeological fieldwork on the site of a Scheduled Ancient Monument (SAM 199) at the National Memorial Arboretum near Alrewas, Staffordshire (SK 1854 1460). The site lies just to the north of the quarry at Whitemoor Haye (Fig. 2). The fieldwork, undertaken in October 1997, involved the recording and reinstatement of a test pit accidentally dug into part of the monument by engineers working on behalf of the Arboretum.

The monument is positioned on the west bank of the River Tame near to its confluence with the River Trent. Cropmark evidence indicates the presence of a large multiple ring ditch consisting of a number of concentric circular features, which lay on a raised gravel terrace. The site was scheduled in 1969. Subsequent aerial photography (Leicester Museum 3325/6 and 3364/14) suggested a larger and more complex site consisting of four concentric circles of ditches or pits plus a pit centrally positioned in the monument (Fig. 8). The SMR entry refers to the monument as a possible henge.

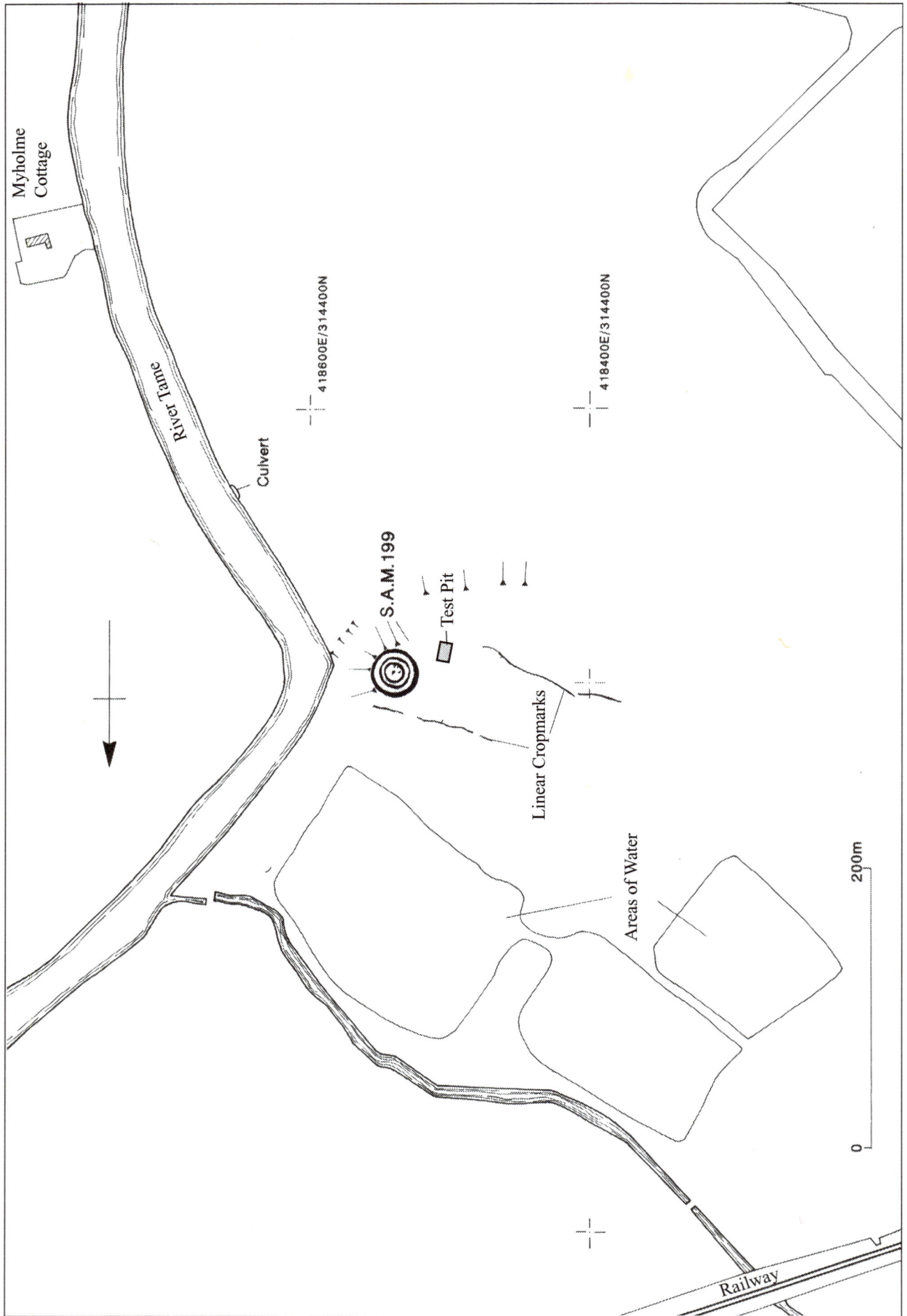

Fig. 8: Plan of National Memorial Arboretum Site

Myholme Cottage

River Tame

Culvert

418600E/314400N

418400E/314400N

S.A.M.199

Test Pit

Linear Cropmarks

Areas of Water

Railway

0   200m

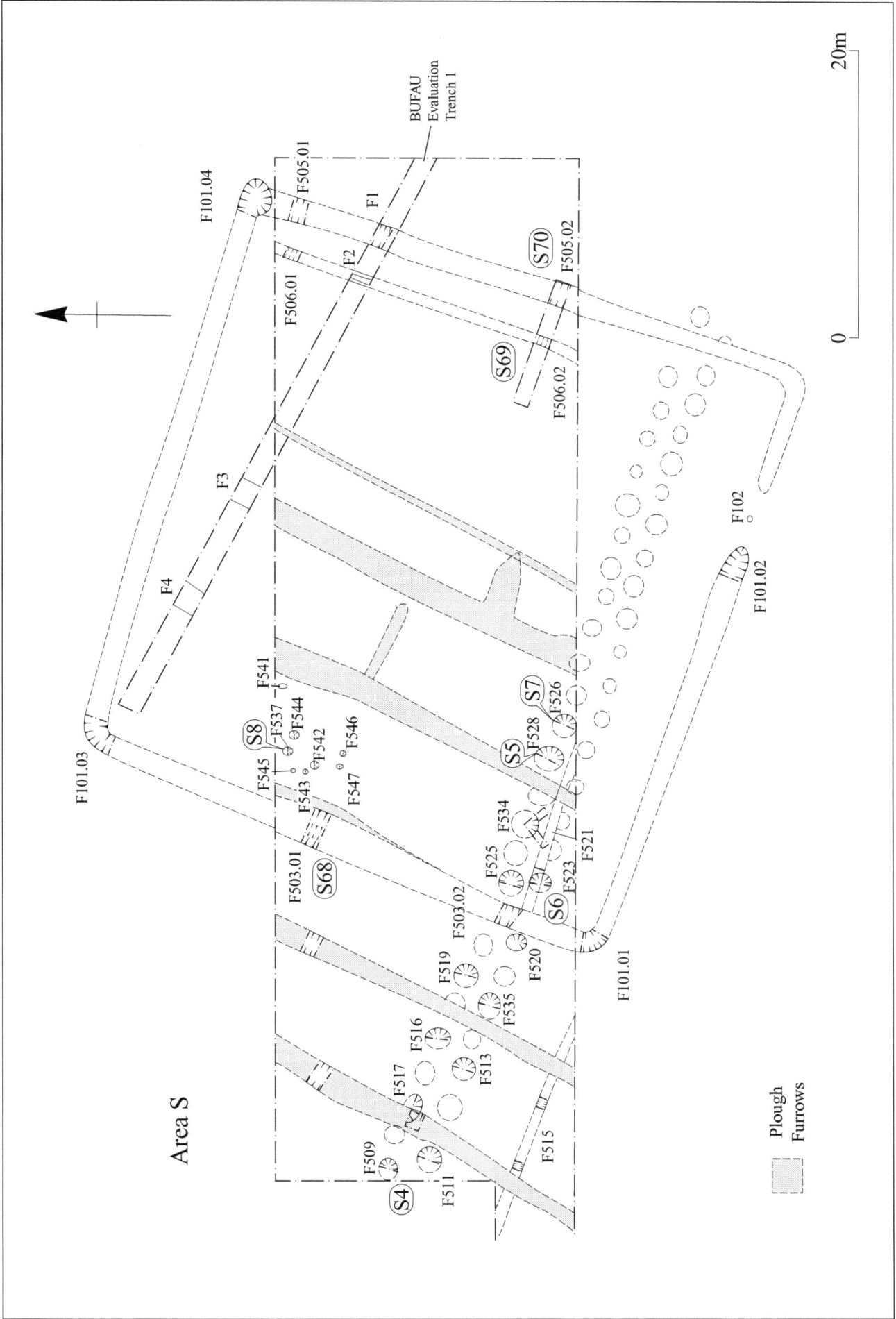

Area S

F101.04
F505.01
BUFAU
Evaluation
Trench 1
F1
F2
S70
F505.02
F506.01
S69
F506.02
F3
F4
F101.03
F102
F101.02
F541
F537
F544
S8
F545
F543
F542
F547
F546
S5
S7
F526
F528
F534
F525
F521
S6
F523
F503.01
S68
F503.02
F519
F520
F516
F535
F517
F513
F515
F509
S4
F511
F101.01

Plough
Furrows

0   20m

Fig.9: Area S: Plan of all excavated features

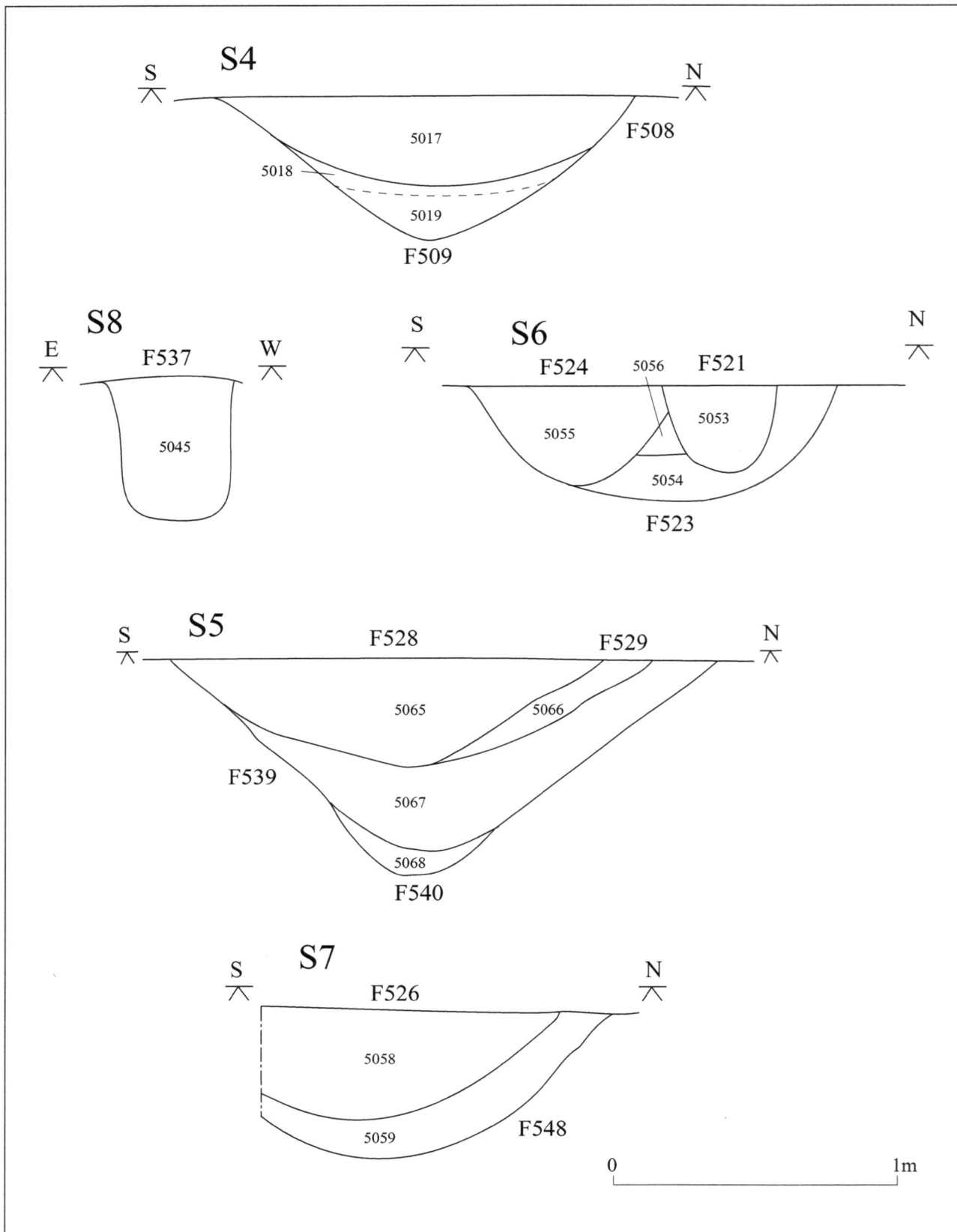

Fig. 10: Area S: Period 2 pit sections

The area around the monument has been subject to gravel extraction by Lafarge Aggregates Limited. Prior to this work, English Heritage and the quarry operators agreed on an area to be excluded from operations in order to preserve the monument. Following gravel extraction the area around the monument became the site of the National Memorial Arboretum. The test pit was excavated in the southwestern corner of the Scheduled Ancient Monument and disturbed part of a Beaker vessel. This was recovered in November 1996, and sent to Stoke-on-Trent Museum where a preliminary identification was made by Dr. Carol Allen.

The objectives of the fieldwork were to carry out salvage recording of the damage to the monument arising from the excavation of the trench and to survey the monument and its surrounding area. The excavated trench was approximately 1.2m deep, 2.8m long and 0.75m wide. It was cleared of collapsed topsoil and plant growth, taking care not to further damage the monument. The natural subsoil comprised orange sandy gravel and was overlain by 0.3m to 0.4m of brown silty topsoil. The sandy gravel was cut by a single feature (F101), 0.6m wide and 0.3m deep. It had a V-shaped profile and was filled with a brown silty sand. The feature was visible in both long sections, suggesting a linear ditch, orientated east-west. It contained two fragments of possibly Roman pottery, two pieces of flint and one tile fragment. Sieving of the soil displaced from the trench produced eight sherds of prehistoric pottery, two pieces of tile, five pieces of flint, one piece of clay pipe and one piece of Post-Medieval bottle glass.

Discussion

The only feature visible in the section contained pottery of Roman or later date. Consequently, it seems likely that this represents a linear feature dating to the Romano-British period or later. No prehistoric material was recovered from the sections of the trench apart from a single worked flint flake. The Beaker pottery that was recovered from the initial pit, and from the sieved soil, clearly must have originated from a small discrete pit or feature that has been completely destroyed during the excavation of the test pit. Clearly, this pit must have been located close to the northwest facing section where the large fragment of pottery was initially observed. It seems likely that the last remaining trace of the pit was lost following a localised collapse of the section when the pottery fell out in November 1996. Only part of the vessel was recovered. It seems highly unlikely that any fragments were missed during the sieving of the excavated spoil heap. Consequently it seems probable that only part of the vessel had been buried in the pit. No fragments of bone were recovered during the sieving process.

Period 2 Iron Age

Pit Alignments

Area S (Fig. 9)

The pit alignment in Area S ran approximately northwest to southeast and consisted of two lines of staggered, circular pits (Plates 4 and 5). With the exception of three pits (F516, F520 and F525) all had been re-cut once, with F540 re-cut three times (Fig. 10, S5). The original cuts of the pits were bowl shaped and varied in diameter between 2.2m and 1m and, in depth, between 0.9m and 0.4m (Table 1 and Fig.11). In general, primary and secondary deposits of silt-sand, often containing some burnt and heat-cracked stones, were visible in the profiles of these pits, although later deposits may have been obscured by the re-cuts. The only original cut containing datable artefacts was F509, where the secondary silt-sand deposit (5018) contained prehistoric pottery of Iron Age date (Fig. 10, S4).

The re-cut pits were also bowl shaped and had a similar range of diameter to the original cuts, but were shallower, between 0.6m and 0.15m (Table 2). Again they had been filled with one or two deposits of silt-sand. Prehistoric pottery was recovered from F519 (the re-cut of F533), F534 (the re-cut of F538) and F526 (the re-cut of F548; Fig.10, S7); this all appeared to be Iron Age in date. The brown silt-sand deposit (5058) within F526 contained a large percentage of heat-cracked stone and charcoal fragments.

Pit F540 had been re-cut by F539, which had subsequently been re-cut by F529 and finally by F528. Three re-cuts of a pit had not been observed elsewhere in the pit alignment and there was no obvious reason as to why this particular pit had been re-defined more times than the others. Pit F511 (the re-cut of F512) was the only pit to have evidence of a post-hole (F510) cut into it, and this probably post-dated the pit alignment as it was cut into the top of the silted up pit.

The pit alignment was observed during the watching brief continuing beyond the excavated area, both eastwards and westwards, and some pits were sampled. These had been heavily truncated during the soil stripping process and yielded no further information to that obtained during the area excavation. Trench R2 of the 1995 Tempus Reparatum evaluation (Fig. 4) contained 12 oval-shaped pits (Lupton 1995, Sec.4.2.24-27), which were on the same alignment as the pits excavated in 1998-99, and would suggest that they continue down to the River Tame.

Table 1: Dimensions of Original Pits from Area S

Pit	Diameter (m)	Depth (m)
F509	1.4	0.6
F512	1.5	0.6
F514	1.44	0.56
F516	1.5	0.42
F518	2.2	0.54
F520	1.4	0.35
F523	1.25	0.8
F525	1.0	0.4
F527	1.0	0.6
F530	1.25	0.8
F533	1.7	0.5
F538	2.0	0.54
F540	2.0	0.9
F548	1.70	0.65

Table 2: Dimensions of Re-Cut Pits from Area S

Pit	Diameter (m)	Depth (m)
F508	1.4	0.3
F511	1.3	0.5
F513	1.44	0.15
F517	2.2	0.4
F519	1.4	0.45
F524	0.5	0.3
F526	1.6	0.46
F528	1.7	0.4
F529	1.9	0.4
F535	1.2	0.6
F539	2.0	0.8

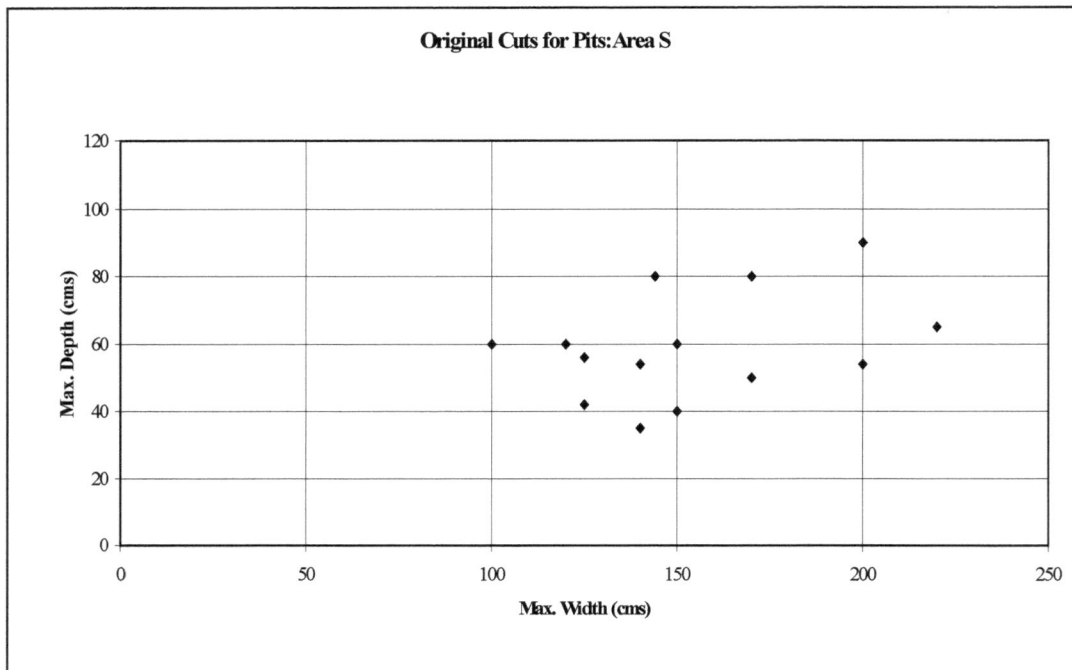

Fig. 11: Area S: scatter diagram of the dimensions of the original cuts of Period 2 pits

Cluster of Post-Holes (Plate 6)

Approximately 15m northeast of the pit alignment, was a group of small post-holes, (F537 and F541-47) generally circular in shape with steep sides and flat bottoms, ranging in diameter from 0.15m to 0.50m and in depth from 0.14m to 0.55m (Table 3). There was no definite pattern to the position of these post-holes, although they possibly formed some sort of curved structure. However, the pottery from F537 (Fig. 10, S8; Plate 7) indicates that a special deposit was made in one of these holes.

Table 3: Dimensions of Post-Holes from Area S

Post-Hole	Length (m)	Width (m)	Diameter (m)	Depth (m)
F537	0.75	0.45		0.55
F541			0.5	0.36
F542			0.5	0.19
F543			0.25	0.14
F544	0.75	0.55		0.25
F545			0.15	0.18
F546			0.35	0.19
F547			0.33	0.17

Pottery

The only primary deposit of pottery was in one of the pits of the pit alignment, F509. This comprised relatively small portions of the rim (12%) and base (15%) respectively from two ellipsoid jars of Iron Age date (Fig. 36, 1 and 2). An important group of three vessels of similar ellipsoid or globular form, but varying in size, was found in the re-cut F526 of pit F548 (Fig. 35, 1-3). These were represented in larger proportions than the vessels from F509 (see *Prehistoric Pottery*, below). The pottery was moderately abraded, but many conjoins could be detected, and the average sherd weight for these deposits was high at 31g. Also from F526 was a flint core fragment, probably of Bronze Age date, although it could have been part of an Iron Age industry. If Bronze Age, then this piece may have been residual, or intentionally deposited as an heirloom (see *Worked Flint*, below). Two other pits within the main alignment contained small amounts of pottery. F519 (the re-cut of F533) and F534, (the re-cut of F538) produced one and six sherds respectively, of average sherd weight 7g. The sherd from F519 was of a similar fabric to the vessels from F509 and F526 and may have come from a comparable jar type. The F534 pottery included five sherds in this fabric plus one very small fragment in the sandy fabric 4. All were of Iron Age date. F519 also contained a stone rubber, made from an erratic deriving from Scottish or Lake District granites (see *Worked Stone*, below). The pits within the double alignment which contained artefacts were all situated in the northernmost row. They were not clustered together but occurred at irregular intervals along the alignment.

The deepest of the post-holes in the cluster north of the pit alignment, F537 (Plate 7), contained a large pottery deposit, similar to that found in pit F526, except that only one large globular jar was represented (Fig. 36, 3). The average sherd weight in this case was 16g.

Dating Evidence

A radiocarbon date (Beta-135227) was obtained from pit F526, context 5058, which produced a calibrated date of Cal BC 400 to 155 at 2 sigma. A further radiocarbon date (Beta-135226) of Cal BC 410 to 340 and Cal BC 320 to 205 at 2 sigma was obtained from 5045, the primary fill of F537 (see *Appendix 1*).

Area T (Fig.12)

The double pit alignment in this area was very similar to that observed in Area S, with which it ran parallel. It consisted of two rows of circular pits running approximately east-west across the area (Plate 8), although there did appear to be some interruption of the sequence of pits in the area where they were cut by the Period 3 droveway ditches. Although the rows of pits ran parallel to each other, they were slightly staggered, in that the southern pits tended to be located in the gaps between the northern pits. The pits were similar in nature on both the east and west sides of the droveway, with a bowl shape and usually filled with two episodes of silting, with an average diameter of 1.40m and maximum depth of 0.50 to 0.60m (Fig. 13, S9-S16; Table 4 and Fig. 14). There was only one pit (F131), which had any evidence of a post-hole within, in the form of a small, circular re-cut in the base of the pit. On the west side of the droveway only a limited number of the northern pits were sampled, as they had been disturbed by a modern land drain which would have resulted in contaminated samples.

Whilst there was a gap in the area later occupied by the droveway, at least when seen in plan, there were three pits (F115, F111 and F128) which were cut by the droveway ditches, F105, F109 and F110 respectively (Fig. 13; S12, S14 and S15). There also appeared to be two inter-cutting pits (F132 and F133) in the central area of the droveway, of which the earlier pit (F133) had very similar characteristics to the other pits in the prehistoric alignment (Fig13; S13).

Although there were clear stratigraphic relationships in the pit sections, there were no artefacts recovered and, therefore, little chance of any associated dating to clarify the associations. Its similarity to the pit alignment from Area S suggests that it belongs in an Iron Age context.

Table 4:   Dimensions of Pits in Area T

Feature	Diameter (m)	Depth (m)
F100	1.38	0.49
F101	1.53	0.57
F102	1.65	0.62
F103	1.88	0.54
F104	1.26	0.52
F106	1.15	0.39
F107	1.54	0.42
F108	1.45	0.34
F111	1.40	0.44
F115	2.00	0.56
F116	1.20	0.44
F117	1.48	0.60
F120	1.50	0.51
F122	1.40	0.49
F125	1.42	0.56
F128	1.20	0.65
F129	1.38	0.51
F130	1.18	0.45
F131	1.31	0.48
F133	1.24	0.54

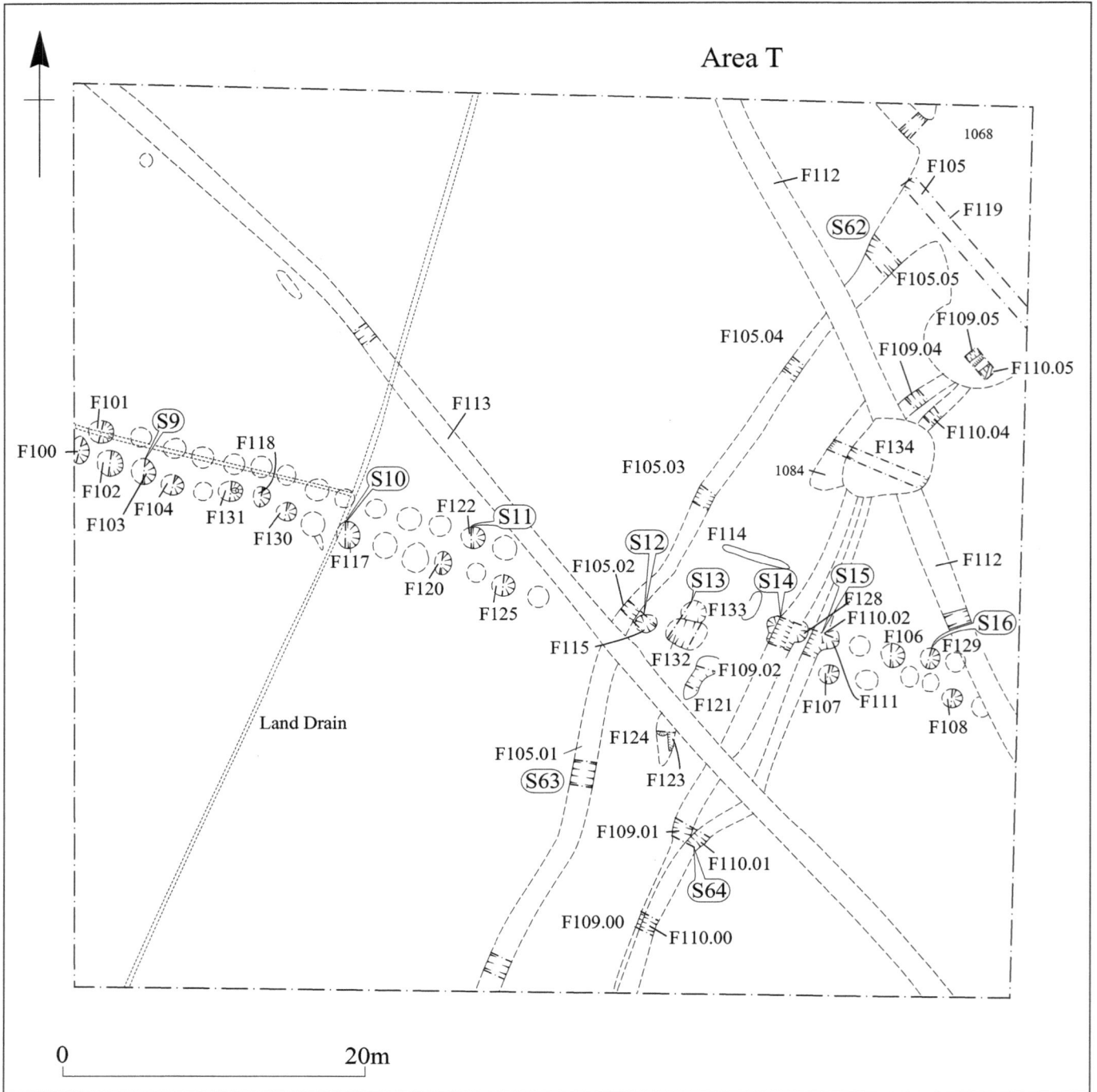

Fig. 12: Area T: Plan of all excavated features

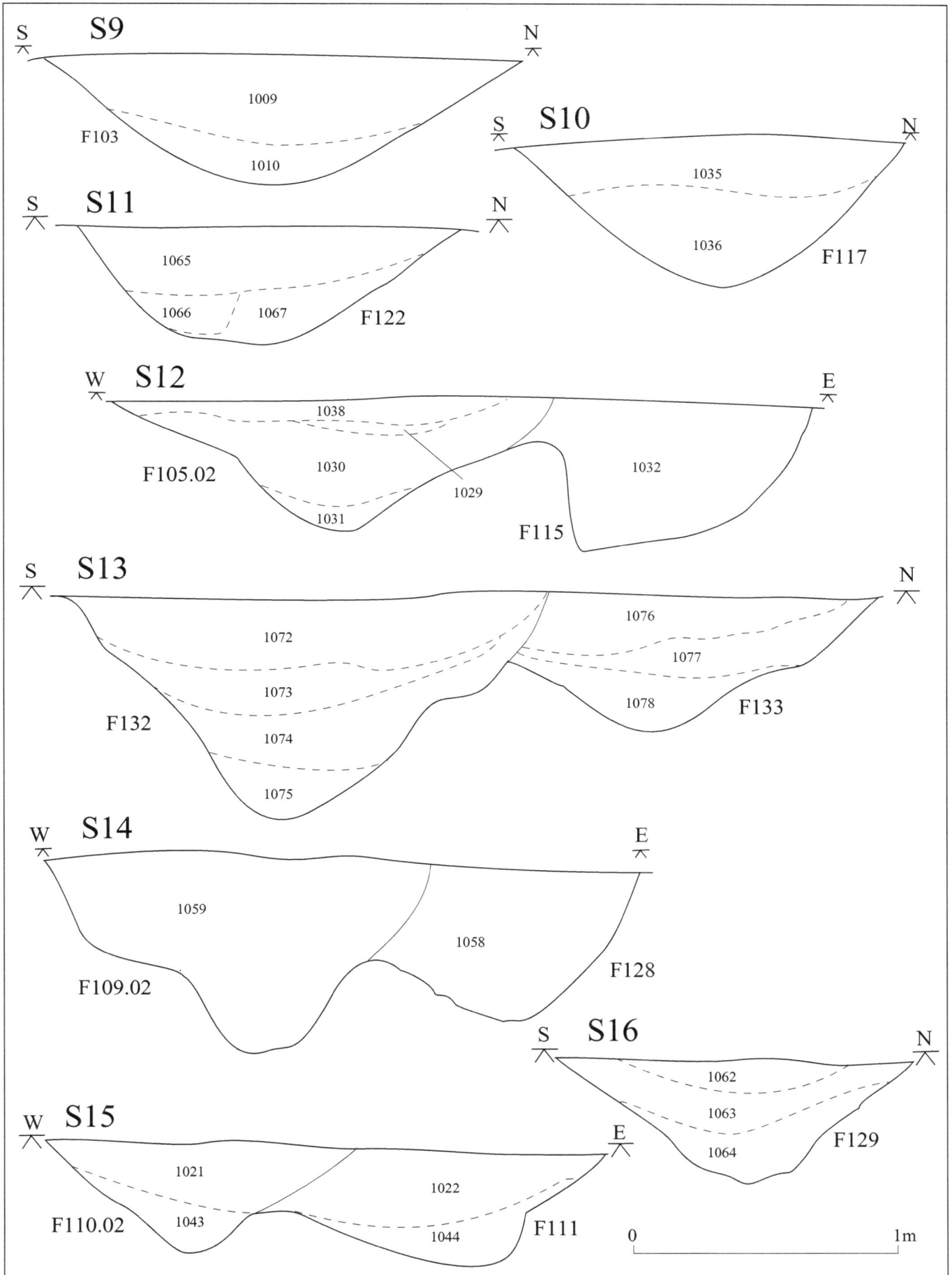

Fig. 13: Area T: Period 2 pit sections

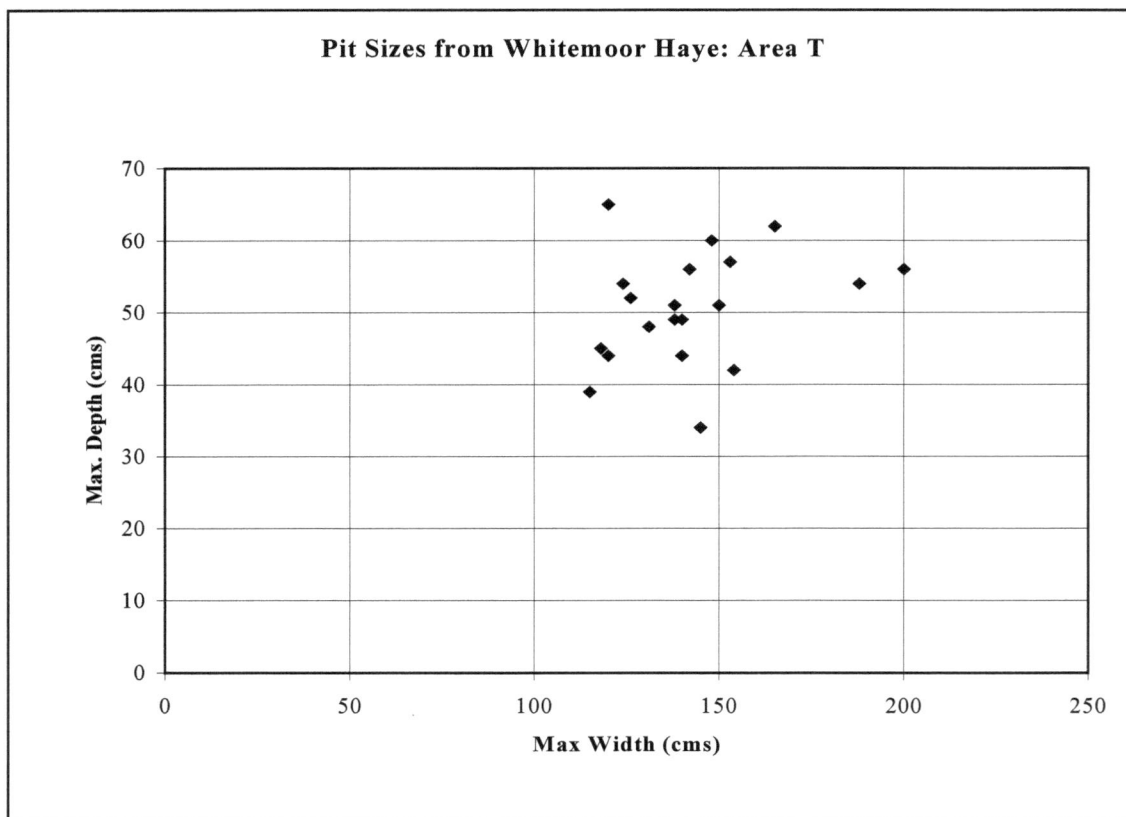

Pit Sizes from Whitemoor Haye: Area T

Fig. 14:   Area T: scatter diagram of dimensions of Period 2 pits

Watching Brief Area T

The double pit alignment identified in Area T continued across the site as originally identified from the aerial photographs, and could be seen continuing up to the eastern extent of the phase 2 stripping (see Fig. 44), with the likelihood that it continued into the adjoining, unstripped field, parallel to the alignment identified in Area S. Where the pits were excavated, and had not been truncated, they were bowl shaped with an approximate depth of 0.50m and width of between 0.90 and 1.40m. They had been filled with two distinct episodes of silting.

Triple-ditched System

Area F (Fig. 15)

Two of the ditches (F800 and F802) belonging to an east-west triple-ditched boundary system had an east-west parallel alignment and terminated within the area. There was a further length of ditch (F806), just beyond the eastern terminal of the more northerly of the two ditches, which was only 0.26m deep with a shallow U-shaped profile and flat bottom. F800 and F802 had similar profiles, but were deeper than F806 (Fig. 16; S19 and S20). The northernmost of the two larger ditches (F802) had evidence of a shallower U-shaped re-cut (F807), 0.22m deep. A continuous ditch (F801) was aligned southwest to northeast across the

northwestern corner of the area. It had a U-shaped profile with a flat bottom, and was between 0.50 and 0.60m deep (Fig. 16; S17 and S18).

Immediately south of the terminal of F800 were two possible pits (F813 and F805). The latter had a circular shape, with shallow sloping sides to a flat bottom, at a depth of 0.28m. The fills of this feature had a high sand content, which may lend itself to a geological interpretation rather than an archaeological one. Northeast of this pit was a larger, ovoid, flat-bottomed pit (F813), which was 0.69m deep (Fig. 16; S21). It had received three re-cuts (F812, F811 and F810) of similar shape but of lessening depths.

Dating Evidence

There were no datable artefacts recovered from any of these features and the placement of these features in an Iron Age context is based on evidence from a 1992 evaluation trench (No.18) (see Fig. 4). The cropmark plot clearly shows the triple-ditched feature running east-west across the southern half of the quarry, and the ditches were also identified during the phase 2 topsoil strip watching brief in 1999, to the southeast of the former location of Area B (Fig. 5). The 1992 evaluation trench sampled the relationship between these ditches and the north-south, droveway, ditches and the report concluded: "The trial trench was able to clearly demonstrate

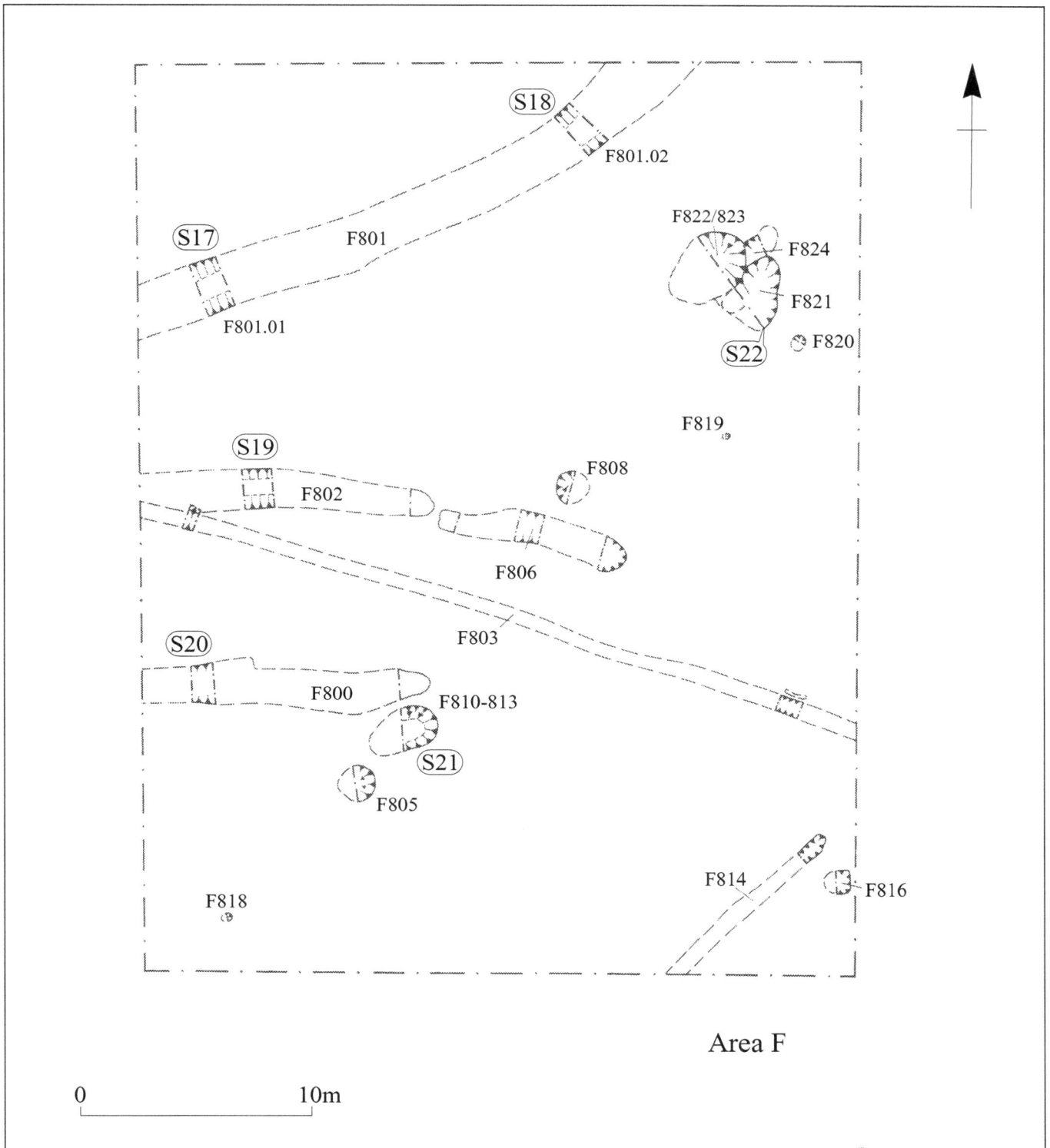

Fig. 15: Area F: Plan of all excavated features

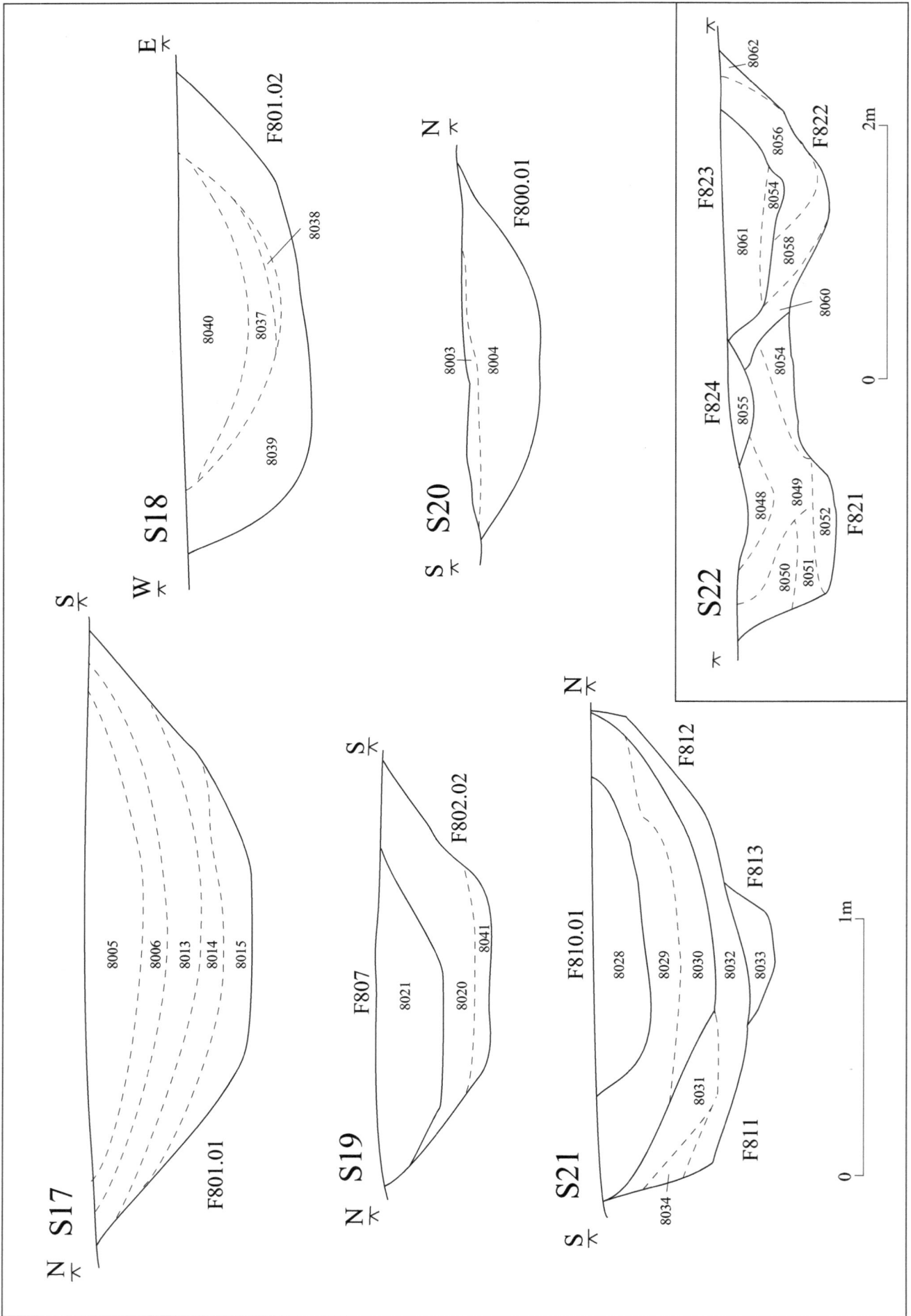

Fig. 16: Area F: Period 2 ditch sections

that the eastern arm of the north-south double ditch system post-dated the east-west triple ditched system" (BUFAU 1992, Appendix III).

Enclosures and Structures

Area R

A single pit, F615, from this area may date to Period 2. It had similar dimensions, and a similar shape and profile, to F612, identified as a Beaker grave. It was also filled with a similar charcoal-flecked silt-sand (6022) (Figs. 6 and 7; S3). The Period 2 dating is suggested by two small, abraded sherds of pottery in an Iron Age fabric type from context 6022, although these could have been intrusive or residual.

Area A (Fig. 17; Plate 9)

The Main Enclosure

The main enclosure, which contained four structures, appeared to have been defined in three distinct stages: an original ditch (F486), a re-cut of this ditch (F468), and finally the excavation of four large pits (F467, F487, F445 and F456) located at a terminal and on the corners of the enclosure. A small gully (F452), cut by the northern terminal of the main enclosure entrance, which continued eastwards until it met with the easternmost droveway ditch, may have been an earlier boundary or enclosure ditch (Fig. 18; S28).

The original main enclosure ditch (F486) was V-shaped, with a surviving depth of between 1.0m and 1.2m, and had silted up with a number of different sand and gravel deposits (Fig. 18; S23 to S28). The bottom fill of the ditch was a dark grey silty clay, which appeared to have been subjected to periods of water-logging (contexts 4132, 4179, 4193 and 4194). In the southwest corner this ditch had cut what appeared to be an earlier, bowl-shaped pit (F472; Fig. 21). The extent of this feature was not fully examined due to the high level of ground water within it.

The re-cut (F468) had a shallower, U-shaped profile and in section appeared to have had a flat bottom with straight sides. In all the excavated profiles, F468 had a similar width and depth, between 0.44m and 0.77m, and was filled with similar silt-sand and gravel deposits, with some slumping of the natural sand-gravel in these sections. The surviving northern terminal of the enclosure ditch, which defined an entrance in its eastern side, appeared to belong to the re-cut phase and was rounded. The later digging of one of the large pits (F445) had destroyed the southern terminal of the enclosure ditch (see Fig. 20).

Only 11 sherds of pottery were found in the excavated segments of the main enclosure ditch. Most were fresh and of fair size (average sherd weight 12g). A large rim and shoulder fragment from a bowl came from the ditch re-cut, F468/4150 (Fig.37, 4); this probably dates from the Early Iron Age. Also from the ditch came the only pottery with granodiorite inclusions − three abraded wall sherds from F454/F468. F486/4143 contained a fragment of upper quern,

made from Millstone Grit or Coal Measures arkosic sandstone (*see Worked Stone*, below).

Structure 3

Structure 3 within the enclosure comprised a 12.0m diameter ring gully (F421) with an entrance on the eastern side; the western side was cut by a later, Romano-British, feature (F415) (Fig.19; S29). The ring gully had a U-shaped profile and was between 0.20 and 0.40m deep. Internally, there was a number of possible post/stake-holes (F424-F425, F431-F432), all circular or sub-circular in shape, ranging in diameter from 0.28 to 0.40m, round bottomed and between 0.12 and 0.16m deep (Table 5). A centrally-located, sub-circular feature (F433), 0.28m deep, contained silt-sand deposits rich in charcoal, which may indicate that it was the remains of an oven or hearth. A small linear gully (F409), 0.50m wide and 0.30m deep with vertical sides and a flat base, cut the ring gully and appeared to terminate within the confines of Structure 3; it continued eastwards, where it was cut by the ring ditch of Structure 1.

Table 5: Dimensions of Features Associated with Structure 3

Feature	Length	Width	Diameter	Depth
F424			0.32	0.16
F425			0.32	0.12
F431			0.28	0.13
F432			0.4	0.12
F433			0.75	0.28
F434	2.7	0.3		0.11

Thirteen sherds of Iron Age pottery were found. The majority was fresh but sherd weights were highly variable. From the ring gully there were large unabraded sherds from half of the base of a jar (Fig.37, 10) and rim, shoulder and body fragments from a necked burnished jar (Fig.37, 6). These were probably deposited at the time of abandonment of the structure. There were also small wall sherds from post-hole F422.

Structure 1

The ring ditch of Structure 1 (F413) had an outer diameter of c.15.0m, with a gap on the eastern side. The ditch had a U-shaped profile and varied in depth from 0.18m to 0.50m; it was generally deeper at the rounded terminals than on the western and southern sides (Fig. 19; S30-31). Internally, there were a number of circular post-holes (Table 6): F401 and F408 spanned the entranceway and, centrally located, there was a further cluster of post-holes (F400, F402-F404), centred on F402. The silt-sand fill of this feature contained a central patch of burnt clay, which may be indicative of an oven or hearth lining. To the north, there was another cluster of post-holes (F406, F410-F411 and F441). These post-holes were generally circular, between 0.50m and 0.95m in diameter and round or flat-bottomed, with a depth of between 0.05m and 0.31m. The linear gully (F409) noted above was also identified within Structure 1, where it appeared to terminate near the southern terminal of the ring gully, though it was truncated by this later feature. No pottery was found in this structure but there was a probable rubbing stone made from Leicestershire granodiorite from pit F441 (see *Worked Stone*, below).

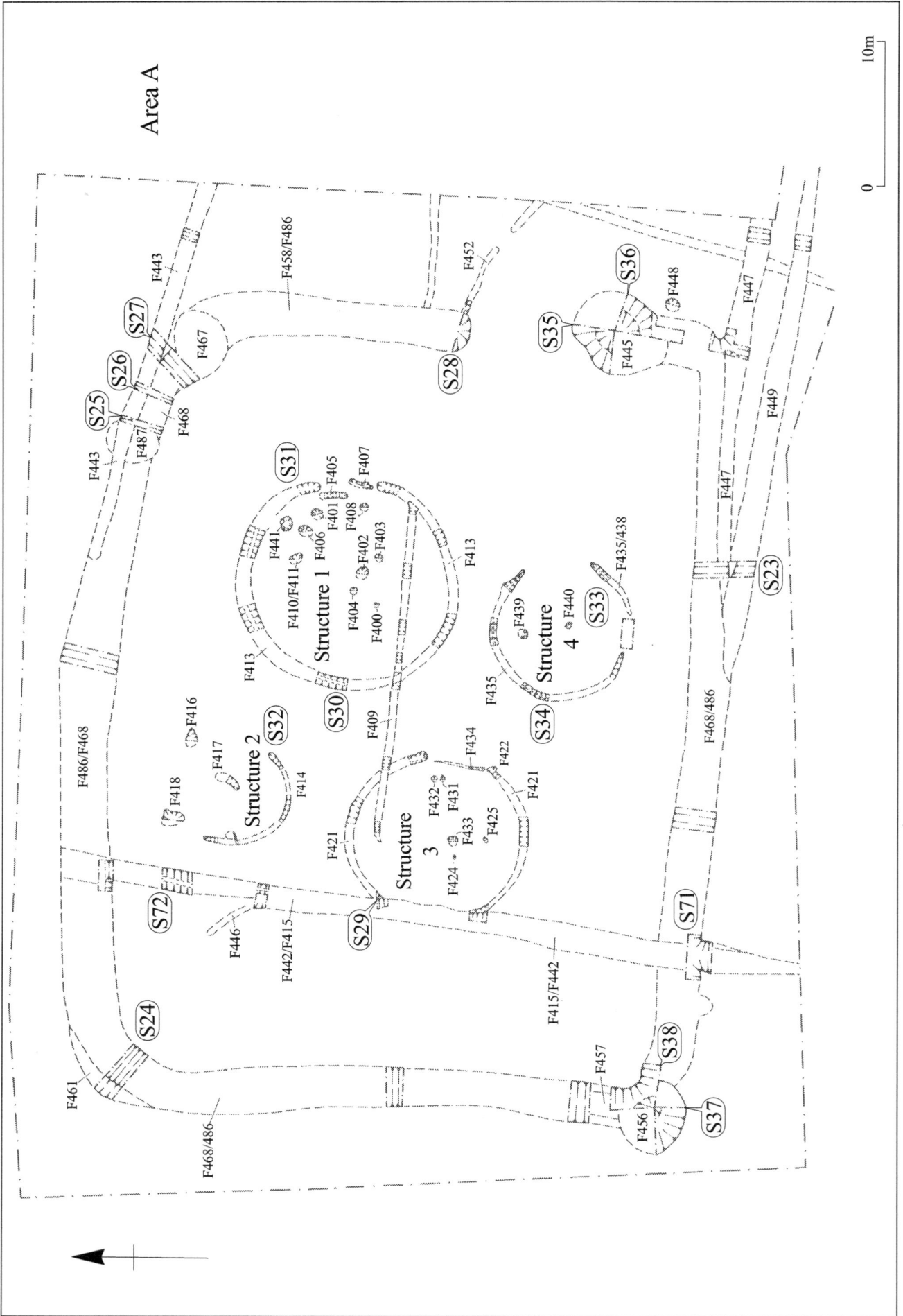

Fig. 17: Area A: Plan of all excavated features

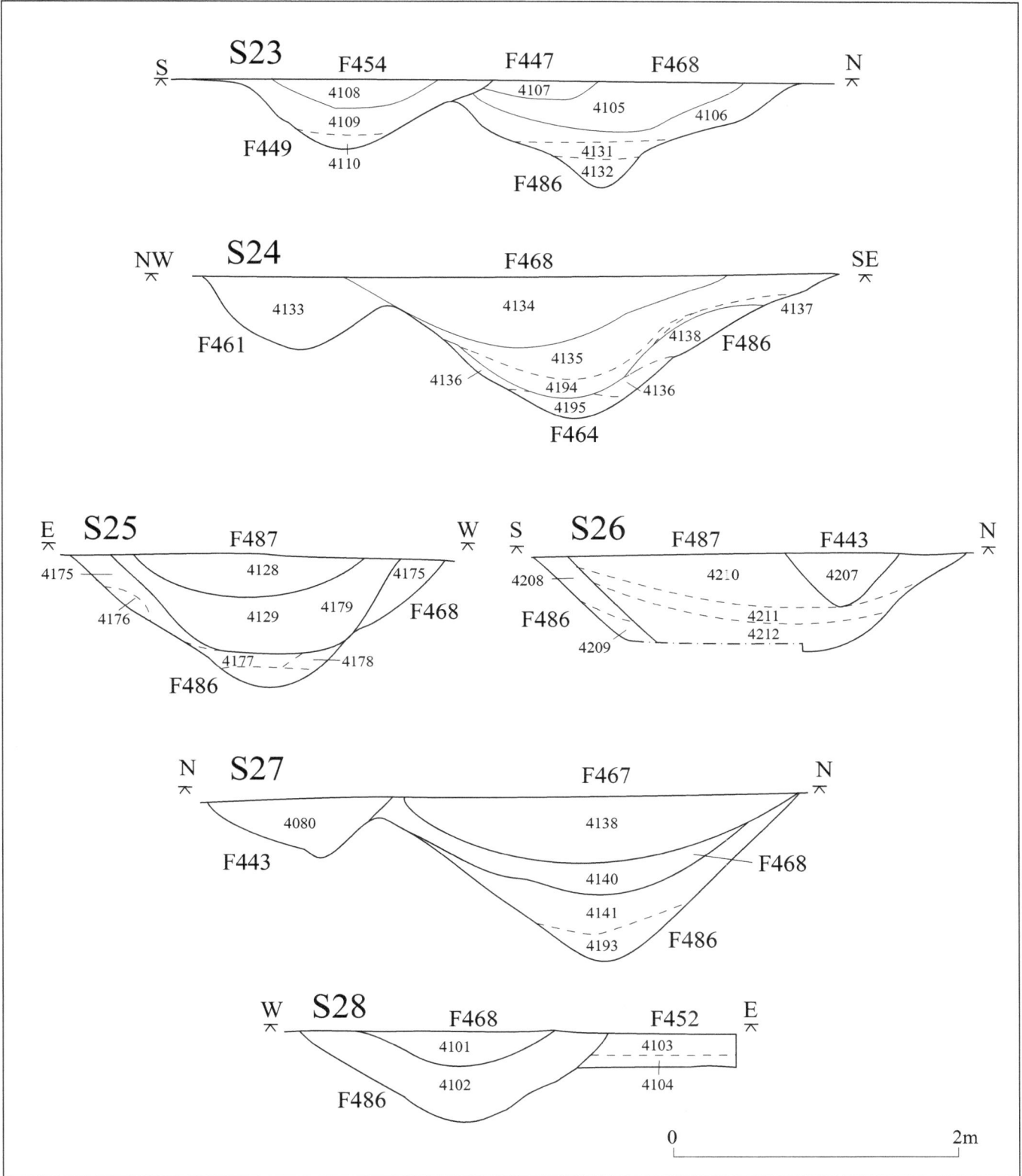

Fig. 18: Area A: Period 2 enclosure ditch sections

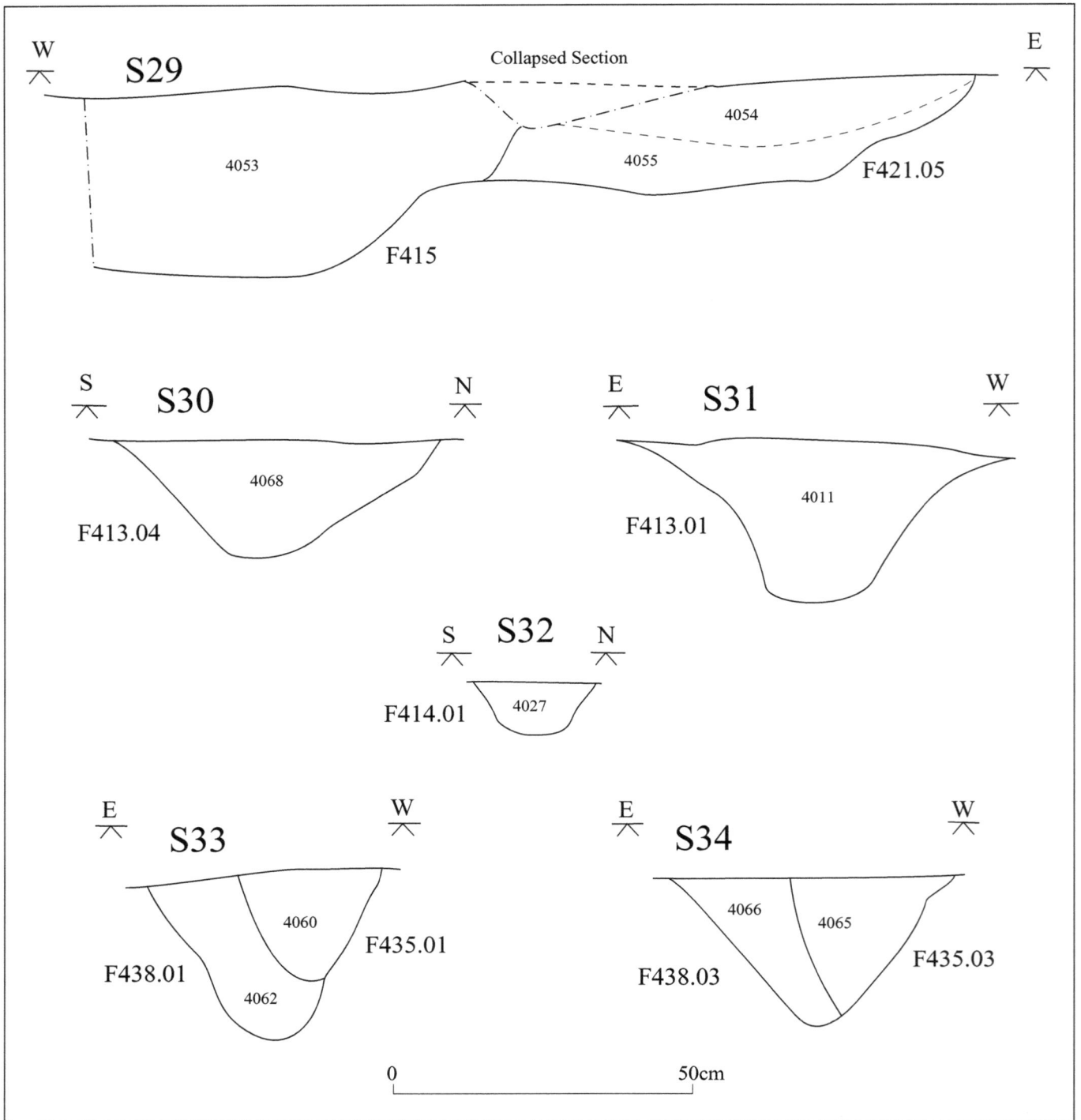

Fig. 19: Area A: Period 2 structures sections

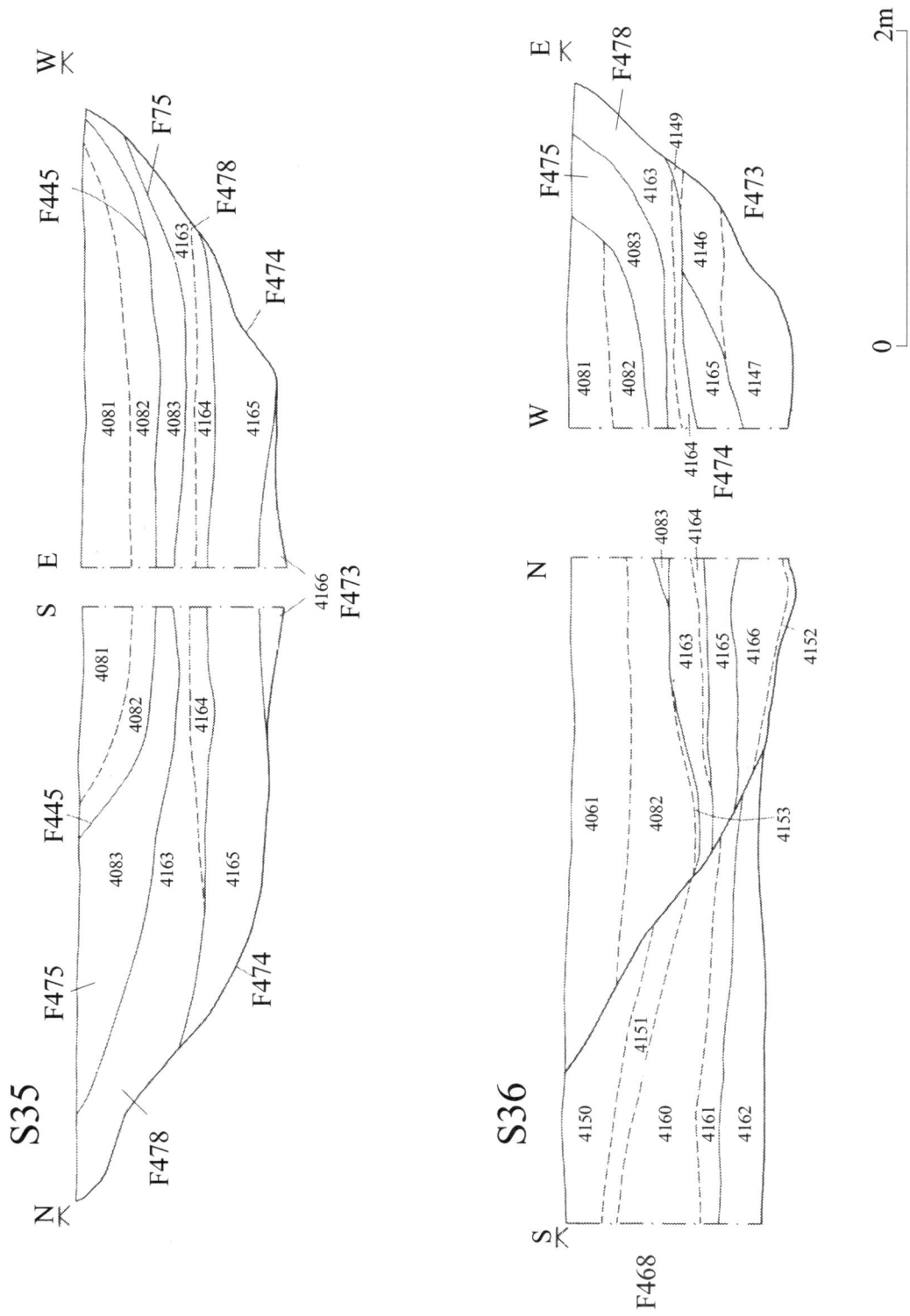

Fig. 20: Area A: Period 2 pit sections

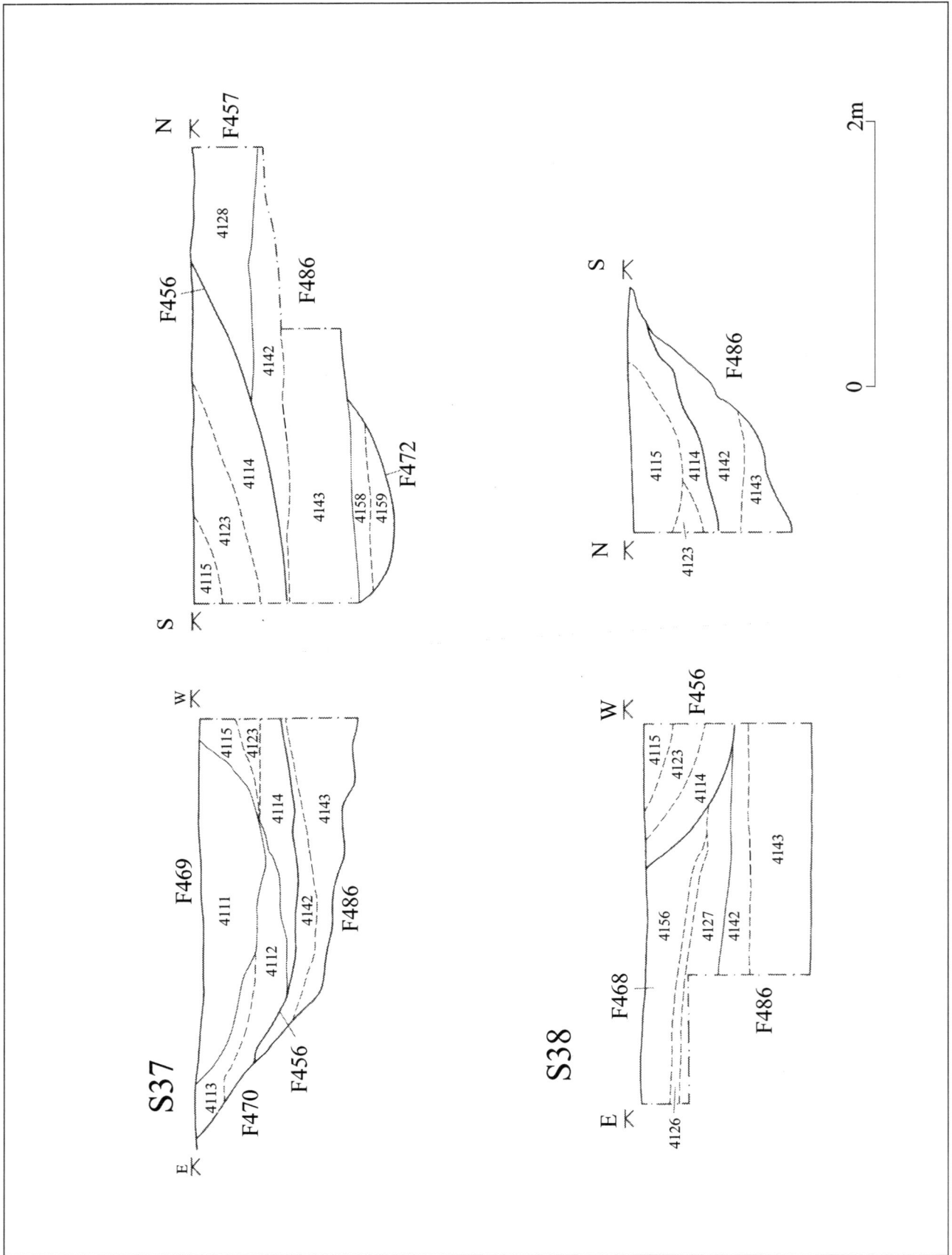

Fig. 21: Area A: Period 2 pit sections

Table 6: Dimensions of Features Associated with Structure 1

Feature	Length	Width	Diameter	Depth
F400			0.5	0.3
F401			0.75	0.28
F402			0.8	0.3
F403			0.55	0.2
F404			0.51	0.05
F405	2.5	0.45		0.25
F406			0.95	0.2
F407	1.8	0.4		0.3
F408			0.65	0.15
F410			0.43	0.21
F411			0.91	0.31
F441	1.2	0.9		0.9

Structure 2

Structure 2 was much more insubstantial, with only parts of the defining ditch (F414) surviving. This was U-shaped in profile, with a depth of between 0.06m to 0.20m and, if complete, a diameter of approximately 7.0m (Fig. 19; S32). The southern terminal appeared to be intact and there was a rounded end to this semicircular ditch on the western side. Three irregular features (F416, F417 and F418) were recorded in the vicinity of Structure 2, but their shape and the deposits contained within them were more consistent with geological rather than human activity.

Structure 4

There was more of the 10.0m diameter ring gully (F435) surviving from Structure 4, and although there was a gap in the southern side the northern terminal appeared to have been plough damaged. The ring gully had a U-shaped profile and was between 0.15m and 0.30m in depth. In the southern terminal and western side sections there was evidence of an earlier ditch (F438) of similar shape and width, but slightly deeper (Fig. 19, S33-4). However, as it was not evident in all the sections, it would not appear to have been a complete ditch. There were two internal post-holes - one (F439) contained a large percentage of small burnt stones and the other (F440) was located approximately centrally within the structure (Table 7).

Table 7: Dimensions of Features Associated with Structure 4

Feature	Length	Width	Diameter	Depth
F439			0.5	0.2
F440			0.5	0.24

The only finds from Structure 4 comprised a large proportion of the base of a large Iron Age pot, found in the terminal of the ring gully (F435.01). This fresh material was probably deposited when the structure was abandoned.

The Later Enclosure

The last phase of the main enclosure was characterised by the digging of four large pits (F467, F487, F445 and F456) and stretches of the later enclosure ditch (F468) may have remained in use (see Fig. 17).

F445, at the south terminal of the enclosure ditch, was the last re-cut of a series of five pits (Fig. 20). The first of these (F473) appeared to be bowl-shaped and contained two waterlogged fills. It was cut by another bowl-shaped pit (F474). In turn, this had been cut by further pit (F478), which was cut by another (F475). The final re-cut of this pit (F445) was shallow and had silted up with a lower fill of grey/brown silt-sand (4082) and an upper fill of orange/brown silt-sand (4081). To the southeast of this large pit was a smaller, circular feature (F448), which at 0.10m deep was possibly a truncated pit that could have been associated either with the large pit or the enclosure ditch as it contained pottery of Iron Age date.

The fifth and latest re-cut of the pit contained mainly unabraded sherds of medium size (average sherd weight 7g). These included rims from two large ellipsoid jars, body fragments from a large vessel with fine brush scoring and part of an everted rim jar (Fig. 37, 7, 8 and 9); they indicate a Middle Iron Age date. The final recut also contained a single unretouched flint flake, which probably was residual. From the upper fill (context 4081) there were two sherds of Iron Age pottery, one sherd of Romano-British date and a deposit of briquetage.

The bowl-shaped pit (F456; Fig.21) cut into the southwest corner of the enclosure ditch was filled with three layers of silt-sand (4114, 4123 and 4115). Cut into the western half of the pit was another bowl-shaped pit (F470) which, in turn, was cut by another pit (F469), of similar shape and filled with a grey/brown silt-sand deposit (4111). The bowl-shaped pit (F456) cut both the enclosure ditch and a short length of U-shaped ditch (F457), 0.30m deep and filled with re-deposited natural sand and gravel (4128). This may have been a deliberate backfilling of this segment of the enclosure ditch in order to create an entrance to the north of the open pit.

Two bowl-shaped pits (F467 and F487) were located on the northeast corner of the enclosure ditch. They were approximately 5.0m apart and appeared to have diameters of 3.5m (F487) and 4.0m (F467) and a depth in excess of 0.60m, although they were not fully excavated (Fig. 8, S25-26 and S27).

Relationship of the Structures and Enclosure

No direct stratigraphic relationship existed between the enclosure ditches and the structures, nor between the structures themselves. The gully F409 cut Structure 3 but was cut by Structure 1, therefore Structure 3 must be the earlier. This still provides a number of possible chronologies and relationships. Taking into account the fact that such structures commonly appear as hut pairs then Structures 2 and 3 could be paired, to be replaced later by Structures 1 and 4. If these hut groups are accepted then F486, the original enclosure ditch, could have enclosed Structures 2 and 3 and the re-cut enclosure ditch, F468, could have surrounded the second hut group, Structures 1 and 4.

The pits dug into the last enclosure ditch seem to correspond with a later use of the enclosure for agriculture and probably not human occupation. The pits and their re-cuts were

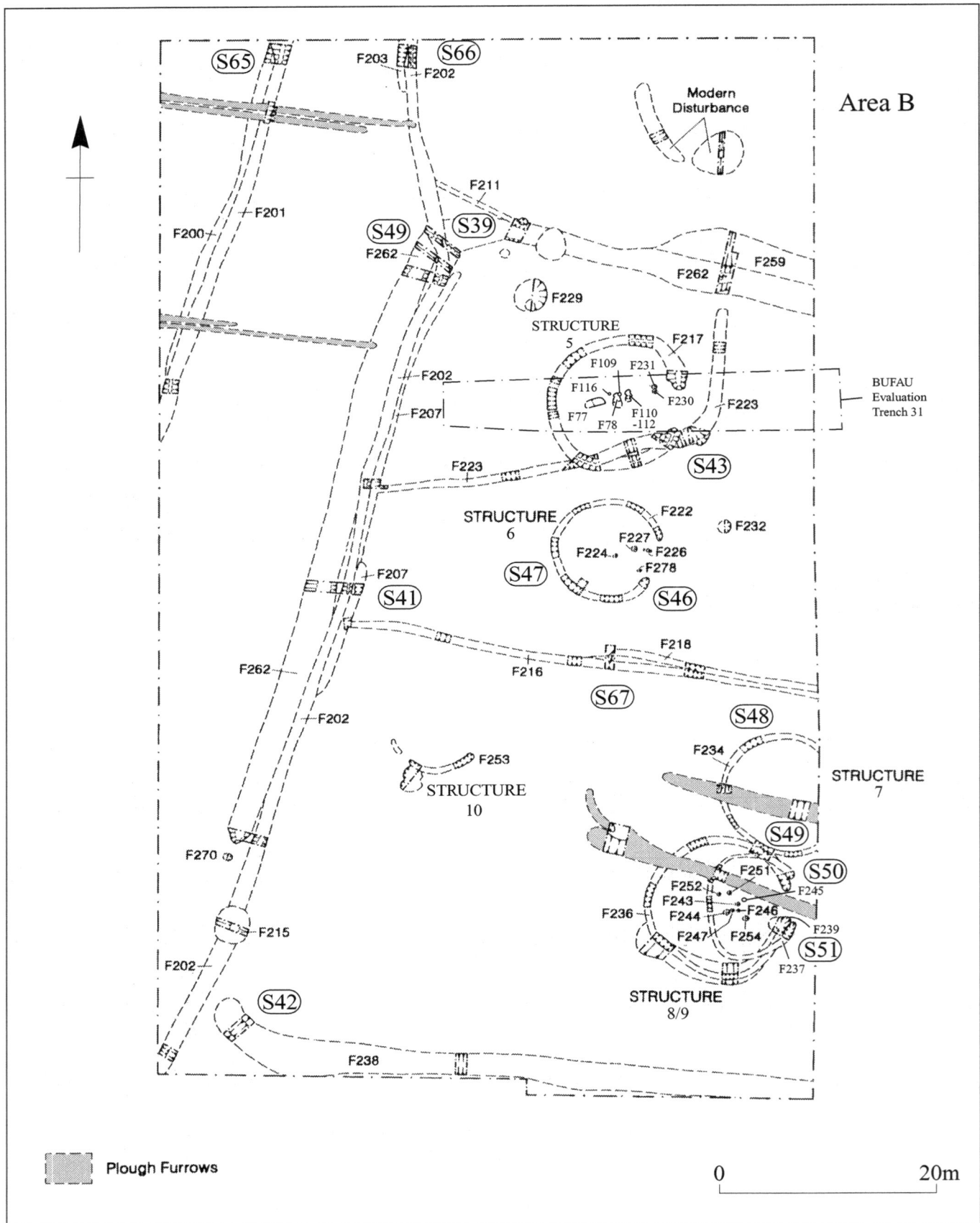

Fig. 22: Area B: Plan of all excavated features

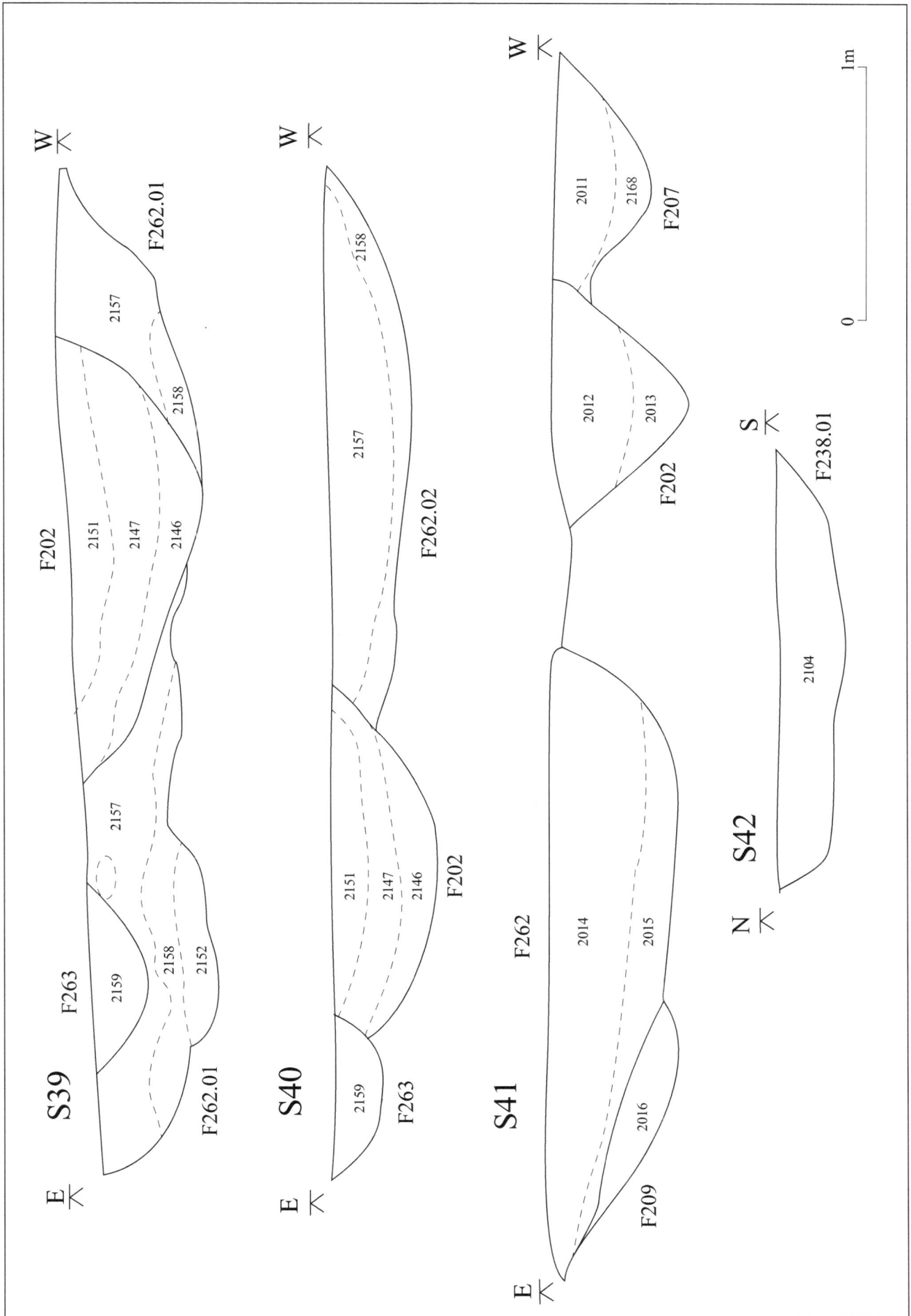

Fig. 23: Period 2 enclosure ditch sections

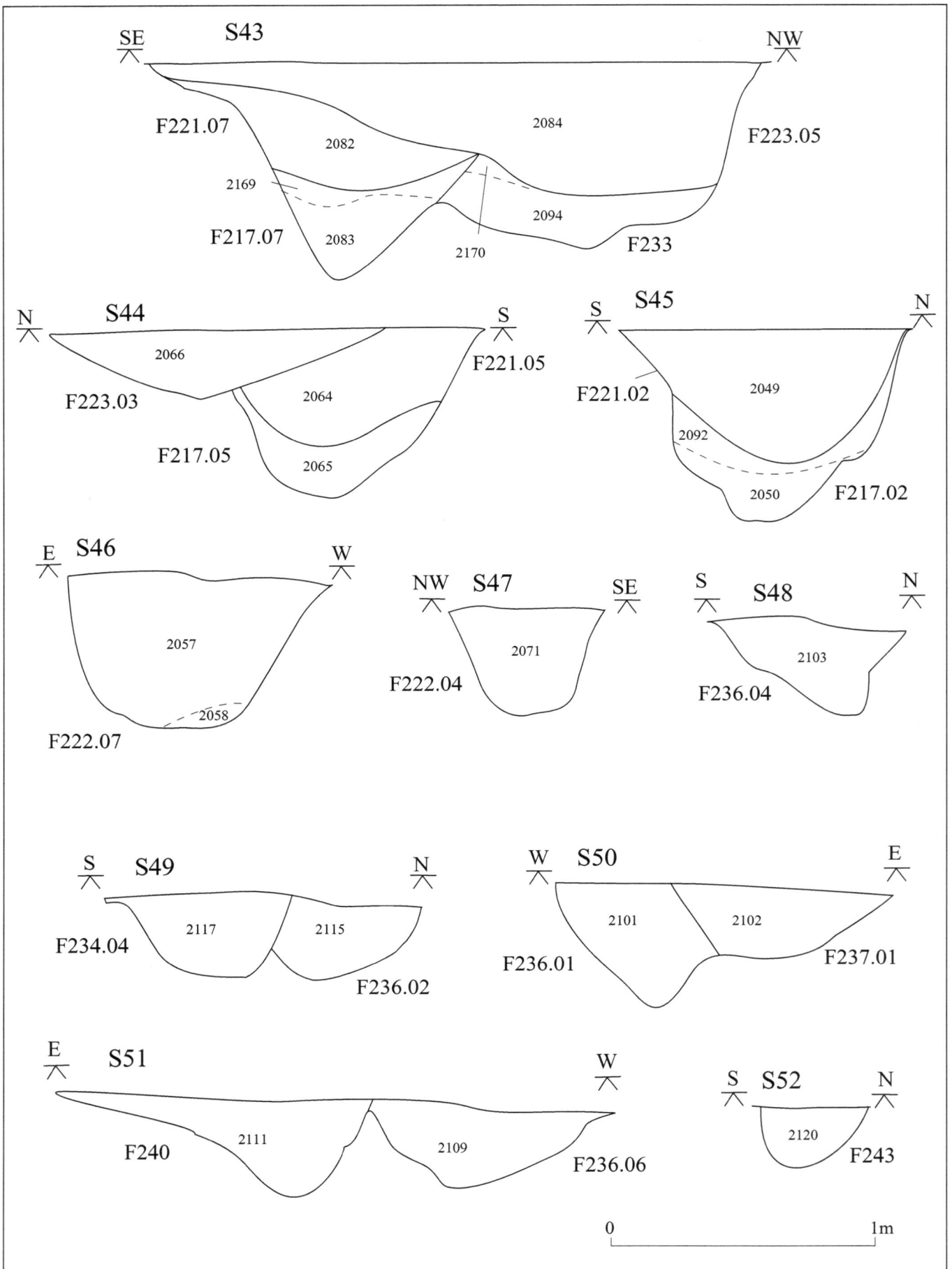

Fig. 24: Area B: Period 2 structures sections

probably watering holes and may have continued to be used in this form into the Romano-British period. The environmental evidence from F473 (context 4166) included both plants and insects. Analyses of these (see *Insect Remains and Waterlogged Seeds* below) suggest that these pits contained water; there was little evidence of human activity.

Area B (Fig. 22; Plate 10)

Enclosure

Only half of the enclosure which surrounded the structures in this area was excavated; the other half lying in the adjoining unexcavated area and only partially recorded during the watching brief. The enclosure had an entrance in the southwest corner. The earliest ditch dug in the construction of the enclosure was F259, on the northern side of the enclosure. It had a shallow U-Shaped profile, 3m wide and 0.8m deep. It was cut by F262, on the northern and western sides, which had steeper sides, a flat bottom and a depth c.0.40m, although it was a lot deeper, 0.90m, on the western edge of excavation (Fig.23, S39-40). There was also a narrow ditch (F211), which appeared to join the enclosure ditch at its northwest corner and was cut by a later ditch (F202). It had a V-shaped profile and was 0.50m deep. The southern extent of the enclosure was defined by a similar ditch (F238), which was more U-shaped (Fig.23, S42). South of the northern terminal of the enclosure ditch was a truncated circular pit (F270), 0.80m in diameter and 0.10m deep. There were no finds from the enclosure ditch fillings excavated. Within the interior of this enclosure ditch were six structures.

Structure 5 (Plate 11)

Structure 5 had a ring ditch defining its outer limit, which had a diameter approaching 13.0m, with an entrance in the east side, 3.6m wide. The original cut of this ditch (F217) had steep sides and a flat bottom, although there was a more pronounced V-shaped profile at the terminal sections. The original ditch had been re-defined with a shallower, U-shaped ditch cut (F221), which was filled with similar silty sand deposits (Fig.24, S43). Several internal features within Structure 5 were identified in Trench 31 of the 1992 evaluation, including a possible hearth (F78), which contained a pottery sherd dated to the Iron Age, a deep pit (F109) and several shallower pits (F110, F111 and F112) and post-holes (F113, F114 and F115) (BUFAU 1992, Appendix III). The subsequent area excavation identified two further inter-cutting stake-holes (F230 and F231). To the northwest of Structure 5 was a bowl-shaped pit (F229) which contained a sandy deposit (2086) rich in burnt and heat-cracked stones; this may have been associated with either Structure 5 or the surrounding enclosure ditch (F262).

A few sherds of Iron Age pottery were recovered from both phases of the ring gully. These included fragments from a rounded shoulder, possibly of Early Iron Age date, in the earlier gully. One small piece of Early Bronze Age pottery, possibly from a Beaker, occurred as a residual item in the later cut.

Table 8: Dimensions of Features associated with Structure 5

Feature	Length	Width	Diameter	Depth
F230			0.4	0.25
F231			0.5	0.18
F78	1.7	0.9		N/A
F109			0.3	0.7
F110			0.3	0.5
F111			0.3	0.3
F112			0.3	0.3

Structure 6 (Plate 12)

Structure 6, directly south of the first structure, had a very similar form to it, with a circular ditch (F222) of 9.5m diameter and U-shaped profile (fig.24, S46-7). There was a 3.6m wide entrance in the eastern side and the fills of the ditch were silt sands. Internally there were several possible post/stake-holes. Two of these (F226 and F228) were located either side of the entrance, while another (F224) was located approximately centrally. Five metres to the east of Structure 6 was a truncated pit, only 0.13m deep, which may have been associated with it.

Table 9: Dimensions of Features Associated with Structure 6

Feature	Length	Width	Diameter	Depth
F224			0.15	0.14
F226	0.7	0.37		0.10
F227			0.5	0.22
F228			0.5	0.12
F232	1.5	1.1		0.13

Structure 7

There were inter-cutting structures further south, Structures 7 to 9, of which structure 7 was the earliest. Both of these structures were similar to Structures 5 and 6, circular with an entrance to the east (the entrance to Structure 7 was assumed to lie outside the excavated area). The ditch (F234) of Structure 7 had a diameter of 11.5m, with a shallow U-shaped profile and a depth of between 0.20 and 0.30m (Fig.24, S49). It was filled with a brown silt-sand deposit. There was no evidence of internal features, which may be due to a plough furrow that ran through the middle of the structure. One small, fresh Iron Age sherd was found in the fill of the ring gully F234.

Structures 8 and 9

Structure 8 was 13.0m in diameter and was defined by a deeper U-shaped ditch (F236), averaging 0.40m in depth. This ditch was cut by a sub-circular gully (F237, Structure 9), that seemed to be a smaller version of the original ditch, with an entrance on the eastern side and a much shallower and narrower U-shaped profile (Fig.24, S48, S50-51). Located at the southern terminal of Structure 8 was a bowl-shaped pit (F239), possibly associated with the later ring gully (F237) as it cut the southern terminal of the earlier ditch. Internally, there was a cluster of post/stake-holes (F243-247, F251-F252 and F254), located approximately centrally, the deepest of which (F254) was 0.33m deep, although they were mostly around 0.2m deep. They were all circular and ranged in diameter from 0.25m (F246) to 0.66m (F244) and were filled with a silty-sand and gravel deposit. It

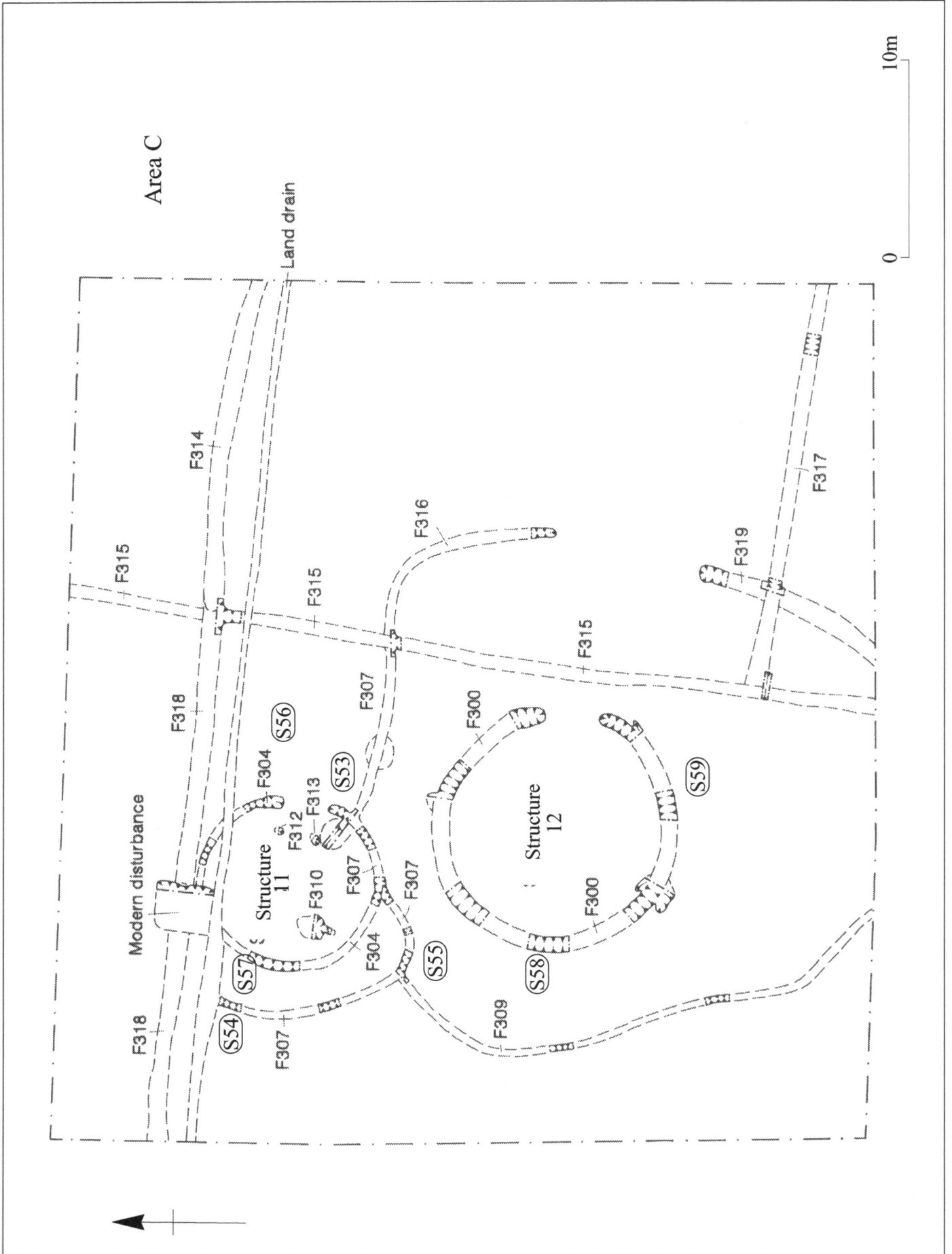

Fig. 25: Area C: Plan of all excavated features

was difficult to determine any pattern to these features, or to assign them to Structure 8 or Structure 9. A single large, but moderately abraded, sherd of Iron Age pottery was found in the terminal of gully F237.

Table 10: Dimensions of Features Associated with Structures 8 and 9

Feature	Length	Width	Diameter	Depth
F243			0.4	0.25
F244			0.66	0.25
F245			0.25	0.1
F246			0.25	0.18
F247			0.4	0.12
F251			0.4	0.22
F252			0.4	0.18
F254			0.45	0.33

Structure 10

To the west of Structures 8 and 9 was a semicircular ditch (F253), which may have been the ploughed-out remains of sixth structure of similar construction. It had a U-shaped profile, 0.25m deep.

Relationships between the Structures

Stratigraphic relationships show that Structure 9 cut Structure 8 which cut Structure 7, and that Structure 5 was of two phases. Occupation is likely therefore to have been long lived. Structures 5 and 6 may have formed a pair of buildings similar to those postulated for Area A. Structures 7, 8 and 9 were successive and may have been related to other structures beyond the margin of the excavation area to the east.

Area C (Fig.25; Plate 13)

Enclosure

Structure 11 was surrounded by a curvilinear ditch, which appeared to form an enclosure around it. The U-shaped enclosure ditch varied from 0.15m to 0.40m in depth and was made up of F316 and F319 on the eastern side of the enclosure, with a 7.0m wide entrance in this side and slightly bulbous northern and southern terminals. The northern side of the enclosure was defined by F307, which cut across the ditch of Structure 12 and turned north, where the end of the ditch was obscured by the cut for a modern land-drain (Fig.26). The western limit of the enclosure (F309) appeared to be the earliest ditch, as it was cut by F307, and it may have continued to form the southern extent of the enclosure, which was presumed to be outside the excavated area but was not identified during the watching brief.

Structure 11

Structure 11 comprised a ring gully (F306), c.9.0m in diameter, with an entrance on the eastern side. In the interior of this structure were two post-holes (F312 and F313), either side of the entrance, just behind the terminals, and a sub-circular feature (F310) with a possible channel leading into it. There was also an area of disturbed soil just to the west of the southern ditch terminal, which appeared to be root

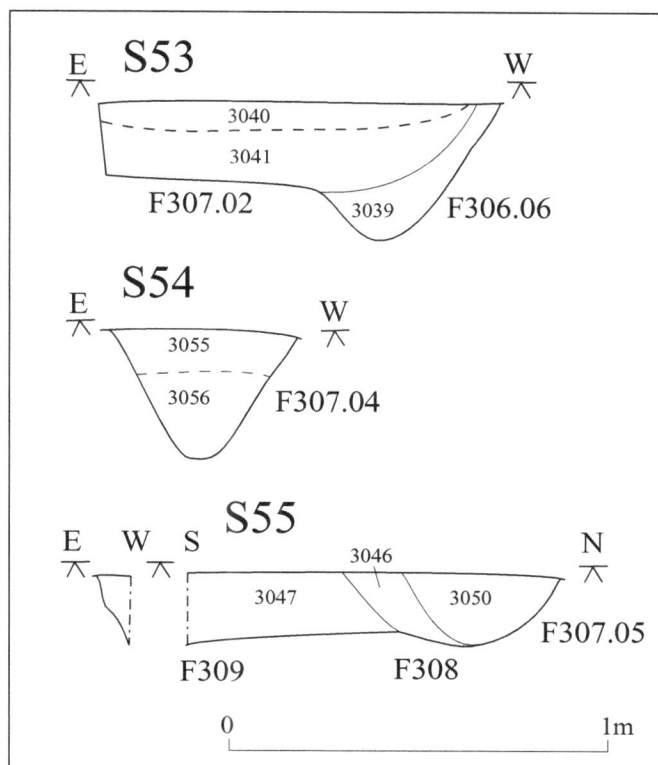

Fig. 26: Area C: Period 2 ditch sections

disturbance. The original, circular ditch (F306) was between 0.30 and 0.45m deep with a sharp, V-shaped profile. This ditch had been re-cut in one section with a U-shaped ditch (F305) of 0.25m depth (Fig.27, S57). The ditch had been finally redefined in the form of a shallow U-shaped ditch (F304) that had a sharper V-shaped profile in two sections (Fig.27, S56). The terminals were rounded, although the northern terminal was slightly bulbous.

Table 11: Features Associated with Structure 11

Feature	Length	Width	Diameter	Depth
F310	1.21			0.24
F312			0.44	0.15
F313			0.40	0.33

Structure 12

Structure 12 comprised a ring gully (F300), 13.0m in diameter, again with an entrance on the eastern side. No internal features could be identified. The ring gully had a V-shaped profile, 0.50 to 0.60m deep, and was predominantly filled with a brown sandy-silt deposit. Its terminals were rounded. This original ditch had been re-cut twice, although not visibly at the terminals. The earlier re-cut (F301) was U-shaped with an average depth of 0.40m, and the final re-cut (F302) had a similar profile but was not as deep (Fig. 27, S58-9). In some sections, the cut for the final re-cut (F302) had obscured that for the earlier one (F301). Four sherds of undiagnostic Iron Age pottery were found in the fill of the ring gully.

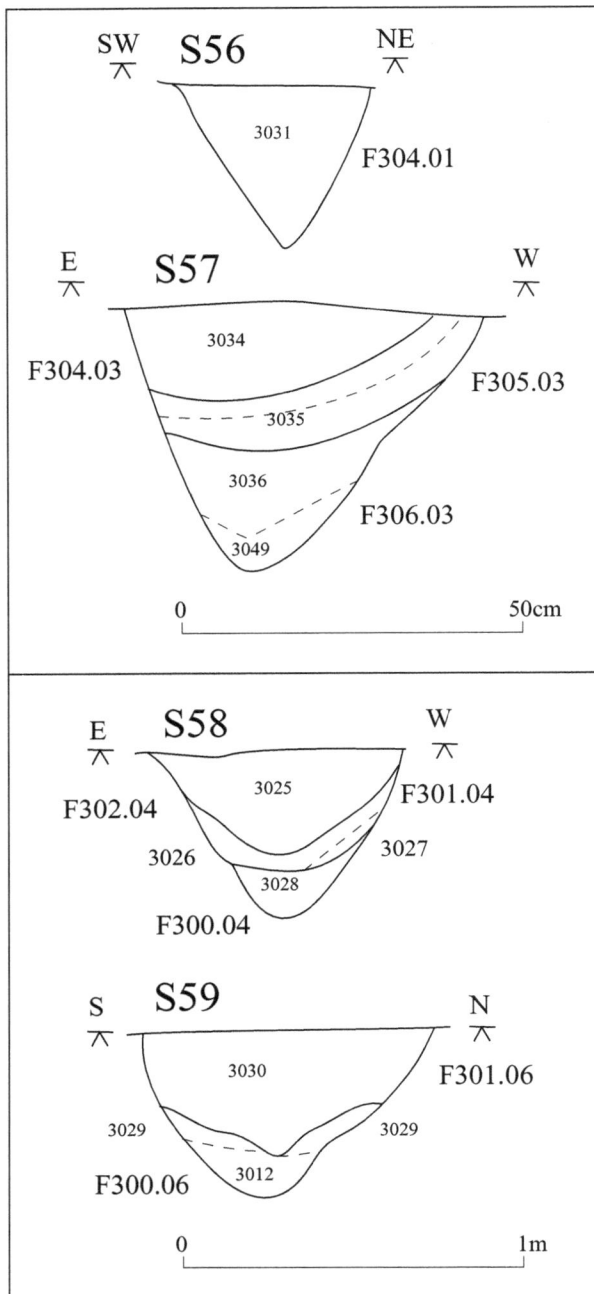

Fig. 27: Area C: Period 2 structures and sections

12 continues to exist, but a more likely explanation is that it has been abandoned or annexed as part of the enclosure.

Watching Brief (Fig. 44)

To the east of an undated enclosure (F910) was an irregular semicircular ditched feature (F913), U-shaped in profile and generally not more than 0.30m deep, although the western terminal was 0.55m deep. A gully (F917) cut across this, although the square cut and humic fill of the former suggested that it was of modern agricultural origin. A few pottery sherds of Iron Age date were recovered from an excavated section of the ditched feature (F913.02), but there was insufficient evidence to determine the function of this feature, although it did not appear to be a plough-damaged hut circle.

Of the other unassociated features identified during the topsoil stripping of this phase, the most notable was a 2.5m-diameter bowl-shaped pit (F903) of 0.90m depth and filled with three layers of silt-sands. The lower fill (9006) of this pit contained sherds from three Late Bronze Age/Early Iron Age vessels and the upper fill (9005) sherds from at least five Iron Age vessels. A small post-hole (F904) was found directly southeast of this feature, but otherwise there were no associated structures or enclosures in its vicinity. The unabraded material from the lower fill (9006) was of average sherd weight 15g. It included fragments from a high-necked jar, a small ellipsoid vessel and a round shouldered jar (Fig. 37, 1, 2 and 3). Also from this layer came a discoidal flint scraper, apparently of Beaker/Early Bronze Age type. This may have been a residual item, or could have been deliberately deposited as an heirloom, or possibly could have been manufactured in the Iron Age period (see *Worked Flint*, below).

A small amount of intrusive material was recovered from pit F903 (9005), in association with the Iron Age vessels. The intrusive material comprised a Black-Burnished ware straight-sided dish and a Central Gaulish (Lezoux) Drag. 18/31, both of mid 2nd-century AD date.

A separate feature, F923, a 1.5m-diameter bowl-shaped pit of 0.52m depth and filled with three layers of silt-sands (9039, 9040 and 9041) was located between excavation Areas A, B and C (see Fig. 44). The upper grey clay-silt (9039) contained the upper stone from a beehive quern, made from Coal Measures quartz arenite (see *Worked Stone*, below).

Period 3 Romano-British

Droveway

The cropmark plot suggested the existence of an approximately north-south aligned droveway running throughout the length of the Whitemoor Haye quarry concession (see Fig. 45). This droveway appeared to be defined by single or, in some places, double ditches on the east and west sides. Evaluation trenches in 1992 and 1995 identified parts of the droveway but failed to date it or more

Relationship between the Enclosure and Structures

Although the artefactual evidence was inconclusive, the stratigraphic relationships suggest possible sub-phases for time, defined by the original ditches of F306 and F300, but not surrounded by any form of enclosure ditch. Phase (ii) saw the redefinition of Structures 11 and 12 in the form of the re-cut ditches, F301 and F304. In Phase (iii), Structure 11 had its final redefinition, in the form of the ditch F302 and is surrounded by an enclosure ditch, F307, F309, F316 and F319. In this phase, it is possible that the phase (ii) Structure

34

closely identify its function. It was more extensively investigated during the 1997 and 1998 area excavations and the subsequent watching brief.

Area S (see Fig. 45)

An access route excavated to allow the machines passage in and out of Area S during its initial strip, without disturbing the surrounding crop, revealed three parallel north-south ditches. Two ditches, F500 and F501, seem to relate to the continuation of the droveway ditches identified in Areas B and T, and during the watching brief. The easternmost of these (F500) was 3.9m wide and 0.3m deep, with a shallow U-shaped profile. The second (F501) had a much steeper V-shaped profile (Fig. 28). Measuring 1.6m wide and 0.48m deep, it had been filled with two distinct silt deposits.

Area T (see Fig. 12)

The western side of the droveway was delineated by a V-shaped ditch (F118), 0.40m deep, on a north-south alignment. This had been cut by a later, U-shaped ditch (F105), with a shallower, 0.30m deep, profile, but following the same course as the original ditch (Fig. 29; S62 and S63). The only stratified artefacts from the whole of Area T came from a section of the original ditch (F118), from a brown silt-sand (1041). A small V-shaped linear feature (F119) ran parallel with the ditch re-cut (F105) in the northeastern corner of the area, and disappeared in F105.04. This may indicate that this ditch was earlier than both the re-cut (F105) and the original ditch (F118). On the eastern side of the droveway was a double ditch marking its edge. The earlier of these ditches appeared to be the westernmost (F109), although it was difficult to differentiate between the very similar fills of both ditches. This ditch had a U-shaped profile, with a general depth of 0.30m (Fig. 29; S64). The later ditch (F110) had a very similar profile and depth to the earlier one.

Dating Evidence

Three sherds of Central Gaulish (Les Martres-de-Veyre) samian from a Drag 37 bowl were recovered from ditch F118.04 (1041). These were dated to AD100-125/130 and have an average sherd weight of 10g.

Area B (see Fig. 22)

Two ditches that demarcate the north-south droveway were identified in this area. On the western side was a U-shaped ditch (F200), 0.40m deep, cut on its eastern side by another U-shaped ditch (F201), 0.50m in depth (Fig. 30; S65). F201 was filled with a grey/brown silt-sand and gravel deposit (2002). The other side of the droveway was delineated by a similar ditch (F202), approximately 10.0m east of F201. In the north of this area there was the remainder of a small V-shaped ditch (F203) which ran parallel to the eastern ditch (Fig. 30; S66). The northern sections of the eastern ditch were 0.40m deep, with steep sides and a flat bottom, whereas the southern sections had a slightly deeper V-shaped profile. In the southwest corner of Area B was a bowl-shaped pit (F215), 1.0m deep, cut into the eastern droveway ditch. It is noticeable that the eastern ditch of the droveway changes its course to run parallel with the earlier enclosure ditch (F262).

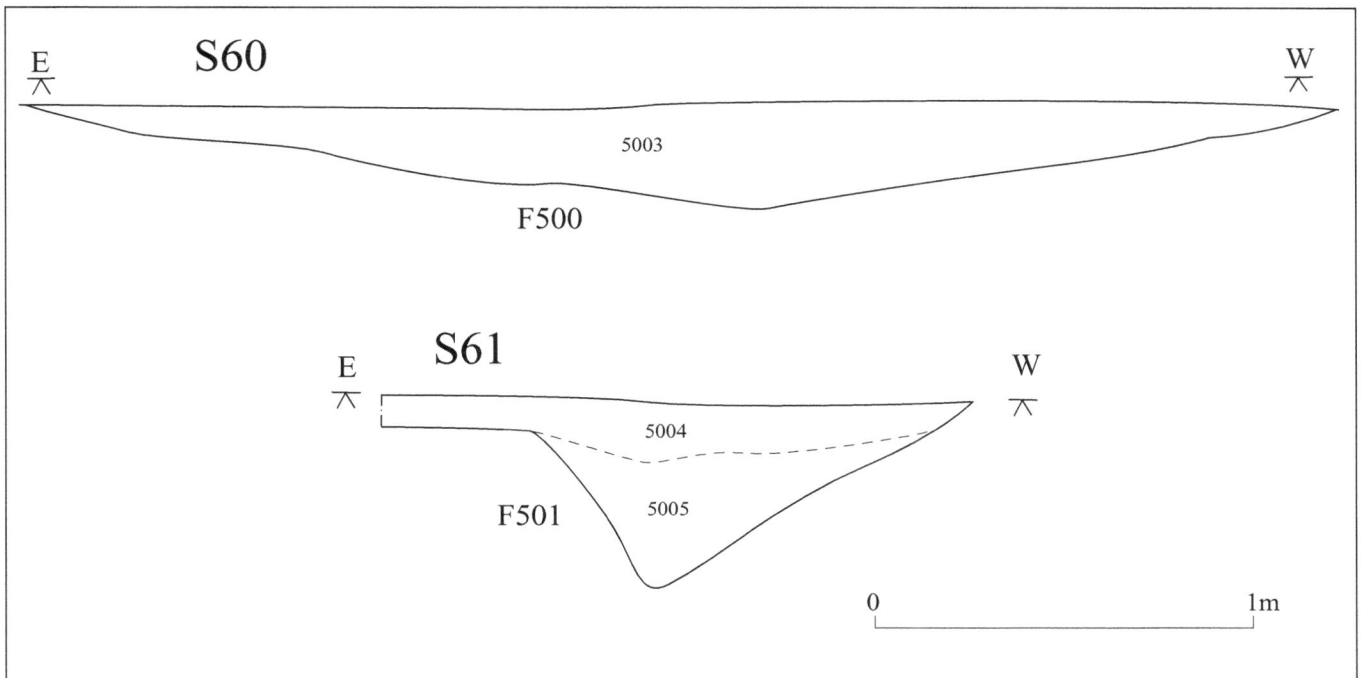

Fig. 28: Area S: Period 3 droveway ditch sections

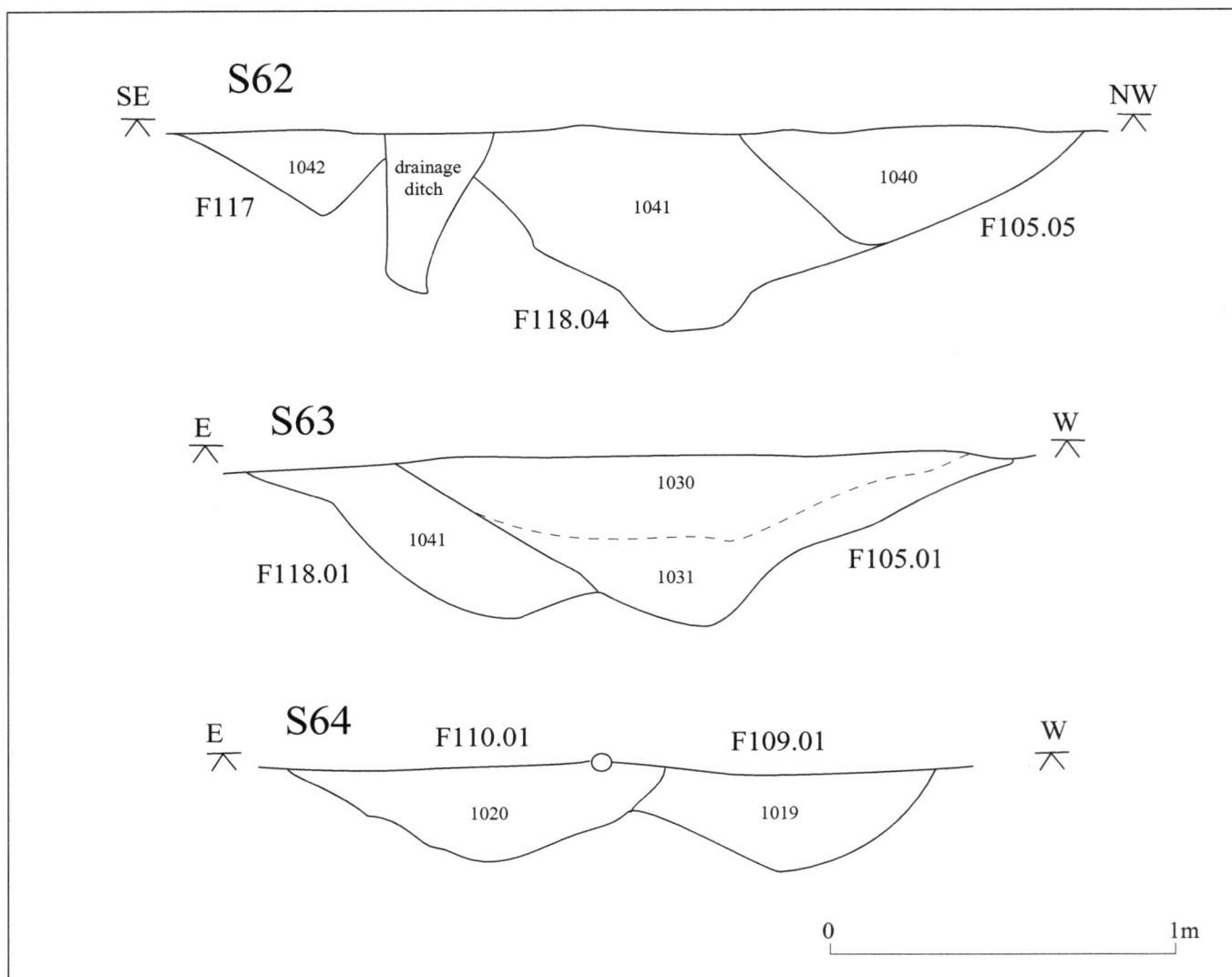

Fig. 29: Area T: Period 3 droveway ditch sections

There was evidence of an earlier ditch (F207) that ran in the same direction as the enclosure ditch's western side for approximately 40m, and appeared to have a flat-bottomed profile, 0.20m deep, with steep sides. This, however, was cut by eastern ditch of the droveway (F202) along the majority of its length (see Fig. 23; S40 and S41).

Some 85 sherds, with an average sherd weight of 10g, could be assigned to features from within Area B. All of the feature sherds derived from ditch F201, along with 80% of the Area B pottery. Severn Valley ware comprised some 65% of the pottery recovered from F201. This assemblage could be dated to the mid 2nd/late 3rd century AD. Diagnostic pieces comprised three wide-mouthed jars with pointed bead rims in oxidised Severn Valley ware and a single Black-Burnished ware cooking pot with near upright or slightly everted rim. Two sherds of Derbyshire coarseware with evidence of external sooting were recovered from F201 (2002). Other datable material included three sherds of Central Gaulish (Lezoux) samian also dating to the mid-late 2nd/early 3rd century AD. A small quantity of Black-Burnished ware, reduced Severn Valley ware and residual southwest

England/south Wales (Caerleon) mortaria was recovered from ditch F200. A small amount of coarse sandy white ware (P04.1) was recovered from ditch F200.02 (2006) and could be dated to the 2nd century AD.

Area T Droveway Interior (see Fig. 12)

A number of irregular-shaped features lay within the interior of the droveway (F114, F121, F123, F124, F132 and 1084) and may have been associated with some repair to the route, especially as the grey sandy-gravel fill of these features was unique to the interior of these ditches. It is also a possibility that this group of features represent the remains of a gateway structure, if the Iron Age pit alignment represented a boundary, which was still respected in this period. F124 is the only surviving post-hole and F121, F123 and F114 may possibly be the remains of a rectangular gully. The large pit F132 remains an enigma, but could still be associated with a gateway. The evidence from these features supports either interpretation. F123 and F124 contained single sherds of Post-Medieval pottery; these were probably intrusive.

36

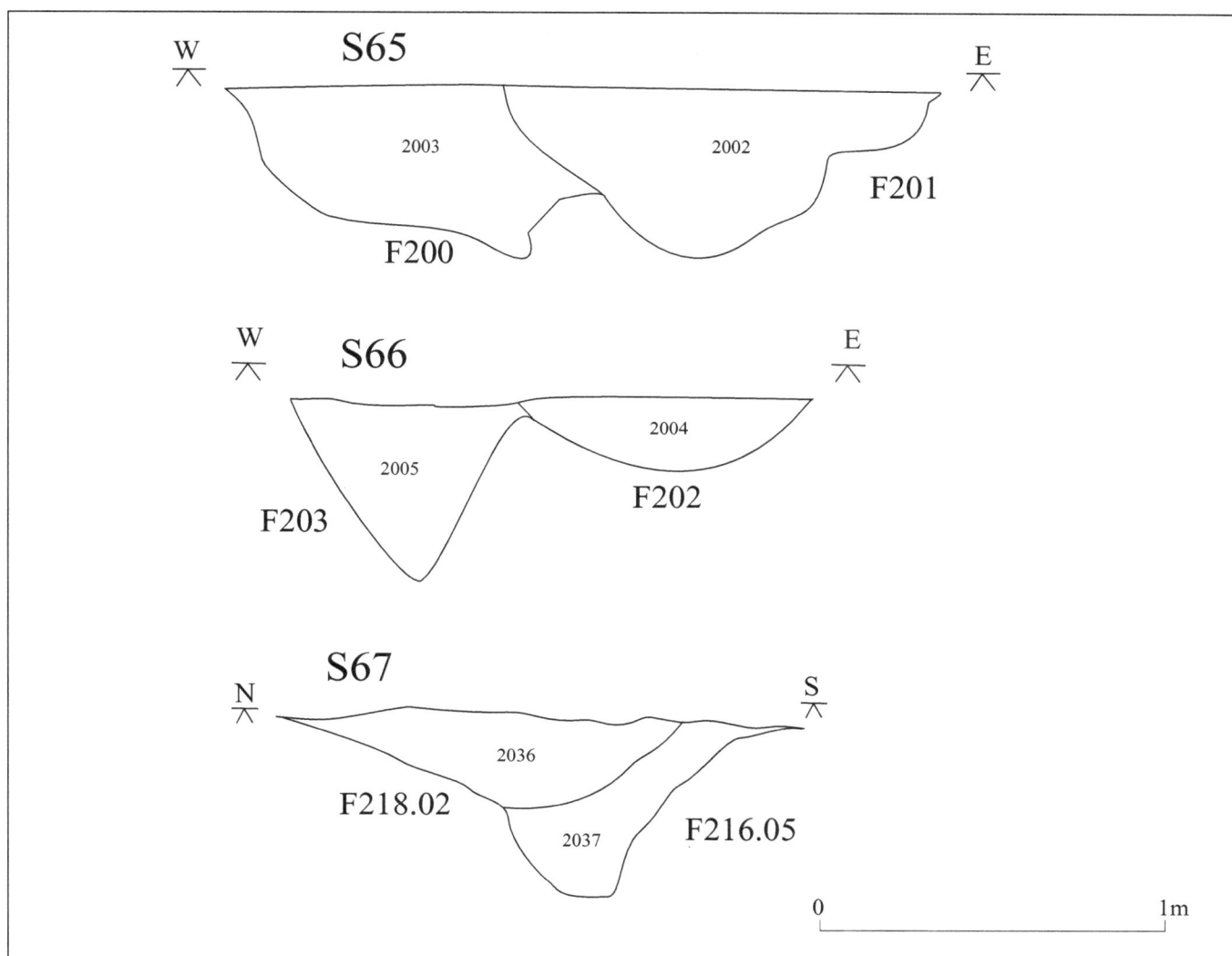

Fig. 30: Area B: Period 3 droveway ditch sections

Pit F132 cutting F133, had an ovoid shape, with steep sides to a depth of 0.90m, which might suggest that this particular feature was a small section of ditch more closely associated with the droveway ditches than the pit alignment.

Enclosures and Boundaries

Area S (see Fig. 9)

A small ditch, F521, lay on the same alignment as the pits, perpendicular to the direction of both the Romano-British ditches and the Post-Medieval plough furrows. It had a U-shaped profile, 0.60m wide and 0.25m deep, and was later than the re-cuts of the pit alignment and appeared to be cut by F503, the Romano-British ditch.

The westernmost of the Romano-British ditches (F503) had a similar alignment to the Post-Medieval plough furrows, as did all the ditches from this period. It had a V-shaped profile, was 0.9m deep and filled with three layers of silting in the northern section (F503.01) and two in the southern section (F503.02) (Fig. 31; S68). A smaller ditch (F506) to the east had a steeper U-shaped profile in its northern section

(F506.01) than in its southern section (F506.02), although the depth remained constant at 0.30m (Fig. 31; S69). It was filled with a brown silty sand, with a small percentage of stones. Parallel to this ditch was a third (F507) similar to the westernmost ditch (F503) and between 0.68m and 0.86m deep. This original ditch had been re-cut by a shallower U-shaped ditch (F505) which was filled with three different layers of brown silt-sand (5012, 5013 and 5014) (Fig. 31; S70).

A total of 76 sherds, with an average sherd weight of 21g, was recovered from three ditch sections within this area. The southern section of ditch F506.02 produced 42 sherds of Romano-British pottery. Several diagnostic forms were recognised, a Black-Burnished ware cooking pot, with near upright or slightly everted rim (Fig. 39.3) and three reduced Severn Valley ware forms: a curving-sided bowl with pointed bead rim (Fig. 39.5), a necked jar with simple bead rim and a necked jar with an everted rim. Ditch F505.02 produced two dateable forms: a lid-seated (bell-mouthed jar) with an internal ridge or ledge on which a lid might rest in Derbyshire coarseware, and a Mancetter-Hartshill bead and curved flange mortaria (Fig. 39.13) dated to 165-180 AD.

37

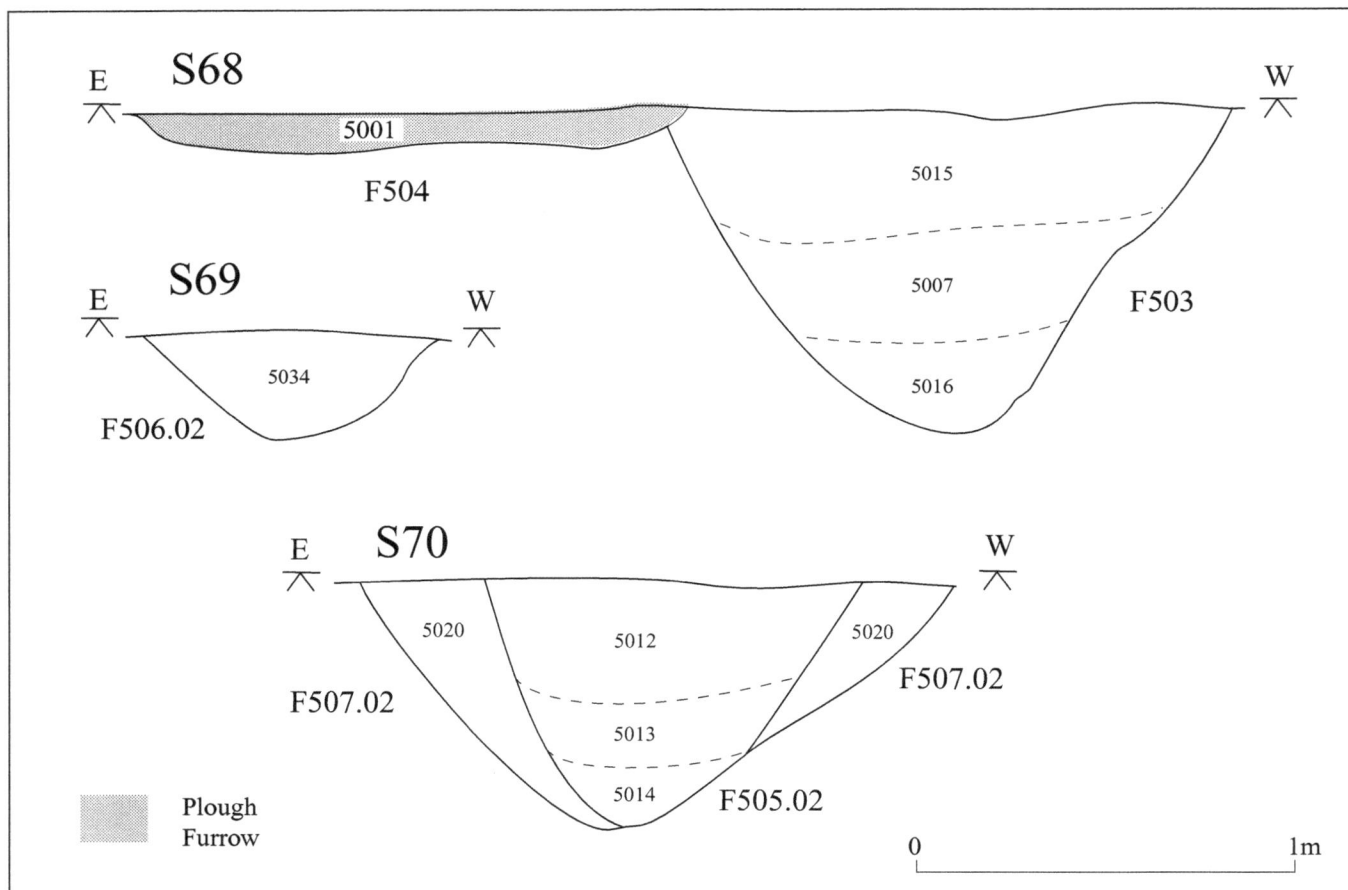

Fig. 31: Area S: Period 3 enclosure ditch sections

Additionally, a single sherd of Central Gaulish (Lezoux) samian could be dated to 150-200AD. Seven sherds showing evidence of external sooting were recovered from F505.02 and F506.02. From the westernmost ditch F503, no datable rim forms were recognised, although a single sherd of East Gaulish (Rheinzabern) samian from a Drag 31 bowl was dated to 150-225AD.

Watching Brief

Excavations and observations during the watching brief revealed the full extent of F503 and F505, which defined a rectangular enclosure with an entrance on the southwestern side (Fig. 9). This enclosure closely matched that observed from aerial photographs and subsequently located on the cropmark plot. Two ditches, F1 and F2, sampled in the 1992 Evaluation Trench 1, also relate to the enclosure ditch. The enclosure measured 40m northeast to southwest and 42-3m in an approximate east-west direction. Excavated sections revealed shallow U-shaped ditches at the corners of the enclosure (F101.01, F101.03 and F101.04), filled with two layers of silt-sand, and a rounded terminal, F101.02, with a steeper U-shaped profile on the western side of the entrance. A truncated stake-hole (F102) was located in the middle of this 4m wide entrance, and may have been part of a gate assembly of some description.

A New Red Sandstone quern fragment was found in F101.02 (see *Worked Stone*, below).

Pottery

A total of 158 sherds was recovered from Area S under watching brief conditions. Thirty-eight percent of the pottery recovered comprised Black-Burnished ware. A small quantity of seven sherds of Derbyshire coarseware was recovered from F101.01. No diagnostic pieces were recovered from this ditch section. Some 51 sherds were recovered which demonstrated external sooting.

Very small quantities of oxidised, reduced and grog tempered Severn Valley wares were recovered from F101.02. Three dateable forms were recognised. These are two cooking pots with upright and slightly everted rim (Fig. 39.4), and a curving-sided bowl with bead rim. Additionally, two lid-seated (bell-mouthed) jars with an internal ridge or ledge on which a lid might rest (Figs. 39.6-7) were recorded, along with a curving-sided bowl with bead rim (Fig. 39.8) and a wide-mouthed jar with everted rim (Fig. 39.10). A single residual sherd of South Gaulish (La Graufesenque) samian was recovered and could be dated to 70-100 AD. This was associated with a single sherd of Dressel 20 amphorae and a greyware of probable local source. Overall this feature could be dated to the mid-late 2nd/early 3rd century AD.

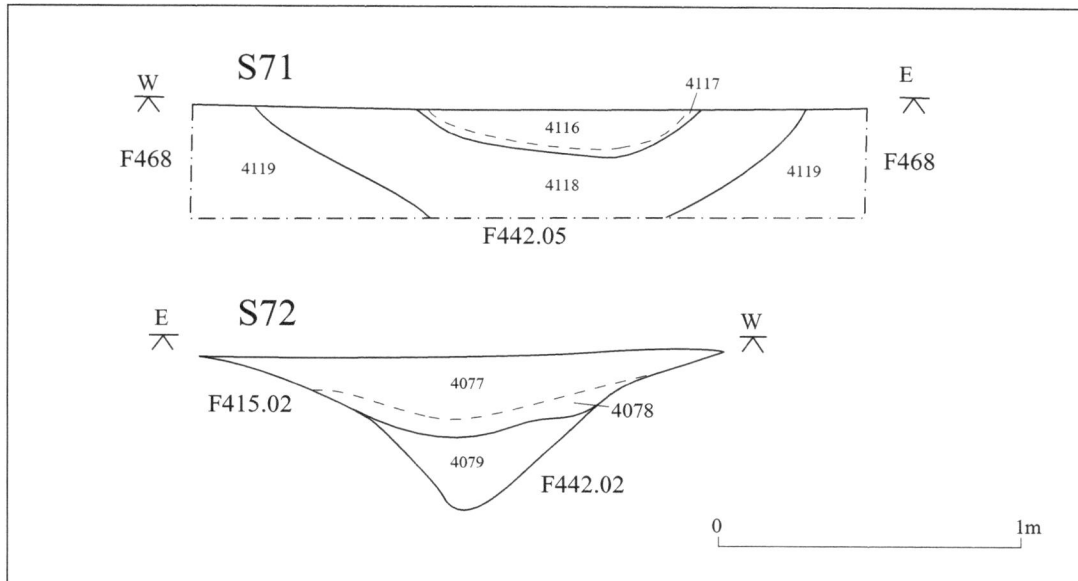

Fig. 32: Area A: Period 3 enclosure ditch sections

Area A (see Fig. 17; Plate 9)

A series of ditches in this area were possibly associated with the Romano-British field system and droveway. A U-shaped ditch (F442) ran north-south across the enclosure and continued south beyond the excavated area. It had been re-cut by a shallower ditch (F415), 0.35m deep and of similar profile (Fig. 32, S71-2). Both ditches were filled with similar silt-sand deposits. The ditches cut a smaller linear channel (F446), of possible geological origin, and the western side of Structure 3 (see Fig. 19; S29).

In the northeast corner of the site there was another ditch of Romano-British date (F443), aligned east-west. It appeared to terminate in the enclosure ditch, had a V-shaped profile and was filled with an orange/brown silt-sand and gravel deposit. In the southeast corner were two more Romano-British ditches (F447 and F449), which were also east-west aligned and continued beyond the eastern edge of the excavated area. What appeared to be the earlier of the two (F447) had to the east a U-shaped profile, but this became wider and shallower as it approached the enclosure ditch. The later ditch (F449), with a shallow U-shaped profile, cut both the earlier ditch and the enclosure ditch. Both ditches were filled with silt-sand deposits.

These ditches (F443, F447 and F449) may have joined with open lengths of the Iron Age ditch, F468, to form a rectangular enclosure with F415 and the westernmost droveway ditch. A

group of briquetage fragments were found in the fill of ditch F447.

A total of 16 sherds, with an average sherd weight of 28g, were recovered from this area. Only two diagnostic rim forms were recognised, both are wide-mouthed jars with simple everted rims and occur in reduced Severn Valley ware and a calcite-gritted ware from ditch F443. Three sherds of Derbyshire coarseware with evidence of external sooting were recovered from ditch F449 (4093). Other undiagnostic material was recovered from ditches F415, F445 and F455. The small volume of pottery from this area dated to the mid-late 2nd century AD.

Watching Brief

During the topsoil stripping to the east of Area A, the continuation of these ditches were observed; in particular where the westernmost droveway ditch (F926) was cut by or cut F443, F447 and F449 (Fig. 45). Ditch F447 appeared to be cut by ditch F926, whereas both F443 and F449 cut F926. This corroborates the stratigraphic evidence obtained from the area excavation where F447 was earlier than F449. It may have been the case that F447 was dug to form an earlier enclosure, which was later superseded by the rectangular enclosure formed by F415, F443, F449 and the droveway ditch F926. The evidence also suggests that this enclosure was constructed later than the droveway itself.

39

The evidence from Area A and the associated watching brief strongly suggests that the main enclosure existed over several hundred years from the Iron Age until well into the Romano-British period. The function of the enclosure changed throughout this period from a domestic-based enclosure to one of solely agricultural use, although the principal activity would have been farming throughout this period.

Area B (see Fig. 22 and Fig. 45)

An earlier ditch (F207), which apparently formed part of the sequence of ditches defining the eastern side of the droveway, was joined at right angles by two east-west aligned ditches (F216 and F223). The latter, of U-shaped profile and 0.35m deep, cut across Structure 5 and turned north until it terminated just before the enclosure ditch. The more southerly (F216), with a V-shaped profile between 0.40 and 0.70m deep, continued eastwards, where it and appeared to turn into a double ditched feature, being accompanied by a shallow gully (F218) (see Fig. 30; S67).

Area C (see Fig. 25)

Area C was traversed by a series of straight ditches, the earliest of which (F317) was located in the southeastern corner. It had an east-west alignment with a U-shaped profile and cut across one of the enclosure ditches (F319) before terminating at the point where it was cut by a north-south aligned ditch (F315). This latter ditch had an almost identical profile and fill, and ran right across the excavated area, again cutting one of the enclosure ditches (F316).

A single sherd of Derbyshire coarseware of 2nd century date was recovered from ditch F315.01 (3062), that was aligned north-south. The sherd weight of 4g suggests that this sherd is more than likely residual. These two linear ditches, together with a third, undated ditch (F314/F318), which cuts across ditch F315 at right angles, may all form part of the Romano-British field system. However, if the sherd is residual, then it is possible that they were part of the Post-Medieval agricultural landscape; the available evidence is inconclusive.

Period 4 Post-Medieval

Plough Furrows

The remains of plough furrows were observed in several areas, generally with a north-south alignment, although there were some east-west examples in Areas B and F. The degree to which they had truncated earlier features varied, although they appeared to be particularly deep in Areas S and R.

Other Features

Area F (see Fig. 15)

Located east-west across the centre of this area was a gully (F803), which was later than F802, and had a V-shaped profile with a depth of 0.33m. The similarity of its dark

brown sandy silt fill to the topsoil may suggest that this was a modern agricultural feature.

Area R (see Fig. 6)

In the south of the area was a small gully aligned east-west (F600/F601) that had a small break of less than 1.0m in the middle of it. With a depth of 0.12m and width of 0.30m, it seemed likely that this was the remains of a former fence line or drainage channel. There were several irregular features that appear to have been associated with this gully, both on its northern and southern sides, of which only two (F624 and F605) gave any indication that they may have been archaeological in nature. The former (F624) had a bowl shape and was 0.27m deep. The only indication that it may have been archaeological was a higher percentage of charcoal flecking in its brown sandy fill (6033) than in the other features. The latter (F605) was a small circular feature, with a pointed base, 0.20m deep, which may have been a stake-hole.

A second linear feature (F608) ran east-west under the southern limit of excavation of Area R and may have been a field boundary, which would explain the root disturbance to its north.

These features combine to form a possible fence line and associated bank and ditch, which ran parallel and within a few metres north of an existing trackway.

Dating Evidence

A number of iron objects, nails and copper alloy objects were recovered from the features associated with the gully F600-1, and, although heavily corroded, their survival in such alkaline conditions would indicate that they were deposited in the Post-Medieval period.

Area T (see Fig. 12)

The Post-Medieval activity was characterised by two roughly parallel ditches (F112 and F113) with a northwest to southeast alignment but slightly converging in the southeast. Brick rubble of 19th- or 20th-century date was included in the finds recovered from lengths of F113. A large bowl-shaped pit (F134) also cut F109, F110 and F112.

Undated

Area C (see Fig. 25)

A north-south linear ditch (F315), tentatively dated to the Roman period, was cut at right angles by a 1.0m-wide east-west aligned ditch (F318 and F314). The two ditches may be elements of either a Romano-British or Post-Medieval field system.

Area F (see Fig. 15)

A possible pit (F808) lay immediately to the north of a short segment of ditch (F806) associated with the triple ditch system. It contained a single burnt sherd of Central Gaul (Lezoux) samian. This could be dated to 120-200 AD. The feature had a bowl shape and was 0.52m in depth. A further feature (F816), in the southeast corner of Area F, may have been a truncated, shallow, flat-bottomed, circular pit. This pit was next to a narrow gully (F814), aligned northeast to southwest. A possible isolated post-hole (F818) lay in the southwest corner of the area.

In the northeastern corner of Area F was a large oval pit (F822) which cut an irregular-shaped feature (F821), which may have been tree root disturbance or geological activity that pre-dated the pit (see Fig. 16; S22). The silted up layers of the pit were cut by a smaller pit (F823) of similar shape. Both these pits were cut by a small linear feature (F824) aligned southwest to northeast, with shallow sloping sides to a depth of 0.20m, which could only be seen in a 4.0m length and may have been caused by modern agricultural disturbance. To the south and southeast of the pit were two possible shallow post-holes (F820 and F819), both of which may have been associated with the pits.

Area R (see Fig. 6)

A number of features (F616/617, F623, F625 and F626) cut in the same vicinity as the central pits may have been archaeological in nature. However, their irregular shape and the nature of their fills, combined with the absence of datable artefacts, make it very difficult to associate these features with any particular period of activity. A small gully (F622) was cut in the northwest corner of the area. Aligned approximately southwest to northeast and 0.16m deep, it contained an orange sandy gravel deposit, which was difficult to distinguish from the surrounding natural sand and gravel. This may indicate that F622 was geological in origin.

Area S (see Fig. 9)

Ditch F515, in the southwest corner of the area, had a similar alignment to both the pit alignment and the Romano-British enclosure. It had a shallow U-shaped profile, 0.6m wide and 0.25m deep, and could be associated with either Romano-British or later agricultural activity.

Watching Brief (see Fig. 44)

An enclosure, to the northwest of Area A, had a trapezoidal shape with the southern ditch running into the limit of the Phase 2 topsoil stripping. The ditch (F910) which defined this enclosure was generally U-shaped in profile with a depth of between 0.30 and 0.88m, and was filled with a grey-brown sandy silt. The variation in the recorded depth of this feature was due to the degree of truncation inflicted by the machining. A possible entrance was identified in the western side, defined either end by the rounded southern and northern terminals of the enclosure ditch. No internal archaeological features were recorded and, with no artefacts recovered from the ditch itself, it was impossible to date or adequately characterise this feature.

THE FINDS

Worked Flint *by Lynne Bevan*

Six items of humanly-worked flint were recovered, comprising a scraper (9006/F903), a retouched flake/possible arrowhead blank (1082/F83), a core fragment (5058/F526) and three unretouched flakes (Trench 20/1000, Trench 32/1016, and 4082/F445). This small collection is not chronologically-diagnostic, although the retouched flake/possible arrowhead blank might represent an early stage in arrowhead manufacture. If this was the case (and the fragment has not been sufficiently modified to be certain) it is most likely that a barbed and tanged arrowhead of Beaker/Early Bronze Age date was the intended form. While scrapers are not generally chronologically-diagnostic, discoidal forms like the one recovered are generally associated with the Beaker/Early Bronze Age period. The core fragment, from which broad flakes have been detached from three platforms, also appears to be of Bronze Age date. However, in this instance, dating of both the scraper and the core is problematic since they were both recovered from Iron Age features.

Based upon the thin compacted remnant cortex visible on some of the fragments, the material used was pebble flint from a secondary source, probably local river gravels or boulder clay deposits. The flints were all small in size, and with the exception of the scraper and retouched flake/possible arrowhead blank, consisted of knapping debris. Two of the flakes terminated in hinge fractures suggesting that the flint, in common with most flint from secondary deposits, was of an unpredictable quality. It is equally possible that the flint was struck during the Bronze Age when flintworking techniques were in decline (Ford, *et al.* 1984), or even that the flint (excluding the possible arrowhead blank of Beaker/Early Bronze Age date) was worked during the Iron Age. This possibility is supported by the fact that two of the flints - the scraper and one of the flakes - were found in pit fills containing Iron Age pottery (see Prehistoric Pottery, below). Although these two flints might have been residual, an Iron Age date cannot be ruled out and there are numerous examples of Iron Age sites with potentially contemporary lithic assemblages. For example, an Iron Age date has been proposed for an assemblage from Fisherwick (Smith 1979, 67-68, Fig.19) containing a similarly-shaped scraper to the one in this collection, which was also made upon a core rejuvenation flake. In addition, at Aston-upon-Trent, May interpreted a small flint assemblage recovered from the excavation of an Iron Age square enclosure, possibly a barrow, as being of Iron Age origin, rather than being residual, earlier material (May 1970, 16-18). At the Middle Iron Age settlement site at Wanlip, Leicestershire it was felt that a proportion of the large lithic assemblage was contemporary with the settlement. This was based upon the low incidence of residuality and the poor technology employed in the knapping process (Cooper and Humphrey 1998).

At the assessment stage it was suggested that the flint might have been deliberately deposited in certain features as an act of 'structured deposition' (Richards and Thomas 1984; Hill 1993) rather than as the result of casual discard. Certainly, the discovery of the scraper in a bowl-shaped pit of Early-Middle Iron Age date (F903) with Iron Age pottery suggests that it might have been deliberately deposited, whether or not it was of Early Bronze Age date or contemporary with the pottery. Research has been conducted upon the curation of prehistoric lithic material in Roman votive contexts (Ferris and Smith 1996) and the possibility that earlier stone tools were collected and deposited by Iron Age people, perhaps as potential 'antiques' with magico-religious, or even ancestral, connotations, should not be over-looked here. Similarly, the rough core fragment, which was found in a pit (F526) of the Area S pit alignment, again with Iron Age pottery, might have entered the archaeological record in the same way. However, in view of the uncertainty regarding the dating of the flint, the possibility of structured deposition has yet to be adequately demonstrated among this small collection.

Catalogue (none of the material has been illustrated)

1. Scraper made on a substantial core rejuvenation flake of opaque beige flint, roughly discoidal in shape and worked around c. 80% of its circumference. Length: 40mm, width: 30mm, thickness: 8-12mm. F903, 9006.

2. Retouched flake/possible arrowhead blank, a roughly triangular shaped, translucent brown flake. Length: 23mm, width: 25mm, thickness: 6mm. F83, 1082.

3. Flake of translucent orange-brown flint terminating in a hinge fracture. Length: 23mm, width: 25mm, thickness: 7mm. Trench 32/1016.

4. Primary flake of translucent yellow-brown flint. Length: 11mm, width: 18mm, thickness: 4mm. Trench 32, 1016.

5. Flake of translucent light brown flint, terminating in a hinge fracture. The flake is almost complete. Length: 25mm, width: 33mm, thickness: 5mm. F445, 4082.

6. Core fragment, with flake detachments from three platforms, of predominantly translucent light brown flint with partial cream-coloured re-cortication. Length: 34mm, width: 35mm, thickness: 38mm. F526, 5058.

The Prehistoric Pottery *by Ann Woodward, with contributions by Rob Ixer and Alistair Barclay*

Neolithic and Early Bronze Age

A total of 238 sherds weighing 1148g was recovered from the evaluation trenches and the main excavation. Most of these belonged to a single Beaker vessel found in Area R, but there was also a significant assemblage of Middle Neolithic Peterborough Ware from one of the 1995 evaluation trenches. The distribution of the pottery by period, type and area is shown in Table 12. Also included in this report is a description and discussion of the Beaker found in 1996 on the National Arboretum site, Alrewas.

With the exception of the fragmentary Beaker vessel from Area R, most of the material was abraded, and the overall mean sherd weight is fairly low (5g). The sherds from Areas A and B were probably residual.

Fabric *by Rob Ixer and Ann Woodward*

Four Neolithic or Early Bronze Age fabrics were defined using a hand lens, and the fabrics of the Peterborough Ware from Trenches B and AE and the Site R Beaker were examined petrographically. Full petrographic descriptions may be found in Appendix 2.

Fabric 8. Grog and ironstone inclusions. Beaker.

Fabric 9. Grog and quartz sand inclusions. Beaker and urn.
Petrography (Beaker, Site R, F612): The main fabric and the grog clasts are similar in terms of their plastic and non-plastic ratios and in the composition of the non-plastics; the latter are quartz and a little white mica. A number of grog clasts have grog within them. The raw materials are compatible with a local source from alluvial or glacial sediments or the Permo-Triassic rocks that underlie them. However, there is little that is distinctive petrographically and the pot could have been manufactured anywhere over a wide area in the Midlands.

Fabric 10. Sparse medium and large angular flint inclusions and quartz sand.

Petrography (probably late Neolithic, possibly Late Bronze Age, Trench AE, F86): Angular quartz and quartzite inclusions. The size and shape of the inclusions suggests that they derive from crushed rock, rather than sand. Limonite-rich areas are only minor in extent and a little post-burial gypsum is present. The composition of the inclusions and the clay are compatible with their having come from the local Permo-Triassic rocks or overlying sediments derived from them.

Fabric 11. Sparse but prominent medium and large angular quartz inclusions. Peterborough Ware: Fengate style.
Petrography (Trench B, F059): The non-plastics have a wide size range and comprise rounded quartz and potassium feldspars plus a number of different, highly silicified or silica-rich rocks and some mudstone clasts. If any grog is present it is very minor in amount. All the natural components of the non-plastics are highly resistant minerals and rocks and could be derived from the local Permo-Triassic 'Bunter Pebble Beds' and Mercian Mudstones or from any alluvial or glacial deposits derived from them. The petrography suggests that the pot could have been made locally. Post-burial groundwaters have deposited extensive amounts of gypsum into void spaces and this is a very distinctive and highly unusual feature.

Table 12: Distribution of Neolithic and Early Bronze Age pottery by period, type and area

Area	Feature	Type	Period	Sherd types	No. sh.	Wt. (g)	Mean sherd wt.	Fabric	Abrasion
Eval. Tr.B	059	Peterborough	MN	4 vessels	91	766	8	11	No
Eval. Tr.Z	1000	Peterborough	MN	wall	1	3	3	10	Yes
R	F612	Beaker	LN/ EBA	rim, base, wall	138	303	2	9	No
A	4002	Beaker	LN/ EBA	rim	1	5	5	8	Yes
B	F221.03	?Beaker	LN/ EBA	wall	1	3	3	8	Mod.
B Tr.31	F75	Urn	EBA	wall	2	15	7.5	9	No
Eval. Tr.28	F94	Urn	EBA	wall	4	53	13	9	Mod.
Totals					238	1148	5		

Form and decoration

All diagnostic items are illustrated.

Peterborough Ware *by Alistair Barclay and Ann Woodward*
(see Fig. 33. 1-4)

Feature 059 in Evaluation Trench B, excavated by Tempus Reparatum in 1995, contained 91 sherds (766g) of Middle Neolithic Peterborough Ware. At least four vessels are represented of which three can be assigned to the Fengate substyle and the other to the Mortlake substyle. This pottery was originally assessed by Alistair Barclay. It has been recorded by Ann Woodward and is discussed by Alistair Barclay.

Fig. 33.1. Fengate Ware. Two rim sherds, weighing 96g, from a small bowl. Fabric: sparse large angular quartz inclusions, described in detail above.

Fig. 33.2. Fengate Ware. Two refitting rim sherds, weighing 23g, from the collar of a vessel. The exterior and interior surfaces are decorated with impressed whipped cord maggot impressions; on the interior these form a herringbone pattern. The rim bevel is decorated with finger-nail impressions to form a chevron motif. Fabric: as 33.1.

Fig. 33.3. Mortlake Ware. Two rim and shoulder fragments, weighing 30g, from a relatively small bowl. The rim, neck and body are decorated with zones of zigzag, oblique and horizontal incised lines. Fabric: sparse large inclusions of angular quartz and black rock.

Fig. 33.4. Fengate Ware. Base angle, three fragments, and 82 decorated wall fragments from a thick-walled large bowl. Total weight: 617g. Fabric: as 33.1.

The rim is collared and has a bevel decorated with oblique finger-nail impressions. The exterior surface and that of the lower wall sherds are decorated with narrow horseshoe-shaped impressions, probably made with a hollow bone point, or a cut quill or reed. The base is relatively thick and is of small diameter.

Forms *by Alistair Barclay*

A minimum of four vessels is represented by the rims and the base. Of the two large vessels, one is represented by the rim (Fig. 33,1) and the other by body and base sherds (Fig. 33.4). The rim is heavy and collared (e.g. Smith 1965, fig. 34: PP277-8) while the body and base sherds derive from a vessel with a trunconic profile, a shallow base angle (around 45°) and thickened flat base. The open shallow bowl form is more within the range of vessels classified as belonging to the Fengate substyle. The all-over stab decoration found on both vessels, possibly made with a hollow bone point or stick, is unusual. A third vessel (Fig. 33.3), represented solely by a rim and shoulder fragment, is more typical of the Mortlake substyle. The rim, with its triangular cross-section,

as well as the use of all-over incised lines is typical of this style (eg. Manby 1975, figs. 14-5; Grimes 1960, fig. 75). A similar rim form occurs on a Mortlake vessel from an adjacent site at Fisherwick (Miles 1969, fig. 12). The fourth vessel (Fig. 33.2) is represented by just two refitting rim sherds with impressed whipped cord decoration. The flattened rim bevel and convex profile of this rim is typical of one of the collared forms associated with the Fengate substyle. Despite the limited profile this type of rim is often found on Fengate Ware vessels of more ovoid shape (Manby 1995, fig.52:2, 5-6; Piggott 1962, fig.12, 18; Leeds 1940, pl. 1A, C).

Beaker

Fig. 34.1. Vessel from the National Arboretum. The large fragment of pottery and three sherds recovered in 1996 were viewed initially at the Stoke on Trent Museum by Dr Carol Allen, who identified them as belonging to a late Beaker. These four fragments weighed 330g and a further seven sherds, including one piece of base angle, weighing 53g were recovered during the sieving exercise of 1997. Taking all the pieces together, it has been possible to attempt a reconstruction of the vessel profile. Approximately one half of the Beaker from rim to below the belly is present, with just a few sherds representing the lowest wall and base angle areas. It appears that the rest of the vessel was not present in the presumed discrete feature within which it had been deposited.

The vessel is buff to pale orange in colour and the sandy fabric contains mica flecks and a rare to medium occurrence of large, sub-rounded pieces of grog. The profile displays a long neck, simple rim and weakly shouldered belly. The base is slightly raised. The decoration is executed in tooth-comb technique, the tool employed having been a comb with five 'short' (i.e. almost square) teeth. The most striking element of the rather roughly executed decorative scheme is a zone of tall standing filled triangles on the neck. These are bordered by bands of horizontal tooth-combed lines and ladder zones, with two rows of free-floating diagonal tooth-comb strokes towards the base.

Fig. 34.2. Vessel from Area R, F612. The vessel is buff to grey in colour and the fabric contains small angular quartz grains and abundant grog up to 1mm in diameter. The quartz may have occurred naturally in the clay utilised, or may have been added intentionally (Fabric 9, examined petrographically by R. Ixer). A large proportion of the rim (70%) was present but only 52% of the base. The short, almost vertical neck is surmounted by a simple rounded rim and the relatively high shoulder is quite sharply angled. The centre of the base is slightly raised. The decoration involves three different techniques of incision but is extremely uneven and poorly executed. On the vertical neck there are three wide horizontal grooves. Below this most of the body of the Beaker is divided into horizontal zones by double rows of discontinuous tooth-comb impressions. Within two of the zones thus defined there are rows of standing multiple triangles executed in very rough narrow incisions, probably made with the edge of a sharp flint or a knife.

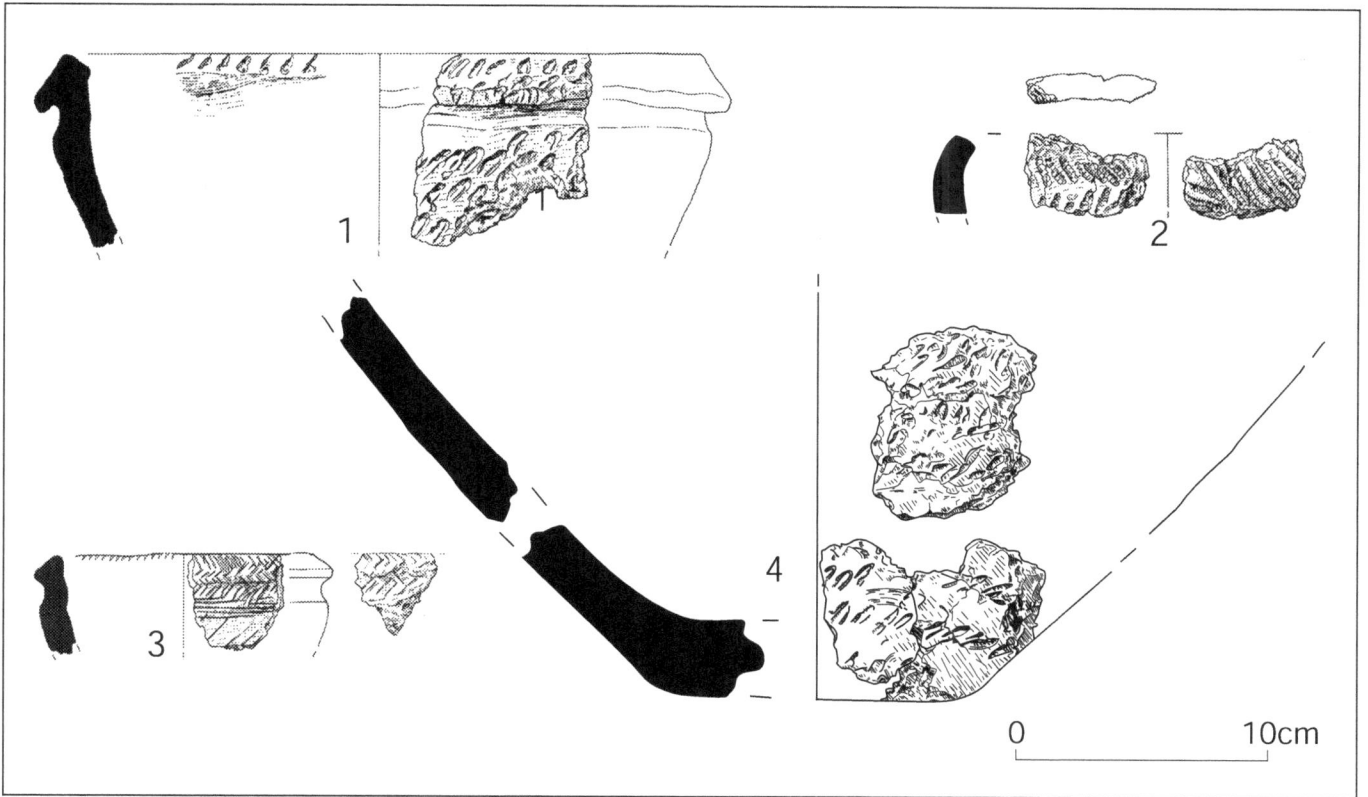

Fig.33: Prehistoric pottery: Peterborough ware

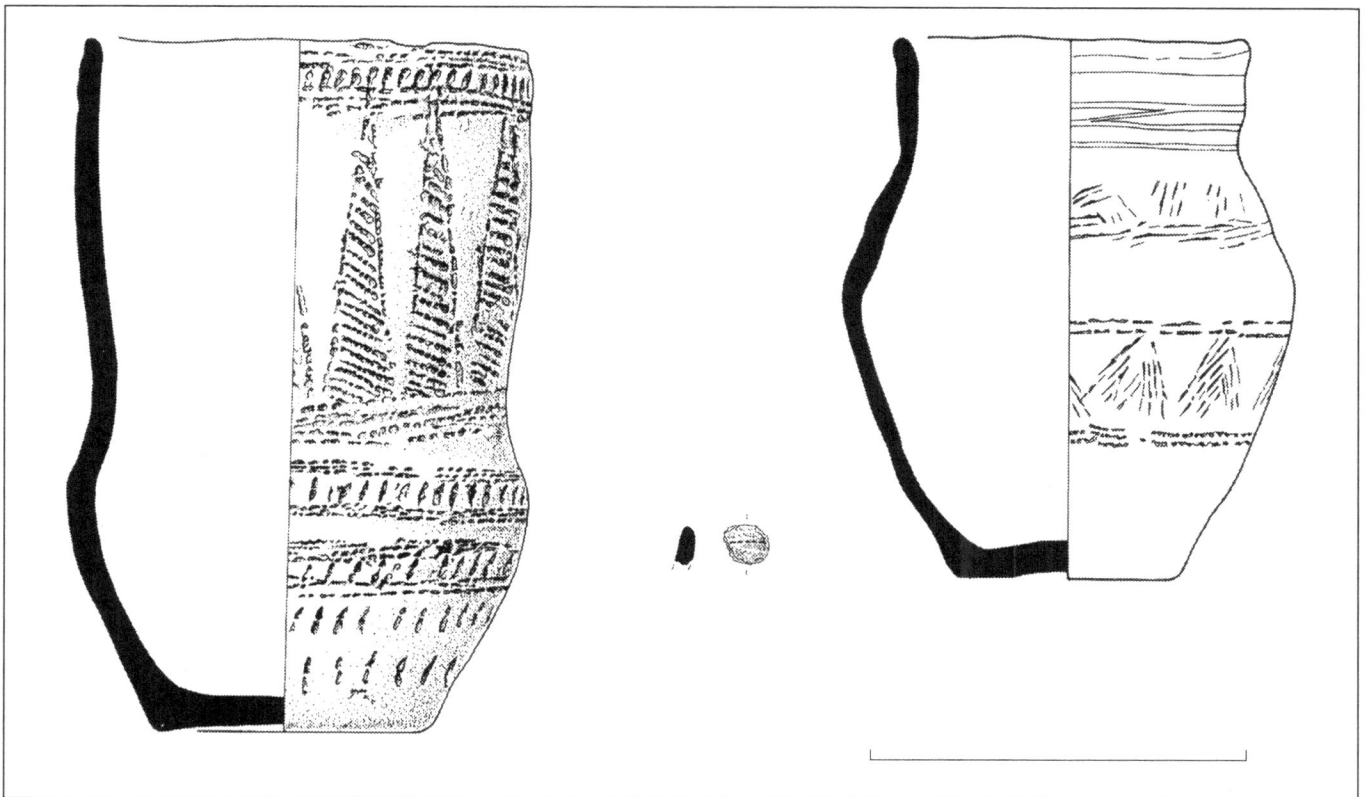

Fig. 34: Prehistoric pottery: Beaker vessels

Fig. 34.3. Sherd from Area A, context 4002. One simple rounded plain rim sherd, black on the outside and red inside. The surface is carefully smoothed. Fabric 8: grog and ironstone inclusions.

Early Bronze Age urns

The sherds from Area B and evaluation Trench 28 were all plain and are not illustrated. All were in Fabric 9: grog and quartz inclusions.

Discussion

Peterborough Ware *by Alistair Barclay*

Other local finds of Peterborough Ware include part of a Mortlake Ware bowl from Fisherwick and decorated body sherds from Lichfield and Fatholme, Barton-under-Needwood (Miles 1969, fig. 12; Barfield 1982, 42 and fig.10; TPAT 1985). All of these finds are associated with occupation rather than funerary sites.

The four vessels from Whitemoor Haye can be placed within the Fengate and Mortlake substyles, supporting the idea that they were in contemporary use. It is acknowledged that the distinction between the Fengate and Mortlake styles is sometimes ambiguous; typologically the two substyles can be seen to merge. There are Mortlake vessels with flat bases and others with collared rims (e.g. Piggott 1962, 33). It is unclear whether this can still be explained in terms of chronological development (see Smith 1968, 16). It is not unusual to find vessels of the two substyles together in the same context suggesting some degree of contemporaneity. The dating of Peterborough Ware needs to be reviewed in the light of recent work on the Fengate substyle by Gibson and Kinnes (1997). Their work indicated that Peterborough Ware was fully developed before the end of the 4th millennium BC. On current evidence it is suggested here that the date range for Fengate and Mortlake Ware may be expected to fall between approximately 3350-2800 cal BC, while Ebbsfleet Ware may still be considered as having slightly earlier beginnings. The fabrics, all of which are dominated by angular inclusions of quartz, are similar to those of other Peterborough Ware vessels known from the Midlands and the upper Thames valley.

Beaker

Both Beaker vessels belong to the Southern style as defined by Clarke (1970), and these form part of the Late Style described by Case in 1977. Following a reassessment of the dating evidence for Beakers in Britain it now appears that the style groups all originated at roughly the same period and Case prefers to use the term 'style 3' rather than Late Style (Case 1993). In terms of the wide-ranging regional groups defined by Case in 1993, the Arboretum and Whitemoor Haye Beakers belong to Group B which, in the Midlands, was current from round about 2000BC.

Grogged fabrics are typical of Beaker vessels in the Trent valley (e.g. Lockington (Woodward in Hughes 2000)) and indeed throughout the country as a whole (Case 1995, 64). However Dr. Ixer's findings concerning the fabric of the

Beaker from Area R are of particular interest. He noted, in thin section, that a number of different grog types are present and that some of the grog clasts may contain earlier grog within them. This indicates that fragments from several different vessels may have been ground up to produce the grog, and that some of these vessels were grogged themselves: in other words, they were probably Beakers also.

Of the more specific decorative motifs represented on the two Beakers, the standing filled triangle and the standing multiple triangle, the latter is much the rarer. Both belong to Clarke's Southern British Motif Group 4, number 29 (Clarke 1970, 427). Within the Midlands, schemes of tall filled triangles, either standing or pendant, are known on S1 vessels from Soham, Cambs., Deepdale, Staffs. and Bakewell, Derbys. (Clarke 1970, figs. 751, 754 and 757). The multiple triangle motif occurs on Beakers at Swinscoe and Wetton, Staffs. (Clarke 1970, figs. 939: type S3 and 861: type S2), and in incised technique on a sherd from Thorpe Cloud, Dovedale, Derbys. (Vine 1982, 333, no.401). Incised decoration is relatively rare on Beaker pottery in the region but does occur on five of the fifteen decorated vessels estimated to have been represented under barrow 4 at Swarkestone (ApSimon 1960, fig.9, 28 and fig.10, 29-35). Wide grooves on the neck can be paralleled on an N2 Beaker from Minning Low and one of S2 style from Youlgrave, both in Derbyshire (Clarke 1970, figs. 529 and 924).

Of particular interest is the fact that in both cases the Whitemoor Haye and Arboretum Beakers were not deposited as complete vessels. Only about half of the Arboretum vessel was present and a little more, at least towards the rim area, of the Area R example. Both Beakers appear to have been deliberately deposited as half-pots. Such a process is highly reminiscent of the deposit of two part-Beakers over the rich metal hoard outside the barrow at Lockington, Leics. (Woodward in Hughes 2000). In that case it was argued that the pots were heirlooms from which fragments had been removed deliberately over time, for use as keepsakes, or for the provision of 'special' grog to be incorporated in new vessels – a procedure that is evidenced by the fabric analysis of the Whitemoor Haye Beaker itself (see above). The extreme wear visible on the Arboretum vessel would add further weight to this type of interpretation – the deliberate deposition of family heirlooms in pits in the vicinity of the early prehistoric ritual cropmark sites.

Most of the Beakers from Staffordshire and Derbyshire derive from barrow or cave contexts in the Peak district, and most of these also belong to Case's Group B. Very few have been found in the gravel areas of the Trent valley and its tributaries (see map in Vine 1982, 275), and these examples, together with those from the Lockington barrow (Woodward in Hughes 2000), provide important additions to the regional corpus.

Urn

The few sherds of Early Bronze Age urns recovered are all plain wall sherds, so it is not possible to determine whether they derive from Collared Urns, Cordoned Urns or any other type. However the nature of the fabric firmly indicates an Early rather than a Middle Bronze Age date. Collared Urns

46

are rare in the county, 11 instances only being listed by Longworth (1984). Similar grog fabrics were common amongst the Cordoned and Collared Urns found at Eagleston Flat, Derbyshire (Beswick in Barnatt 1994, 314), but in the Trent valley there are examples with stone grits from Swarkestone, Derbys. (ApSimon 1960, fig.10, 44) and Willington (Manby in Wheeler 1979, fig.64), and quartzite inclusions in urns from another site at Willington, Derbys.(Woodward and Hancocks in Hughes forthcoming), whilst at Sproxton, Leics. there were Collared Urns with igneous rock inclusions (Clay 1981).

Late Bronze Age/Iron Age

A total of 432 sherds weighing 9194g was recovered from the evaluation trenches, the main excavation and the watching brief (see Table 13). For the area excavated this represents a rather small assemblage. Furthermore, most of the pottery came from two areas only, Area A and Area S. In many areas, there was too little pottery to allow any close dating of the various structures or to inform any interpretations concerning production, function or site status. However, amongst the assemblage, three aspects may be highlighted. Firstly, the semi-complete vessels from some of the features associated with the pit alignment in Site S are probably the result of deliberate deposition, and are of more than regional significance. Secondly, the small Late Bronze Age/Early Iron Age assemblage found in the watching brief feature F903 is a rare occurrence within the Midlands region, and thirdly, the range of diagnostic pieces from Area A allows some chronological and comparative conclusions to be drawn.

Fabric by Rob Ixer and Ann Woodward

Seven Late Bronze Age or Iron Age fabrics were defined using a hand lens, and five samples representing four of the fabric types were examined petrographically. Full petrographic descriptions may be found in Appendix 2.

Fabric 1. Coarse matrix containing much argillaceous material, sparse quartz and a few large, rounded fragments of rock or gravel.

Two samples, belonging to illustrated vessels Figs. 35.2 and 36.3 were examined in thin section.
Petrography: F526, context 5058. A dark natural clay carries small, angular quartz and larger, rounded quartz and potassium feldspar grains with authigenic overgrowths on them, and siliceous rock fragments. All these are constituents of the Permo-Triassic bedrock or could derive from any associated overlying sediments. The origin of the limonitic and grog-like areas is difficult to determine; some are oxidised magnetite clasts but others may be mudstone or grog. This pot could have been locally made.
F537, context 5045. Large, rounded quartz, potassium feldspars and siliceous rock fragments lie within a clean clay. The sand grain size is coarser than in the F526 sample. The limonite areas within the pot range from oxidised magnetite clasts to possible mudstones. The composition of the non-plastics is compatible with an origin from the local Permo-Triassic rocks or any overlying sediments derived from them.

Fabric 2. Similar to fabric 1, but with no large rock or gravel inclusions: the interior surface is usually vesicular.

Fabric 3. Very hard sandy matrix with argillaceous material and rare rock inclusions. Petrography: F903, context 9005 (Early Iron Age). Small, angular quartz grains and rare, larger, rounded quartz clasts are accompanied by large, rounded to irregularly shaped, limonite-rich areas. These range in composition from oxidised, euhedral magnetite to organic matter-rich; they are neither grog nor mudstones. Although the clay could be local, it is not possible to determine whether any of the inclusions have been deliberately added.

Fabric 4. Sandy matrix with sparse large rounded quartz inclusions.

Fabric 5. Fine sandy fabric, no large inclusions.

Fabric 6. Dense irregular and angular ill-sorted medium to large white inclusions. Petrography: F454, context 4119. Deliberate inclusions of angular, altered granodiorite within a clay carrying quartz and trace amounts of white mica, sandstone, and quartzite clasts. The granodiorite, which is

Table 13: Distribution of Late Bronze Age and Iron Age pottery by area

Area	No.sh.	%	Wt. (g)	Mean sh.wt. (g)	burnish	finger treated	scored ware
A	122	28	2407	20	2	2	2
B	7	2	190	27	-	1	-
C	4	1	56	14	-	-	-
R	2	<1	18	9	-	-	-
S	250	58	5840	23	-	1	-
WB	35	8	543	16	-	-	-
Eval.	12	3	140	12	1	-	-
Total	432		9194	21	3	4	2

not local, does not match the granodiorite rubber from F441 (see *Worked Stone*, below), fabric IGSC defined at Swarkestone Lowes, Derbyshire (Elliot and Knight 1999, 129) nor fabric G from Fisherwick, Staffs. (Morris in Smith 1979, 51), all of which have a petrography which matches the Mountsorrel (Leics.) granodiorite. However, the degree and type of alteration, although not unusual, do suggest that the inclusions originated from a Midlands igneous complex, perhaps one of the south Leicestershire diorite outcrops.

Fabric 7. Similar to fabric 3, but with no rock inclusions. Petrography: F445, context 4082. Round to subangular quartz and potassium feldspar both with authigenic overgrowths, opaque clasts, including oxidised magnetite, and siliceous rock clasts are present in a dark clay. Both the clay and the non-plastic components could derive from the local Permo-Triassic or any associated overlying sediments. It shares many characteristics with the samples of Fabric 1 and could have been made locally.

Fabric 3 shows some similarities to the Mercia Mudstone fabrics defined for the Swarkestone Lowes assemblage (Elliot and Knight 1999, 128-9), but appears to be different from Fabric F described from Fisherwick (Morris in Smith 1979, 51). Fabrics 1, 7 and 10 have some affinities with the quartz fabrics QUSV and QUSM from Swarkestone Lowes (Elliot and Knight 1999, 128) but there are differences, notably the presence of potassium feldspars and amount of limonite (ex-magnetite) in the Whitemoor Haye fabrics. It was suggested that the Swarkestone quartz fabrics contained deliberately added inclusions of crushed rock, but at Whitemoor Haye it appears that the added materials were sand rather than crushed rock as the grains are rounded. Fabrics C, D and E from Fisherwick (Morris in Smith 1979, 49-51) may be broadly similar. The solid and drift geology of the site is covered by the memoir for the area around Lichfield (Sheet 154: Barrow *et al..* 1919). Here it is noted that local alluvial deposits in the Hopwas-Alrewas area include reddish silty muds derived from Triassic debris (*ibid*, 193). Such deposits, or others like them, could be the source of the clays for the pots represented in Features 526, 537, 445 and perhaps even 903.

Form and decoration

Almost all of the diagnostic sherds have been illustrated (Figs. 35-37). In all there were only 12 vessel rims and five base angles represented. Using the classification devised by David Knight (1998), the main profile forms present were ellipsoid (ELL) and globular (GLOB), with single examples of the ovoid (OV) and carinated (CAR) forms. There were also two instances of rounded shoulders (RS). Bases were flat (FLT), often with the margin pinched out (FLP). Rims were mainly simple rounded direct (RD), some of them inturned, although a few everted (EVR) examples were also represented.

Formal decoration is totally absent, but various surface treatments do occur. These include burnishing and vertical or diagonal finger smearing (see Table 13). Scored ware of the traditional deeply grooved variety is lacking, but one vessel carried fine brush marks.

Illustrated sherds
Area S
Fig. 35
1. Rim and shoulder, 35%, ELL, fabric 1. F526, 5058.
2. Rim and shoulder, 43%, ELL, base 40%, FLP, fabric 1. F526, 5058.
3. Rim and shoulder, 10%, GLOB, base 41%, FLP, fabric 1. F526, 5058.

Fig.36
1. Rim and shoulder, 12%, ELL, fabric 2. F509, 5018.
2. Base, FLT, 15%, fabric 2. F509, 5018.
3. Rim and shoulder, 37%, GLOB, base, FLP, fabric 1. F537, 5045.

Watching brief and Area A
Fig. 37
1. Tall straight neck, RD rim and RS, fabric 3. WB F903, 9005.
2. Inturned RD rim, fabric 2. WB F903, 9005.
3. RS, fabric 3. WB F903, 9005.
4. Everted rim EVR, concave neck and sharp shoulder (CAR), 13%, vertical finger smearing, fabric 4. F468, 4150, south ditch fill.
5. Inturned RD rim, OV profile, fabric 1. F445.02, 4124.
6. RD rim, concave short neck, 11%, fabric 7, burnished. F421, 4035, structure 3.
7. Tapered everted EVT rim on slight neck, fabric 2. F445.02, 4099, pit cutting enclosure ditch.
8. Inturned RD rim, fabric 2. F445.02, 4099, pit cutting enclosure ditch.
9. Fine brush scoring, fabric 2. F455.01, 4082, pit cutting enclosure ditch.
10. Flat base FLT, 49%, fabric 2. F415, 4053, structure 3.
11. Flat pinched out base FLP, 86%, fabric 2. F435.01, 4060, structure 4.

Deposition

The mean sherd weight for the whole assemblage (21g), and for most individual areas, is relatively high (see Table 13). Most of the pottery (63%) was fresh and unabraded, with 34% moderately worn and only 3% severely abraded. These factors indicated that much of the pottery occurred *in situ*, that residuality is minimal, and that several of the context groups represented examples of deliberate structured deposition. Two main forms of such deposition can be distinguished.

Firstly, large portions of vessel bases occurred in shallow features within Area A (F415, structure 3 ring gully, 49% of vessel base and F435.01, Structure 4 ring gully, 86% of base: Figs. 37, 10 and 11). These could not have been set in these features whilst the building were standing so it seems likely that they had been deliberately placed at the time the structures were abandoned, or later. The second type of deposition involved the placing of large chunks of vessels, both rim to shoulder portions and base fragments, within features associated with the pit alignment in Area S. These deposits included chunks from two vessels in pit F509 (Fig. 36.1-2), and from three vessels in pit F526 (Fig. 35.1-3).

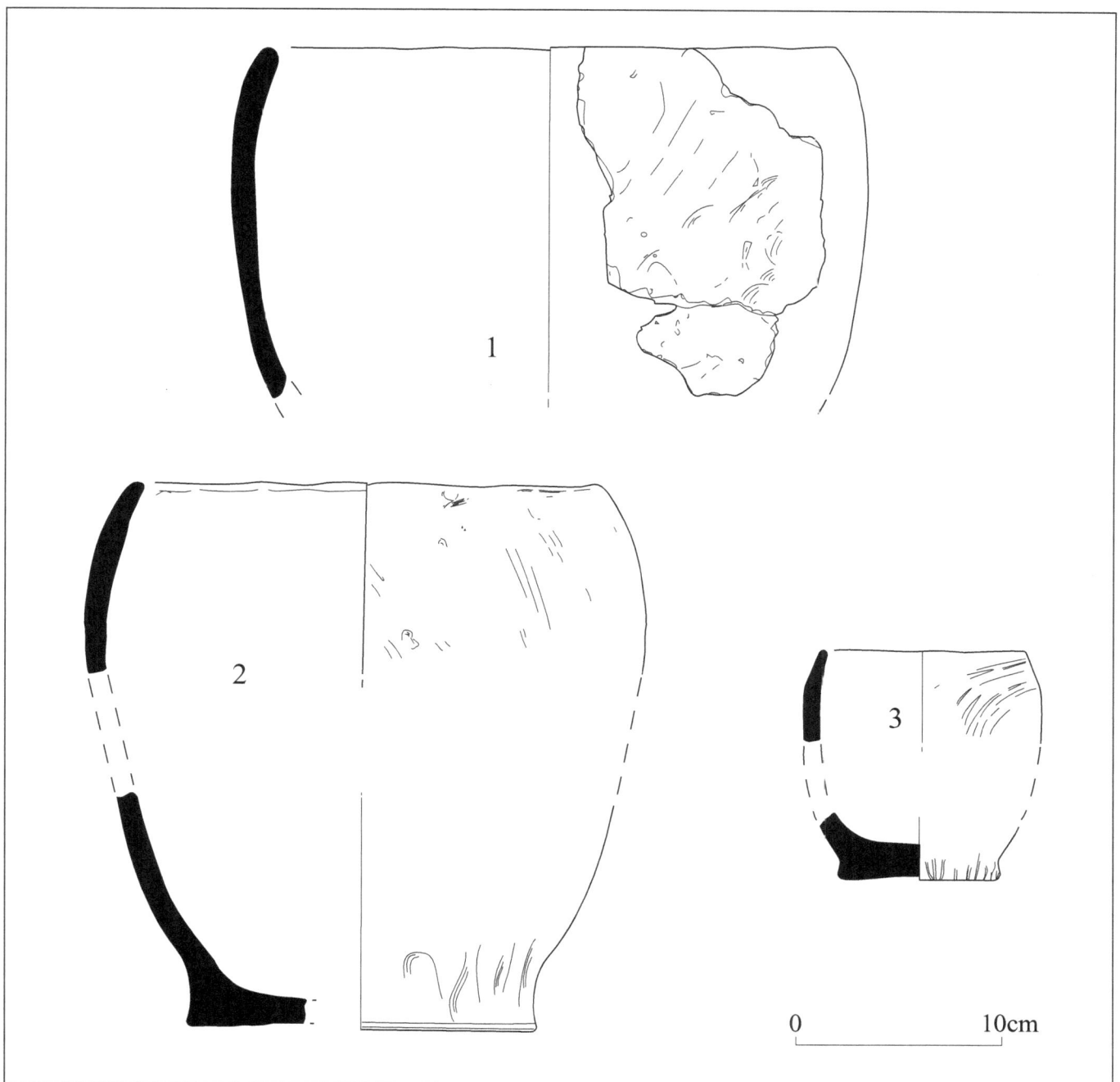

Fig. 35: Prehistoric pottery: Late Bronze Age/Iron Age pottery from Area S, F526 (scale 1:3)

Both these pits lay in the main alignment, whilst large fragments from a further vessel (Fig. 36.3) had been placed in one of the smaller pits, F537, which formed an arc arrangement just to the north of the alignment.

Vessel function

No residues were preserved and no patterns of sooting or use wear were observed amongst this small assemblage. There are few measureable rim diameters, although it seems that large- and medium-sized vessels occur in most of the groups. The only small vessels occurred in one of the pit alignment deposits (Fig. 35.3) and in an Early Iron Age group from a feature excavated during the watching brief (Fig. 37.2).

Chronology

The earliest group of pottery is that from F903 in the watching brief area (Fig. 37.1-3), and the forms can be matched in other Late Bronze Age/Early Iron Age assemblages within the region. High, gently concave and thin-walled necks, and rounded or sharp shoulders, occur at Swarkestone Lowes (e.g. Elliot and Knight 1999, Fig. 17, 7-9) and in Assemblage I (Form II) at Willington (Elsdon in Wheeler 1979), both in Derbyshire, and at Gamston, Nottinghamshire (Knight 1992, Form I). They also occur rarely at Wanlip, although there they are residual items (Marsden in Beamish 1998). The vessel with a concave neck, everted rim, sharp carination and vertical finger smearing (Fig. 37.4) cannot be matched exactly in the

49

smearing (Fig. 37.4) cannot be matched exactly in the regional assemblages but the form and surface treatment seem to be early characteristics. The occurrence of carination amongst selected regional assemblages is shown in Table 14.

This table also shows the occurrence of the main Iron Age profile, rim and decorative forms that are represented at Whitemoor Haye, and three forms which are not: bead rims, finger-treated rims and deep scoring. Ellipsoid and ovoid jars (ELL, OV and GLOB) with inturned rims occur widely and in assemblages dating from the Late Bronze Age to the full Iron Age. The same applies in the case of the expanded base form FLP. Everted rim jars are less common, occurring on only some of the regional sites. Bead rims are a later Iron Age form and do not occur at Whitemoor Haye. However, the absence of finger treated rims and deep scoring may not be indicative of an early date for the assemblage here for at Wanlip absolute dating suggests that all forms of scoring – from light brushing to deep grooves - occurred from the fifth century BC onwards (Marsden in Beamish 1998, 49).

The range of pottery from Whitemoor Haye suggests that the site was occupied from the seventh century BC at the earliest to the second or first century BC. There are no obvious Late Iron Age forms, but there were none at

Table 14:   The occurrence of selected formal characteristics at Whitemoor Haye and in seven assemblages from the region.

Site	Ref.	CAR	ELL, OV, GLOB	EVR	FLP	light brushing only	BEAD	FT rim	deep scoring
Whitemoor Haye	Min. vessels	2	8	2	4	1	-	-	-
Fisherwick	Smith 1979	-	*	*	*	-	-	-	*
Willington Assemblage I	Wheeler 1979	*	*	-	*	*	-	rare	-
Willington Assemblage II	Wheeler 1979	-	*	-	*	-	*	rare	*
Foxcovert Farm	Hughes 1999	-	*	*	*	-	-	-	*
Swarkestone Lowes	Elliot and Knight 1999	*	*	-	-	-	-	*	-
Enderby	Clay 1992	-	-	*	*	-	*	*	*
Gamston	Knight 1992	*	*	*	*	-	*	*	*
Wanlip	Beamish 1998	*	*	*	*	-	-	*	*

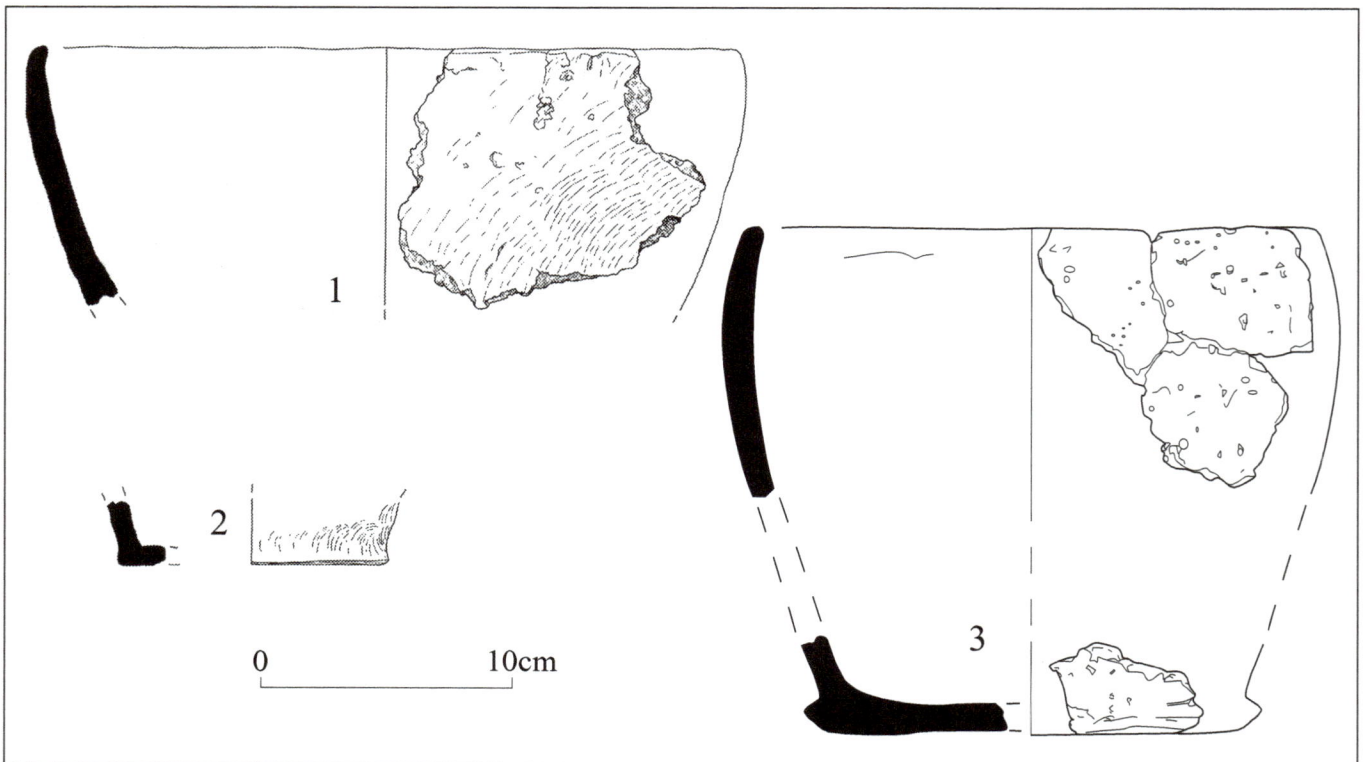

Fig. 36: Prehistoric pottery: Late Bronze Age/Iron Age pottery from Area S, F509 and F537 (scale 1:3)

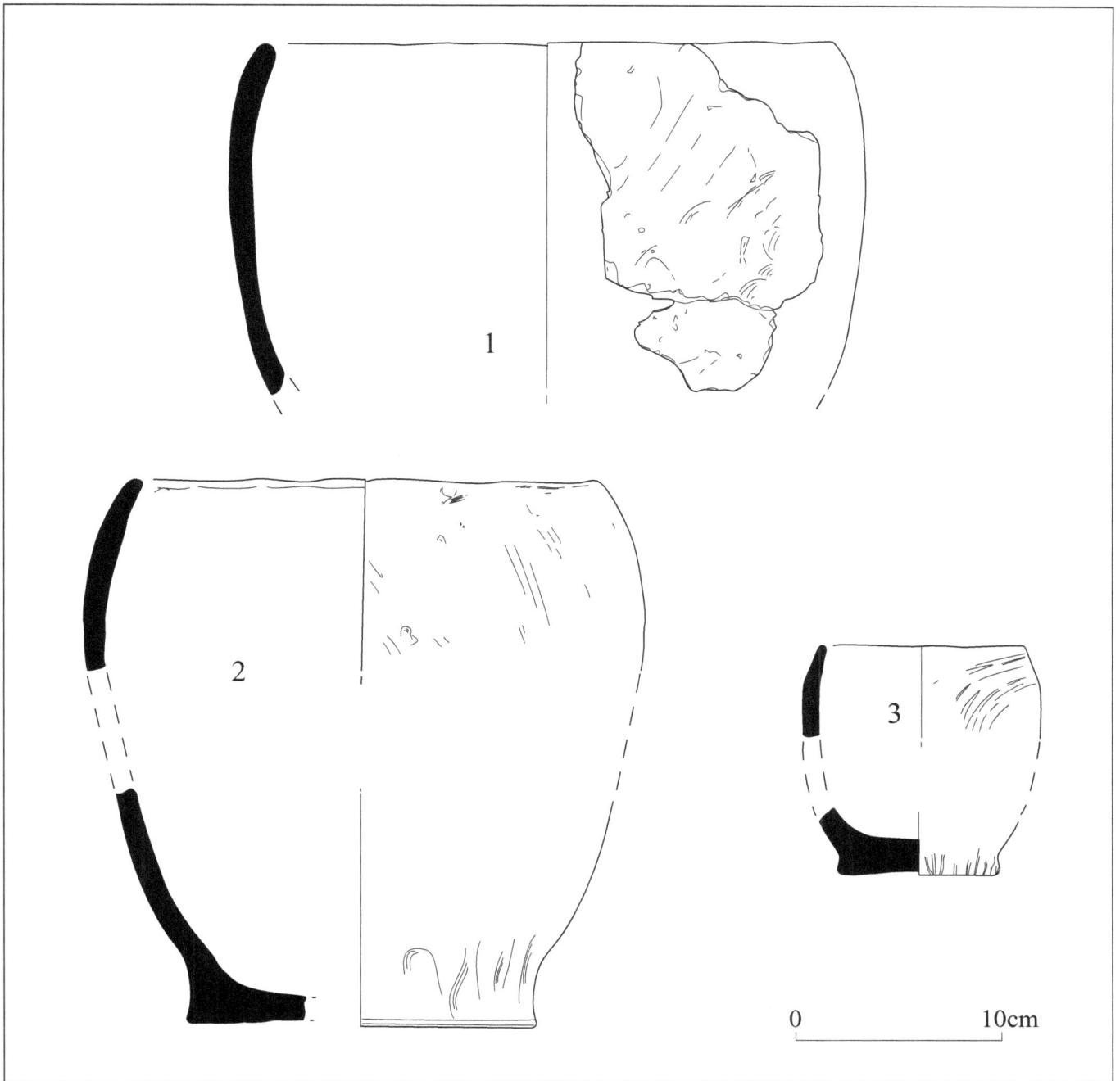

Fig. 37: Prehistoric pottery: Late Bronze Age/Iron Age pottery from Area A and watching brief (scale 1:3)

Fisherwick either, and the radiocarbon dates from there indicated that occupation may have lasted into the first century AD. The two dates from features associated with the pit alignment in Area S at Whitemoor Haye suggest depositions in the fourth or third centuries BC (at one sigma).

Discussion

Apart from providing a rough chronological structure for the excavated features across the site, the assemblage is important in two different ways – the nature of the structured deposits, and the evidence for regional ceramic exchange.

Both forms of structured deposits evidenced on the site have also been recognised elsewhere within the region in recent years. The deposits associated with the pit alignment are rare occurrences, but some fragments of pottery occurred in the upper fills of five pits in an alignment at Swarkestone Lowes (Trench 23), and the one diagnostic rim sherd was from a plain ovoid jar (Elliot and Knight 1999, fig.17, 11). The deposition of the jar bases can be compared functionally with a structured deposit at Wanlip where a pit near to an Iron Age house and hearth had contained a large, repaired, ovoid jar and two smaller vessels (Marsden in Beamish 1998, fig.28, 55-61), along with fragments from four different querns.

Analysis of the pottery fabrics at Whitemoor Haye has indicated that most of the vessels could have been made on or near to the site, but one sherd was found to contain inclusions of granodiorite which may derive from a source in south Leicestershire, but not the Mountsorrel source. This is indicative of the widespread distribution of certain igneous-tempered Iron Age pots in the Midlands. At sites near to the Mountsorrel outcrop much of the pottery includes pieces of Mountsorrel granodiorite, e.g. 82% at Wanlip (Marsden in Beamish 1998). One of the earliest identifications of such material was at Gamston in Nottinghamshire, where it occurred at c.1% (Knight 1992) and recently similar fabrics, from at least five vessels, have been described from Swarkestone Lowes, Derbyshire, upstream from the outcrops and about 25km east of Whitemoor Haye (Elliot and Knight 1999, 129-30). The identification of similar, but not identical, material in Staffordshire significantly extends the known distribution of such traded wares into the West Midlands.

Briquetage *by Elaine L. Morris*

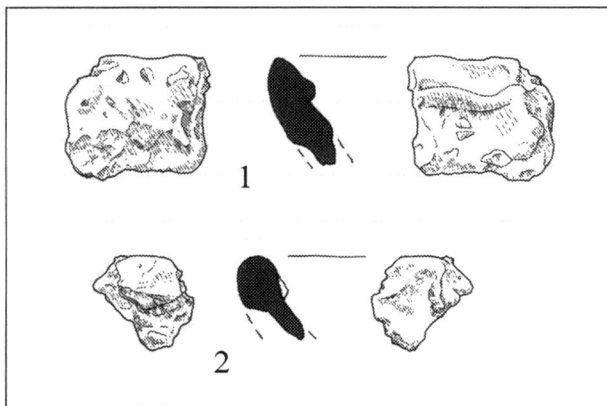

Fig. 38: Prehistoric ceramics: Briquetage (scale 1:2)

A total of 32 pieces (225 grams) of unusual ceramic material, known as Stony VCP, or Cheshire briquetage (Morris 1985), was identified. This handmade, primarily oxidised material is characterised by the presence of a range of angular and rounded glacial drift rocks in the sandy clay matrix. These inclusions have been found to concentrate in the Cheshire Plain area near the brine spring sources of Nantwich, Middlewich and Northwich. This ceramic material represents vessels used to help dry salt crystals and transport the salt from one or more of these sources. Distribution extends over a wide region from Anglesey, North Wales to the Trent and Soar Valleys of the eastern Midlands, during the second half of the first millennium BC (Morris 1994).

Context, Condition and Nature of the Material

The fragments were recovered from three different features in two different areas of the site. Pit F445 in Area A (context 4081) contained a rim, four body sherds and four flakes, while ditch F447.02 (context 4201) contained one rim, 11 body sherds and eight flakes. Excavation of the terminal end of ditch F304.01 (context 3031) of Area C revealed three small body sherds.

Although the mean sherd weight of pieces in this assemblage is small, the presence of flakes in the assemblage, demonstrating the quality of recovery methods, has biased this impression. Amongst the sherds alone (2 rims, 18 body sherds, 182 grams), the mean sherd weight is 9 grams. The surfaces of the sherds are in good condition.

The two rim sherds (Fig. 38.1-2) are typical of the range of types known: one is pinched over and the other rounded. The pinched-over rim displays the very distinctive white 'skin' patches on the exterior surface, which are thought to be salts deposited during the heating and drying process when the vessels are used. The rim and body sherds vary in thickness from 9mm up to 15mm. This variation appears to represent different coils or collars of clay used to construct the open, flared or flower pot profile of the flat-bottomed vessels (Morris 1985, fig. 8). Comparison of the vessel wall thickness found within each context suggests that the different sizes might represent different collars from the same briquetage vessel. This is supported by the recognition that the larger pieces have the same range and density of rock inclusions in the fabric and all the sherds have the same oxidised colour tones. Therefore, it is highly likely that there is only one vessel represented in each of the contexts.

Discussion

The recovery of at least three vessels of Cheshire briquetage at Whitemoor Haye from two different Middle and Middle to Late Iron Age features in the quarry reinforces the discovery and publication of identical material at Fisherwick (Smith 1979). Contrary to Banks and Morris (1979), it is now appreciated that this material was not made in the Tame Valley but rather manufactured in the Cheshire Plain (Morris 1985). The original interpretation that it is most likely to belong to salt-drying and transportation vessels of Iron Age date still holds true. Since that early publication, many more individual sherds representing single vessels and small assemblages have been found on settlement sites in Leicestershire (Elsdon 1991; 1992, fabric E; 1994), Nottinghamshire (Knight 1992) and Derbyshire (Knight 1999; Morris 1999). The wide distribution of these containers holding Cheshire salt (Morris 1985, figs. 9-10) is remarkable and suggests that the quality of the salt was recognised, possibly through the distinctive packaging of the Stony VCP ceramic vessels. The extensive nature of this network (Morris 1994, fig.4a) is complemented by that of the intensive nature of the Droitwich salt network which has also been documented by the distribution of its own distinctive ceramic vessels (Morris 1985, figs. 5-6; 1994, fig. 4b). The distribution of Charnwood Forest pottery from Leicestershire (Knight 1992; 1999), Millstone grit querns from Derbyshire (Samuels 1979; Hughes 1999) and salt in ceramic containers from Cheshire demonstrates an energetic exchange system, or systems, in action during the later prehistoric period in the wider Midlands area of England.

Illustrated Sherds (Fig. 38)

1. Rim, folded-over type; patches of white deposit on exterior; 10-11 mm thick; 4081, pit 445.
2. Rim, rounded type; 12-13 mm thick; 4201, ditch 447.02.

Romano-British Pottery *by Annette Hancocks, with contributions by Kay Hartley and Steven Willis*

Summary

A total of 557 sherds (c.11kg) of pottery with an estimated vessel equivalent (EVE) of 10, was recovered during the fieldwork. Of this material 32% was unstratified or could not be phased. The remaining 68% of the ceramics derived from well-stratified and secure contexts. No preservation bias was observed. Overall the minimum number of vessels represented was 50.

A single Roman phase of occupation, phase 3, was identified and dated to the mid/late 2nd/early 3rd century AD. The stratified assemblage came from some 21 features; these were predominantly ditches. The pottery represented good closed groups of material from seven areas (A, B, C, F, R, S and T). Small amounts of residual material, some Verulamium Region mortaria and some South Gaulish La Graufesenque samian were observed. Overall the assemblage was characterised by the presence of local and regionally imported traded wares, such as Derbyshire coarseware, Black-Burnished ware 1, Severn Valley ware, Mancetter-Hartshill and Little Chester mortaria.

The assemblage was unabraded, with very little fragmentation. This is reflected in the high average sherd weight of 20g for the whole assemblage. This may be indicative of the depositional processes at work on the site. Some 13% of the pottery comprised diagnostic rim forms, with 14.5% decorated body sherds and 5% base angles. The remainder are body sherds.

Introduction

Very little previous work has been carried out at Whitemoor Haye. A small amount of Romano-British pottery was recovered from a similar site at Fisherwick (Smith 1979) and some published groups from Rocester (Leary 1996), Wall (Jones 1998) and Little Chester provide comparative material from key Romano-British type sites in Staffordshire.

Methodology

All of the pottery was studied and analysed by area. The pottery was recorded using the standard BUFAU Roman pottery recording system. Details of this form part of the archive. The fabrics were classified using a site-specific series, which was integrated into the BUFAU type fabric series and cross-referenced, where possible, to the National Roman Fabric Reference Collection (NRFRC; Tomber and Dore 1998). The fabrics are listed and described in Appendix 3. Where possible, precise form types and broad vessel classes (for example bowl, flagon and mortarium) were both recorded (Appendix 4). Other characteristics noted included decoration, evidence for manufacture (wasters) and, if present, repair (rivets and rivet holes). The assemblage was quantified in full: by sherd count, weight (g) and EVE. Only rim Eves are published, but percentages for bases are recorded in the archive. The level of abrasion was not recorded for individual sherds, although general impressions were noted by context during the assessment. The pottery data was analysed using Microsoft Access 97.

Fabrics (Appendix 3)

Table 15 quantifies the percentage occurrence of each fabric type within the overall pottery assemblage.

Some 32 fabrics were defined and occurred in various quantities. The most common fabrics were the regional traded wares, such as Black-Burnished ware 1 (DOR BB1), 23% by count, reduced Severn Valley Ware (SVW G), 15%, and oxidised Severn Valley Ware (SVW OX2), 11%. Amongst the local wares, Derbyshire coarseware (DER CO) was the most common fabric, 14% by count. All of the imported wares comprised 3% by count of the total ceramic assemblage. The assemblage overall was dominated by the regional traded and local wares, with a few key wares noticeably dominating the assemblage. Generally, the local wares, with the exception of Derbyshire coarseware, are poorly defined and could not be readily sourced using the NRFRC handbook or by comparison with published sites such as Rocester, New Cemetery (Leary 1996) or Wall (Jones 1998), both in Staffordshire. The coarsewares do prevail over the fine wares, with reduced wares been more common than oxidised wares. The lack of finewares amongst the assemblage is of particular note and may be an indication of the function and status of the settlement at Whitemoor Haye.

The most commonly represented fabrics by rim EVE by fabric are Black-Burnished ware (21%), followed by reduced Severn Valley ware (18%), Oxidised Severn Valley ware (15%) and Derbyshire coarseware (13%). The remaining fabrics are represented by less than 6% of Rim Eves (Fig. 40).

Table 15: Romano-British pottery: fabric, sources and quantities in assemblage

Fabric Name	NRFRC	Qty	% Qty	Wt (g)	% Wt (g)	Rim EVE	% EVE
A02	BAT AM 1	2	<1	497	4.5	-	-
S01	LGF SA	2	<1	56	0.5	-	-
S02	LMV SA	4	<1	49	0.5	10	1
S03	LEZ SA2	9	<1	148	1	21	2
S04R	RHZ SA	1	<1	4	<0.5	3	<1
TOTAL IMPORTED		**18**	**3**	**754**	**7**	**-**	**-**
B02	DOR BB1	126	23	1225	21	207	21
B03	SOW BB1	9	2	44	<1	13	1
C02	LNVCC	1	<1	17	<0.5	10	1
G02	LNVGW	2	<1	353	3	-	-
G04	SVW G	85	15	1480	14	180	18
JO3	CALGW	2	<1	17	<0.5	16	2
M02a	MAH WH	2	<1	168	1.5	14	1
M02b	MAH WH	2	<1	299	3	26	3
M08	CAR WS	1	<1	15	<0.5	-	-
M09	LCH WH	2	<1	550	5	49	5
O02.1	SVW OX2	63	11	1435	13	147	15
O03.1	SVW ORG	7	1	71	1	-	-
P04.1	GOD WW	8	1	62	0.5	-	-
W06	LNV WH	10	2	157	1	-	-
TOTAL REGIONAL		**320**	**58**	**5893**	**54**	**-**	**-**
F02		5	<1	16	<0.5	-	-
F03		1	<1	8	<0.5	-	-
F09		4	<1	36	<0.5	13	1
G06.4	DER CO	80	14	2207	20	130	13
G07.3		1	<1	15	<0.5	-	-
G08.1		2	<1	66	1	-	-
G09.2		1	<1	5	<0.5	-	-
G09.3		5	<1	29	<0.5	6	1
G09.4		25	5	461	4	58	6
G09.6		11	2	386	3.5	53	5
G09.7		36	6	897	8	49	5
O06.2		1	<1	25	<0.5	-	-
O06.8		47	8	161	1.5	-	-
TOTAL LOCAL		**219**	**39**	**4312**	**39**	**-**	**-**
TOTAL							
POTTERY		**557**	**100**	**10959**	**100**	**1005**	**100**

Forms (Fig. 39)

The forms are presented as a form series within fabrics groups (i.e. the oxidised wares and reduced wares). The illustrated forms are noted in the following catalogue. All are Area S WB03, phase 3 unless stated.

Catalogue

B02 (DOR BB1)

1. BI8.22 Bead and flange rimmed bowl/dish with dropped flange. The majority of surface treated, most commonly burnished inside and wiped outside with a high percentage decorated externally, mainly acute lattice or intersecting arcs (as in this case). Paralleled at Greyhound Yard (Seager Smith and Davies 1993, fig. 151, 360 Type 25), early-mid 2nd-century date.
Fig. 39.1, 9070, F944, diam. 19cm (19%), Area WB02.

2. BI8.31 Flat-rimmed bowl/dish with flat base; majority

of surface treated, most commonly burnished externally, in this case with intersecting arcs. Paralleled at Greyhound Yard (Seager Smith and Davies 1993, fig. 123, Type 22), early-mid 2nd-century date.
Fig. 39.2, u/s, F101.02, diam. 20cm (23%).

3. JK7.2 Cooking pot, near upright or slightly everted rim, often beaded. Burnished on shoulder, neck and rim. Band of acute lattice decoration separating upper and lower portions. Paralleled at Greyhound Yard (Seager Smith and Davies 1993, fig. 122, Type 1, late 1st/early 2nd-century date.
Fig. 39.3, 5034, F506.02, diam. 12cm (100%).

4. JK7.3 Cooking pot or storage jar with everted rim, with bead. Burnished on shoulder, neck and rim. Lower portion of vessel wiped and frequently decorated with a band of acute lattice decoration, separating upper and lower portions. Burnished wavy line around exterior of neck.
Fig. 39.4, 1005, F101.02, diam. 18cm (21%).

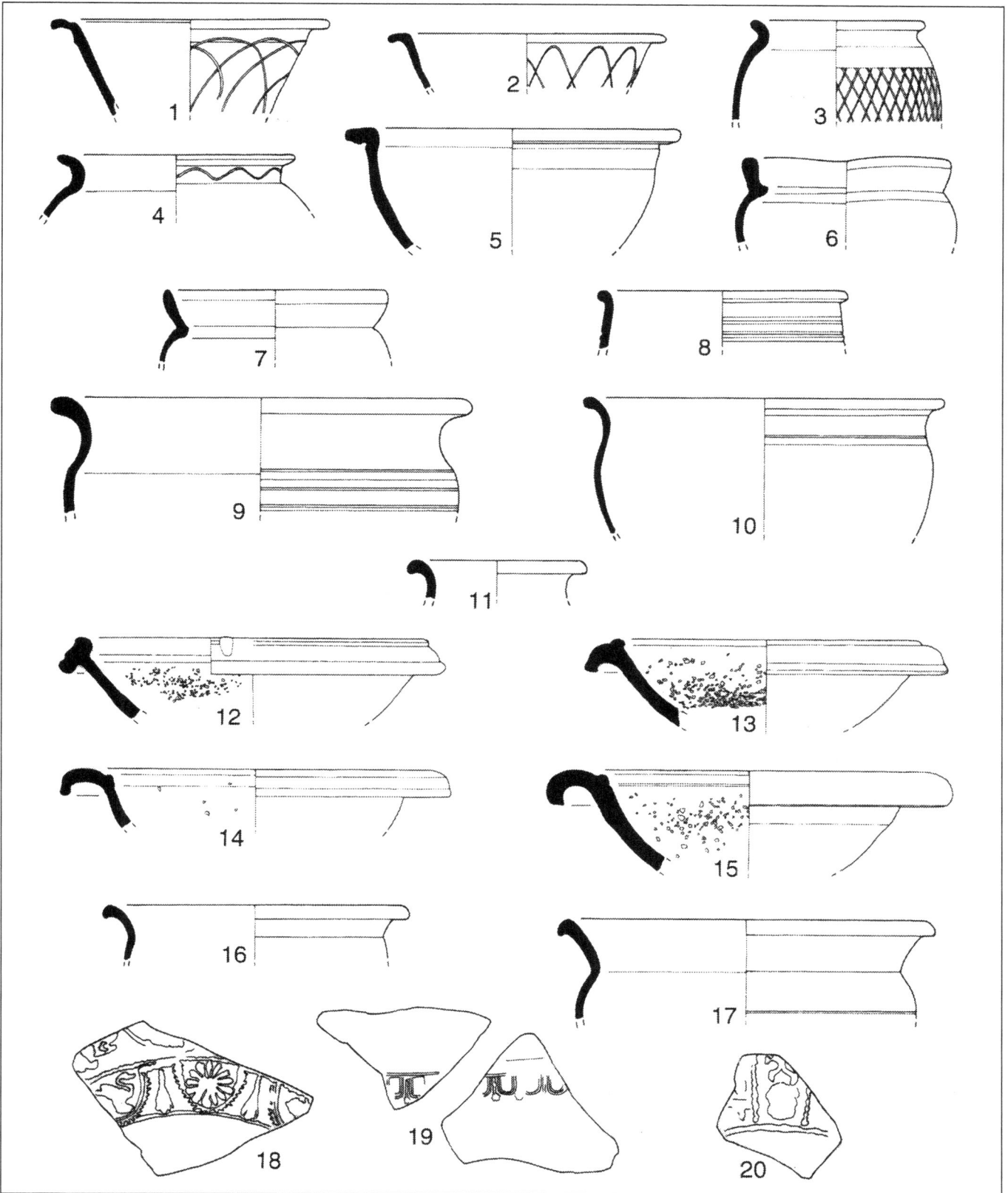

Fig. 39: Romano-British pottery: Coarsewares, mortaria (scale 1:4), Samian (scale 1:2 and 1:1)

G04 (SVW G)

5. BC1.04 Curving-sided bowl with pointed bead rim.
   Fig. 39.5, 5034, F506.02, diam. 24cm (28%).

G06.4 (DER CO)

6. JJ6.05 Lid-seated/bell-mouth jar, with an internal ridge or ledge on which a lid might rest. At its widest point the rim is usually 2/3rds the height of the vessel. This example has a warped rim profile and looks very much like a pottery waster. Form paralleled at Little Chester (Gillam 1939, fig. 2.1).
   Fig. 39.6, 1006, F101.02, diam. 15cm (75%).

7. JJ6.05 Lid-seated/bell-mouthed jar, with an internal ridge or ledge on which a lid might rest. Form paralleled at Bewcastle (Gillam 1939, fig. 2.12) and Rocester (Leary 1996, fig. 22.55).
   Fig. 39.7, 1005, F101.02, diam. 15cm (15%).

G09.6 (local)

8. B1.01 Bowl type with bead rim.
   Fig. 39.8, 1005, F101.02, diam. 18cm (7%).

9. JW7.01 Wide-mouthed jar with everted plain rim.
   Fig. 39.9, 9070, F944, diam. 30cm (20%), Area WB02.

G09.7 (local)

10. JW7.01 Wide-mouthed jar with necked, everted rim.
    Fig. 39.10, 1006, F101.02, diam. 25cm (49%).

J03 (local)

11. JW7.01 Wide-mouthed jar with everted plain rim.
    Fig. 39.11, 4207, F443.04, diam. 12cm (16%), Area A.

O02.1 (SVW OX2)

16. JW1.04 Wide-mouthed jar with pointed bead rim. Webster 1976, fig. 5.23/24, mid-late 2nd/late 3rd century.
    Fig. 39.16, 2002, F201, diam. 22cm (19%), Area B.

17. JW1.04 Wide-mouthed jar with pointed bead rim. Webster 1976, fig. 5.25, 2nd-3rd century.
    Fig. 39.17, unstratified, F101.02, diam. 28cm (22%).

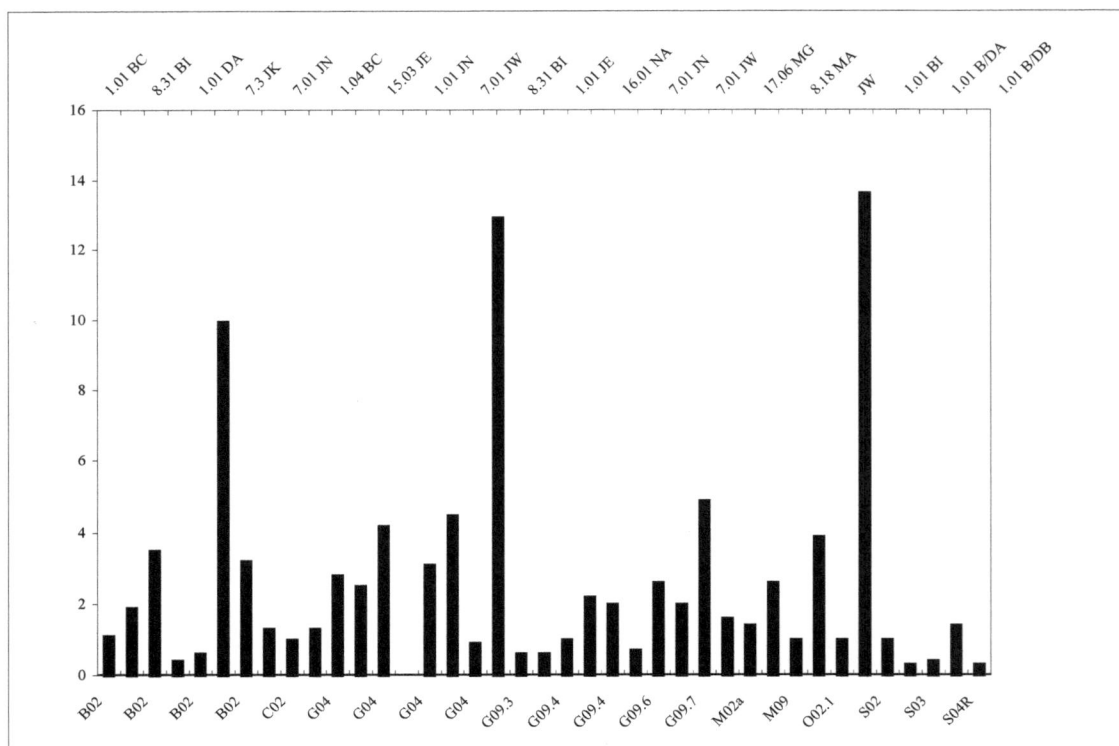

Fig. 40: Romano-British pottery: histogram of form occurrence by fabric

Mortaria *by Kay Hartley*

M02a (MAH WH)

Bodysherd. This is from a well-made thin-walled mortarium in quite hard fabric with the type of trituration grit normal in the Mancetter-Hartshill potteries after *c.* AD140. As a bodysherd it is not strictly datable but these characteristics suggest a date in the third or fourth century rather than earlier. Unstratified

12. MG17.06 A mortarium with triple-reeded rim, wide central zone and upright bead; the left-facing side of the spout survives, formed by breaking the bead and turning the broken ends outward. Mancetter-Hartshill. Optimum date AD180-230.
Fig. 39.12, unstratified, diam. 29cm (14%)

M02b (MAH WHv)

Bodysherd, perhaps from the same vessel as below. 2166, Area B, cleaning layer

13. MA8.05 Enough of this vessel survives to show that it was never stamped. The practice of stamping ceased in these potteries *c.* AD170-180. We do not know whether it ceased overnight in the all workshops there, but that would not be impossible if, as seems likely, it stemmed from a complete reorganisation of the industry there. This rim-profile is associated with the latest generation of stamping potters, especially Maurus and Sennius, who were active *c.* AD150-170. The same form continued in production for at least a brief period after the cessation of stamping and if enough of the spout had survived it could have made it possible to date this mortarium very closely. Its optimum date is AD165-180.
Fig. 39.13, 5013, F505.02, diam. 26cm (26%)

M08 (southwest England or south Wales (Caerleon) (CARWS)

Not illustrated. Incomplete rim-section of a mortarium or segmental bowl. The fragment is too small for any trituration grit to survive. 2003, F200, diam. indeterminate, Area B

M09 (Little Chester)

14. MA8.18 Bead and flange mortaria with flange higher than bead. It would best fit manufacture in the workshop at Little Chester, AD100-130 (see comments for 15 below).
Fig. 39.14, 1057, F064, diam. 29cm (10%), Evaluation Trench 27 1992

15. MA8.19 Bead and flange mortaria with flange higher than bead. The optimum date for this rim-profile is AD100-130. Mortaria of this type (see also 14 above) were made in cream fabrics at both Little Chester and Mancetter-Hartshill during this period. Some potters like Septuminus were, in fact, active at both workshops (Brassington 1971, 53, no. 120). The fabric and trituration grit of this example would best fit manufacture at Little Chester. Heavily worn and slightly singed.
Fig.39.15, unstratified, F101, diam. 29cm (39%), Area T

With reference to Figure 41, the most common vessel class is the wide-mouthed jar (JW), representing some 24% of the rim eve within the assemblage. This form commonly occurs in the regionally traded oxidised and reduced Severn Valley ware fabrics (16% of rim eves), as well as the more locally produced greywares (G09.6 and G09.7). The cooking pot (JK) class comprises the second most common form at 14.5% of the rim eves within the assemblage. Interestingly, this form only occurs in the Black-Burnished ware fabrics B02 and B03 and may be indicative of a military influence amongst the assemblage. On a more local level lid-seated (bell-mouthed) jars (JJ), which only occur in Derbyshire coarseware (DER CO), are represented by some 13% of the rim eve total.

Overall, jars are the dominant vessel class within the assemblage, followed by bowls and mortaria. A few straight-sided dishes are represented. As the sample size is small it was not possible to study the range and variety of rim diameters, by form or fabric, to determine any cultural or functional influences. These are all represented in coarseware fabrics, with the exception of the samian, which occurs in fineware bowl forms (B, B/DA and B/DB). This is very significant in determining the status and function of the site. Coarsewares prevail over finewares.

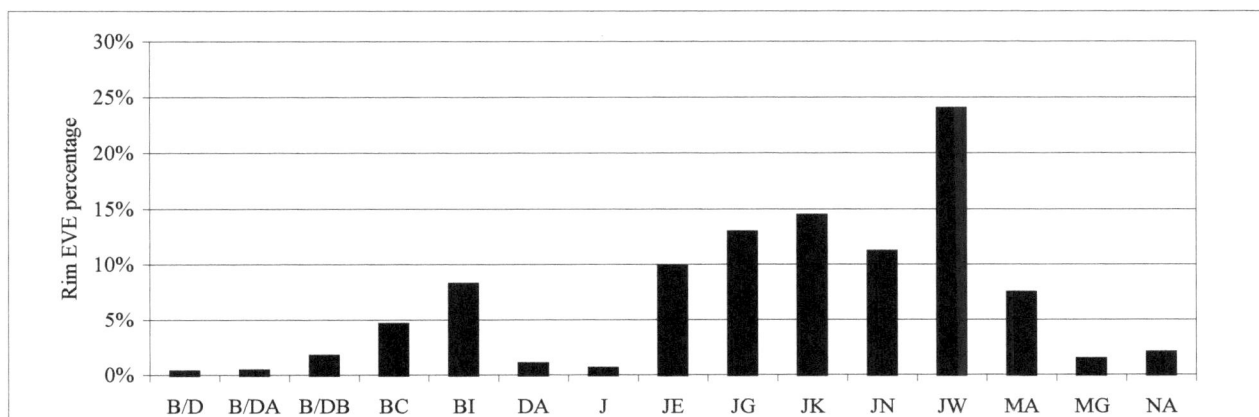

Fig. 41: Romano-British pottery: histogram of percentage occurrence by rim EVE for vessel classes

Treatment and decoration

Some 100 sherds, 18% of the assemblage, demonstrated signs of modification of some sort. Of these, 90% showed signs of external sooting, occurring in only four fabrics: 49% Derbyshire coarseware lid-seated (bell-mouthed) jars, 38% Black-Burnished ware cooking pots, 2% reduced Severn Valley ware and 1% fabric G09.3. A single sherd of Central Gaul Lezoux samian (1%) showed signs of general burning. Nine percent of the modifications showed evidence of being Derbyshire coarseware wasters.

Decorative motifs on the pottery were restricted primarily to the Black-Burnished ware forms. The majority of the vessels demonstrated surface treatment. Most commonly this comprised a burnished inside and a wiped outside, with a high percentage decorated externally, mainly with acute lattice or intersecting arcs. The only other decorative motifs occur on the decorated samian described below. These decorative elements are all chronologically diagnostic and date the assemblage to the 2nd/early 3rd century AD.

Discussion

Only a single phase of Roman period occupation has been identified at Whitemoor Haye. This occupation appears to be datable to the mid-late 2nd/early 3rd century AD. The forms and fabrics identified include locally produced Derbyshire coarseware, in lid-seated (bell-mouthed) forms. This is a distinctive type that has been found on local sites such as Little Chester, Wall, Rocester, Stapenhill near Burton-on-Trent and Margidunum (Gillam 1939). Kay (1962) has noted two sources of manufacture for Derbyshire ware, Hazelwood and Holbrook. The known distribution of the pottery appears to correspond to the line of known Roman roads and lesser-known Roman routes such as Portway. At Hazelwood the occurrence of the 'bell-mouthed' type A, as opposed to rolled (type B) rim jars is (70%:30%). The overwhelming evidence suggests that the bell-mouthed forms were intended to take a lid or wooden stopper. Jones and Webster (1969) revised Gillam's (1939) original dating for the production of Derbyshire coarseware from the late 3rd/4th to the mid 2nd century AD. Production was initially localised with expansion in the late 2nd -early 3rd century due to improved marketing that sent the ware across the northern military zone. Brassington (1980) excavated several Derbyshire coarseware kilns at Derby racecourse and dated these from the Flavian to Hadrianic/Antonine periods. Earlier work by Brassington (1971) suggested that the style of the Derbyshire coarseware vessels had marked affinities with a late 1st-century group from Manduessedum and links with Mancetter-Hartshill potteries. Material from this industry was also recovered from Whitemoor Haye.

In addition to the Derbyshire coarsewares, large diagnostic pieces the regionally traded Black-Burnished ware, in cooking pot and flange bowl forms, and oxidised Severn Valley ware were observed. These date to the late 2nd/early 3rd century and have decorative motifs, such as acute lattice and intersecting arcs, which are all chronologically significant.

There is a small amount of residual Roman material. This includes a sherd of southwest England/south Wales (Caerleon) mortaria from Area B, droveway, 2003 (F200), dated to the 1st century and the South Gaulish La Graufesenque samian from Area T, pit, 1005 (F101.02) and dated to 70-100AD (see below). Overall, however, the ceramic assemblage can be closely assigned to the mid-late 2nd/early 3rd century AD.

A small quantity of intrusive material was recovered during the watching brief from pit F903. This comprised a Black-Burnished ware straight-sided dish of mid 2nd-century date and a Central Gaulish (Lezoux) Drag 18/31 (see below). This feature dated to the Late Bronze Age/Early Iron Age.

What is most apparent is the utilitarian nature of the assemblage. The vessel classes represented amongst the assemblage are commonly associated with food preparation (mortaria, lid-seated [bell-mouthed] jars, cooking pots, bowls) and storage (wide and narrow-mouthed jars). It has been suggested (Brassington 1971) that the Derbyshire coarseware jars were produced as utilitarian containers for beans grown in south Derbyshire. There is a distinct lack of high status tableware such beakers, cups and platters. This is reflected in the lack of regionally traded colour-coated ware and the small quantity of imported samian amongst the assemblage. Black-Burnished ware cooking pots with near upright rims, Severn Valley wide-mouthed jars with pointed bead rims and lid-seated (bell-mouthed) jars in Derbyshire coarseware, dominate this small ceramic assemblage.

Samian *by Steven Willis*

A total of 16 sherds of samian pottery (*terra sigillata*) was recovered. The sherds derive from 13 vessels, with a variety of form types and sources represented. No context yielded more than three sherds. Although a very small number of items, the samian provides significant information with regard to dating activities and site phasing. Overall, the group has a date range of c. AD 70-225, with the majority of the pieces belonging to the second century. Sherds vary greatly in size, presumably reflecting differing taphonomic processes and deposit formation mechanisms operative across the site and through time. The sherds contrast *vis-à-vis* their state of preservation, with some abraded and some showing chemical weathering, while others are in comparatively good condition.

The catalogue lists all samian and adheres to a consistent format, as with the coarsewares above. The decorative details catalogued by Rogers (Rogers 1974) are simply referred to as, for example, Rogers B105, following the standard convention, without quoting the bibliographic reference on every occasion. Similarly, Oswald's typology of figures (Oswald 1936-7) is referred to following convention; for example O.2220 would be his type 2220. The presence of other features such as burning, etc. is also noted.

Catalogue

S01 (SG La Graufesenque)

Not illustrated. Body from a platter, c. AD 70-100. This sherd is from the floor of the vessel, within the footring, and has apparently been trimmed around to produce a disc.
1005, F101.02.

18. Decorated body, from Drag. 37 c. AD 80-100. The decoration is arranged in bands; the lower band is better represented and comprises a festoon inhabited by differing motifs, including a large 13 petalled rosette (Hermet 1934, Pl. 15 No. 65) and the swan O.2220 (Hermet 1934, Pl. 28 No.34.) The festoon itself is formed by semicircular plain ridges with a serrated or leaf edge without (cf. Hermet 1934, Pl. 31 No. 21.). The festoons are divided by trifid leaf/bud pendants with long stems and are poorly defined. Above the festoon is a larger (main) band of decoration, which is here vestigial and abraded; it appears to include a scroll, and a subsidiary bird is also present; the lower vessel wall is unusually thick.
Fig. 39.18, unstratified, from linear between Areas B and C.

S02 (CG Les Martres-de Veyre)

Not illustrated. Body from Drag. 18/31R, c. AD 100-130. In good condition.
9070, F944, Area WB02.

19. Rim sherd and 2 decorated body sherds all from the same vessel, a Drag. 37 c. AD 100-125/130. Part of the ovolo band is present, but weathering has obliterated any other decorative details. The ovolo, which is neatly proportioned, well executed and sharply defined, is cf. Rogers B28, having a single border and a straight, probably corded, tongue which ends in a rosette terminal. This type of ovolo was popular with several Les Martres potters, including Donnaucus, Drusus i, Ioenalis and X-2 (cf. Terrisse 1968). There is a good gloss finish to the vessel.
Fig. 39.19, 1041, F118.04, RE: 0.10, Diameter 20cm, Area T.

S03 (CG Lezoux)

Not illustrated. Rim, from a bead rimmed bowl or dish, potentially c. AD 120-200, though probably c. AD 120-150; stained and weathered.
9070, F944, RE: c. 0.03, Diam. uncertain, Area WB02.

Not illustrated. Body, from Drag. 31R c. AD 160-200.
Unstratified.

20. Decorated body, from Drag. 37 c. AD 140-180. Stained. A small area of abraded decoration occurs, comprising part of a panelled design, perhaps the work of Cinnamus ii. The panels are defined by fine bead borders ending in small roundels; within one panel is the ornamental motif Rogers Q58 (or Q1, if part of a combined arrangement); to the left, in a second panel is an apparent standard, Rogers Q27. Cinnamus ii employed both motifs (cf. Stanfield and Simpson 1958, fig.47 Nos. 18 and 28) though neither is exclusive to him.
Fig.39.20, Unstratified

Not illustrated. Rim probably Drag. 18/31, c. AD 120-150; rather weathered and abraded.
9005, F903, RE: c. 0.04, Diam. 18/19cm, Area WB02.

Not illustrated. Body, form not identifiable, c. AD 120-200.
2002/2003, F201/F200, Area B.

Not illustrated. 2 conjoining body sherds, form not identifiable, c. AD 120-200.
2002/2003, F201/F200, Area B.

Not illustrated. Virtual profile, comparatively large Drag. 31 c. AD 150-200.
5012, F505.02, Rim Eve: 0.14, Diam. 21cm, Base Eve: 0.13, Diam. 12cm.

Not illustrated. Body probably Drag. 37 c. AD 120-200; burnt and abraded.
8024, F808, Area F.

S04R (East Gaul Rheinzabern)

Not illustrated. Rim probably Drag. 31 c. AD 150-225.
5007, F503, RE: c. 0.03, Diam. Uncertain.

Discussion

The quantity of samian recovered during 1997-9 is insufficiently large to permit any quantitative analysis. The material covers a reasonably broad date range. The two earliest vessels are South Gaulish, a platter and a decorated Drag. 37 bowl, indicating a supply to the site in the late first century. It is entirely possible, though, that at this site these vessels were still in use during the early years of the second century; indeed, the platter fragment (from F101.02, 1005, Area S, WB03) was evidently re-fashioned into a disc, which may have prolonged its currency. South Gaulish samian reached a wide variety of sites in the Midlands and northern England, in modest quantities, particularly after c. AD 70. There is some firm evidence that decorated bowls were acquired by rural/indigenous consumers in preference to plain ware form types during the initial decades of the Roman era (cf. Willis 1997). Hence the presence of the Domitianic Drag. 37 from the vicinity of Areas B and C is of interest (Fig. 39.18).

Les Martres-de-Veyre samian, of Trajanic-early Hadrianic date (c. AD 100-130), is also represented by two vessels, indicating sustained consumption of samian during a period when the overall level of samian supply to Britain appears to have been comparatively low. One vessel is a decorated bowl (Fig. 39.19).

As is usual at rural sites of the Roman period in England and Wales, Lezoux samian, of Hadrianic-Antonine date, forms the major part of the collected samian (cf. Table 16 below), with a variety of forms represented. A solitary East Gaulish vessel is present, from Rheinzabern, which is the most frequently represented East Gaulish source in Britain. This item may have arrived, and been consumed at the site, before the close of the second century.

As a whole, there is a comparatively high frequency of decorated to plain ware types present (see Table 16). At other sites this trend can often be taken to be an indicator of higher status, though in this case the sample size is too small and is perhaps collected from too broad an area for this to be considered a reliable index. The main aspect of note, overall, is the sustained supply and consumption of this imported fine ware at the complex through the early Roman period, albeit in apparently small quantity.

Worked Stone *by Lynne Bevan and Rob Ixer*

Five items of worked stone were recovered, comprising the upper stone from a beehive rotary quern (Plate 14), fragments from two other querns (F486/4143 and F101.02), a rubber (F519), and a possible rubbing stone (F441). The upper quernstone from a beehive quern was a particularly fine specimen of this typically Iron Age form of quern. Due to fragmentation among the other querns, the barely-modified nature of the rubber, and uncertainty regarding the identification of the possible rubbing stone, none of the other stone items has been illustrated.

The beehive quern is unusual in that the central hole is slightly off-centre, creating a difference in height, with one side being noticeably higher than the other. Moreover, the quern is equipped with two handle holes rather than the customary one necessary for manual rotation. As well as extensive pecking visible on the outer surface, care has been taken to create the raised outer lip on the edge of the central hole, reminiscent to that of a vessel, which appears to have been created for aesthetic rather than practical, reasons. The

moulded rim is typical of a Hunsbury type A quern (Philips 1950, 76), an example of which has been recovered from Fisherwick, Staffordshire together with parts from two other beehive querns (Samuels 1979, 65-66, fig.17a).

Although the dating of beehive querns is uncertain, this form of quern is believed to have been first introduced during the Early Iron Age and to have continued into the Roman period (May 1976, 137). At Fisherwick, Ancaster (May 1976, 136) and Salmonsbury (Dunning 1977, 114), beehive querns appear to have been used contemporaneously with saddle querns (Samuels 1979, 65). The presence of a stone rubber (Cat. No. 4) and a possible rubbing stone (Cat. No. 5) in this small assemblage suggests that this might also have been the case at Whitemoor Haye, although this cannot be demonstrated contextually.

As with other finds categories such as flint (*Worked Flint*, above) and prehistoric pottery (*Prehistoric Pottery*, above), the possibility of structured deposition (Richards and Thomas 1984; Hill 1993), i.e. that items were deliberated deposited in certain contexts rather than being casually discarded, should not be overlooked here. According to research conducted on the contexts in which they have been found, querns are a class of object that may have been placed as part of ritual or special deposits (Buckley 1991). However, the saddle and beehive querns from various contexts, including the bottom of Iron Age pits, examined by Buckley tended to have been deposited in a complete and useful state (1991, 1). Apart from the beehive quern, which was in a good state of preservation, this was not the case at Whitemoor Haye, since both of the other quernstones were fragmentary, although this does not preclude the possibility of structured deposition since deliberate breakage might have constituted part of the ritual. For example, the manipulation of the fragment in many prehistoric archaeological contexts has recently been discussed (Chapman 2000). At Wanlip, Leicestershire, fragments of four querns from three different geological sources were placed in a single pit (Marsden 1998, 63). Other examples of querns used in identified special deposits are known from other sites including Danebury (Brown 1984) and Gussage All Saints (Buckley 1979 and 1991).

Table 16: The Composition of the Samian Assemblage (items identifiable to generic forms only)

Form Type	South Gaulish (S01)	Central Gaulish - Les Martres (S02)	Central Gaulish – Lezoux (S03)	East Gaulish (S04R)
Decorated Bowls:				
Drag. 37	1	1	2	
Plain Bowls:				
Drag. 31R			1	
Bowl or Dish:				
Specific form uncertain			1	
Dishes:				
Drag. 18/31			1	
Drag. 18/31R		1		
Drag. 31			1	1
Platters:				
Specific form uncertain	1			
Totals:	2	2	6	1

Finds from Iron Age enclosure ditches have exhibited unusual patterning, suggesting that these ditches were singled out as appropriate contexts for structured deposition (see Hill 1993 for discussion). That the larger of the upper quern fragments at Whitemoor Haye was found in an enclosure ditch (F486/4183) might be of relevance. Such boundaries are increasingly accepted as 'representing significant discontinuities in social/symbolic space, and not simply ecological/economic space' (Hill 1993, 65), and it has been suggested that the significance of the enclosure was that in certain circumstances it symbolically defined the social group (Hingley 1984). Other potential instances of structured deposition at Whitemoor Haye include the possible granodiorite rubbing stone from a pit inside a hut (F441) and the non-local biotite granite rubber from a pit in one of the pit alignments containing Iron Age pottery (F519). The possible rubbing stone was complete and useable and the rubber, although broken along its length, was of an unusual and attractive grey, yellow and white mottled material. Its appearance alone suggests that it might have been selected for inclusion in a 'special' deposit. However, as with the small flint assemblage discussed above, while structured deposition among the lithic assemblage at Whitemoor Haye can be regarded as a distinct possibility, the evidence, derived from isolated items among which dating is uncertain, remains enigmatic.

The querns are made of three different fine to medium-grained sandstones. Two are of Millstone Grit/Coal Measures sandstones of Carboniferous age and the third is a New Red Sandstone of Triassic age. The Carboniferous querns are probably regional imports from the Peak District whereas the Permo-Triassic quern may be more local. Querns made of Millstone Grit are commonly reported, as at Fisherwick (Samuels and Smith 1979, 171); those made of New Red Sandstone less so.

The petrography of the granodiorite rubbing stone is close to that of the Mountsorrel granodiorite. This is not true for the biotite granites.

Although there is no exact match between the granite-granodiorite rubbing stone and any of the Midlands intrusive rocks, the degree and type of alteration of this rock would be consistent with a regional (Leicestershire or Warwickshire) source. This is not true for the biotite granite.

Catalogue

1. Upper stone from a beehive quern of fine-grained bedded white sandstone (Coal Measures). A Coal Measures quartz arenite. The finely-worked surface has been extensively pecked. The central hole is off-centre and the quern is considerably higher at one side than the other. The quern is unusual in having two rectangular-shaped handle holes, both of which continue through the walls and into the central hole. One, situated below the shorter side of the quern, would have been more effective for manual rotation. The other is situated to one side of the higher side of the quern. The height ranges from 165mm to 200mm. Basal diameter: 200mm, outer diameter of central hole: 110mm. Dimensions of ?handle holes, upper: 55mm x 40mm, lower: 60mm x 40mm. A very pure, quartz arenite comprising quartz and trace amounts of perthite, microcline, zircon and white mica. The sandstone is matrix supported with much void space. Angular to rounded quartz grains display serrated contacts where they touch and these are accompanied by some grain size reduction. Elsewhere, thin, authigenic quartz overgrowths form euhedral terminations into void spaces. Trace amounts of perthite and microcline are fresh, although other potassium feldspar grains are altered; white mica flakes, opaque minerals, chert, fine-grained sandstone and polycrystalline, metamorphic quartz clasts are all very rare. Minor amounts of fine-grained, white mica/clay minerals lie about the quartz grains. The purity and pale colour of the sandstone suggest that the quern is a Coal Measures sandstone, rather than the local Triassic, sandstone. F 923, 9039. Plate 14.

2. Upper quern fragment of pale-coloured, medium-grained, Millstone Grit or Coal Measures arkosic sandstone, on which part of the central channel for the spindle is visible. This fragment comprises approximately 25% of the original quern. Diameter: 400mm, height: 65mm. F486, 4143. Not illustrated.

3. Quern fragment of fine-grained, pink sandstone New Red Sandstone of Triassic Age on which the remains of part of the central channel for the spindle is visible. All of the original edges have been lost. Length: 100mm, width: 88mm, thickness: 43mm. F101.02, 1005. Not illustrated.

4. Rubber of coarse-grained biotite granite with smoothed lower surface resulting from use. Scottish and Lake District granite erratics including those from the grey Dalbeattie granite are common within the drift of the area. The rock is not local or regional. The object has been broken. Length: 150mm, width: 110mm, thickness: 45mm. F519, 5032. Not illustrated.

5. Possible rubbing stone of a medium-grained granite-granodiorite. Length: 270mm, width: 185mm, thickness: 57mm. It is a plagioclase-potassium feldspar-quartz-brown/green amphibole-biotite rock with trace amounts of apatite and zircon and secondary epidote, chlorite, white mica and deep green amphibole. Graphic intergrowths between perthite and quartz are noticeable and the potassium feldspars include perthite and microcline. Zoned plagioclase, displaying altered cores enclosed within fresh margins, is altered to white mica and epidote. Amphibole alters to epidote and chlorite and biotite to chlorite and secondary biotite. The petrography suggests that this might come from the Mountsorrel complex. F441, 4076. Not illustrated.

ECOFACTUAL EVIDENCE

Plant Macroremains   *by Marina Ciaraldi*

Methodology

The design of the sampling strategy adopted followed the general BUFAU guidelines outlined in the 'On-site guide to environmental sampling'. Bulk samples of 20 litres were collected from datable contexts, while the entire deposit was taken where smaller contexts were encountered. A total of 23 samples was processed using bucket flotation. The light fraction (flot) was recovered on a 500μm sieve while the heavy fraction (residue) was retrieved on a 1mm mesh. The flots were sorted using a standard low-power stereomicroscope while the residue was sorted by eye.

The samples were processed and assessed in two stages. The first assessment was done only on seven samples and none of the samples contained enough charred plant remains to justify further analysis. The processing of more samples was recommended (Moffett 1999). A further 16 samples were processed and their assessment confirmed the general scarcity of charred plant remains. Only three of these samples were recommended for further investigation (Smith 1999).

Two samples come from the fill of hut gullies in Area A (F421.04/4055 and F438.01/4062) and date to the Early/Middle Iron Age (Period 2). The third came from the fill of a ditch in Area S (F505.02/5012) and dates to the 2nd century AD or later (Period 3).

Identification

The plant remains from the three selected samples were identified with the help of a reference collection. Nomenclature follows Stace (1997) for the wild species and Zohary and Hopf (1994) for cultivated plants.

Sample F421.04/4055 was formed almost exclusively of compacted charred straw. Numerous culm nodes and bases were also found. The culm nodes and bases were large enough to be those of cereals, but it was preferred to group them as cereals/Poaceae. A few detached coleoptiles were also found and assigned to the same category. A few cereal grains were found in the deposit but were too poorly preserved to be identified.

Cereal grains from the other two samples were slightly more abundant but equally distorted and damaged. Only one grain from the Iron Age sample F505.02/5012 was tentatively identified as emmer (*Triticum* cf. *dicoccum* Schübl.). The grain presented a high bump above the embryo, a rather curved ventral profile and a tapered tip (Jacomet 1987).

A large chaff assemblage was recovered from the Roman sample F505.01/5012. It was mainly formed of glume bases and rachis internodes. Glume bases that presented a prominent primary keel and tertiary veins and an angle wider than 90 degrees in correspondence to the primary keel were identified as spelt (*Triticum spelta* L.). Glume bases that were either damaged or had no distinctive features were assigned to the emmer/spelt category.

It was possible to identify some of the wheat rachis internodes as those of spelt. They presented the two typical longitudinal lines on the outer edge of the convex surface normally observed in hexaploid wheat (Hillman *et al.* 1996). The absence of rachis internodes joined together suggests that they were not those of bread wheat (*Triticum aestivum* s.l.).

Barley grains were easily identifiable on the basis of their "barrel" shape. Unfortunately they were too corroded and distorted to observe the presence of husk or if their embryo was symmetric. Rachis internodes identified as those of six-row barley (*Hordeum vulgare* L. subsp. *hexastichum*) presented the diagnostic structure and position of the scar.

A single grain and some joint rachis internodes of rye (*Secale cereale* L.) were also found. The grain had the typical elongated embryo and truncated opposite end.

A seed of false flax (*Camelina sativa* (L.) Crantz.) was identified on the basis of its prominent embryo and the size of the seed (1.9 mm length). The size of false flax seeds is intermediate between that of *C.microcarpa* Andrz. and *Camelina alyssum* (Miller) Thell. (Rich 1991). In a small area at the base of the embryo a cell pattern similar to that observed in modern specimens was still visible.

It is impossible to say whether the seed belong to the wild or cultivated form as no fruits were found (Zohary and Hopf 1994).

Discussion

Iron Age assemblage

The two Early/Middle Iron Age samples had a very different plant composition. Despite the scarcity of botanical remains recovered from sample F438.01/4062, the presence of a few chaff and weed seeds suggested that there was some crop processing on site. Noticeable is the presence of a single seed of gold-of-pleasure or false flax (*Camelina sativa* (L.) Crantz.). False flax was probably imported into Europe during the Bronze Age as a weed of flax or cereals and only later started being cultivated as an oil plant. Schültze-Motel (1979) suggests that false flax became widespread along coastal areas of the Baltic and North Sea only during the Iron Age. Latalowa (1998) found seeds of various species of *Camelina* in a 9th-century bundle of flax from Poland. She suggests that this species is one of the weeds that occur typically in flax fields. Only two records from England are known to the author. They were both found from Roman and Saxon deposits in London (Tyers 1988 and Jones *et al.* 1991 cit. in Tomlinson and Hall 1996). The Whitemoor Haye find could therefore be the earliest record from an English site.

Sample F421.04/4055 comes from a hut gully in Area A. The composition is very characteristic as the matrix is mainly formed of compressed charred straw. A good number of culm nodes, culm bases and germinated embryos (coleoptiles) were observed but only a few fragments of charcoal (see *Charcoal*, below). The sample composition is very characteristic and allows an unequivocal interpretation of the assemblage as burnt stable manure. Kenward and Hall (1997 and 1998) mention the presence of compacted straw as one of the indicator groups for stable manure. The aspect of the sample is also similar to that described by Miller (1984) in her experiment on modern charred dung.

The few cereal grains found in the deposit seem to indicate that the straw came from cereals rather than grasses. The low ratio of grains compared to the relative abundance of parts of the culm suggests that it consisted probably of stubble. The occurrence of a good number of culm bases is a clear sign that the stubble was uprooted. The stubble might have been used either as animal fodder or as litter for domestic animals. It is impossible to determine on the basis of a single sample whether the stable manure had been charred because it had been used as a fuel or as a consequence of routine cleaning of the stables.

The poor preservation of the cereal grains did not allow the observation of any sign of digestion of the grains (for instance the "puckered appearance" observed by Charles (1998)), as one would have expected in presence of charred dung.

The presence of cereal/grasses coleoptiles is also of some interest. They have often been interpreted as evidence for malting associated to the production of beer. In this case, however this interpretation seems unlikely. Their presence in the Whitemoor Haye sample is probably related to germination during storage in damp conditions or to the fact that they may represent grains left on the ears after the harvest and germinated in the field as consequence of the late gathering of the stubble.

A very similar plant assemblage has been recovered from a Roman sample at Colchester (Murphy 1992). In that case too, the deposit was interpreted as evidence of animal dung cleaned out from byres and stables and burnt together with spilt fodder and litter. Animal dung was tentatively identified from Gamston, Nottinghamshire, a nearby site of the same period (Moffett 1992). Waterlogged plant remains from horse dung where analysed by Wilson (1979) from the Roman level at Lancaster.

The presence of stable manure in the fill of the hut gully from Area A has important implications for the general interpretation of the area. Its presence seems to suggest that the enclosure may have been used as animal pen. This hypothesis is also supported by the interpretation of the other biological remains from the same area. The analysis of the waterlogged insect and plant remains from a pit feature in Area A (F468/4166) also suggested that animals were present in the area. Insects associated with dung were found in the area (see *Insect Remains*, below) and the possibility that F468 could have been a drinking hole for animals (see *Waterlogged Seeds*, below) has also been suggested.

Roman assemblage

The only sample from the Roman occupation at Whitemoor Haye contained a rich charred plant assemblage. A total of 580 anatomical parts of plants was recovered. The sample is widely dominated by chaff, mainly spelt glume bases (see Fig. 42). High percentages of chaff seem to be common on Roman sites in this region (for instance Tiddington (Moffett 1986), Norfolk Street (Jones 1982) and Salford Priors (Moffett and Ciaraldi forthcoming)). This has often been interpreted as an indication of the use of chaff as fuel. The most common cereal in the Roman sample deposit is spelt, but barley and rye are present too. It is not clear whether these two cereals are independent crops or if they represent contaminants of spelt. The sample clearly represents the waste of cereal crop processing. The high percentage of spelt glume bases and some small-seeded weeds such as blinks (*Montia fontana* sbsp. *minor*), corn spurrey (*Spergula arvensis* L.), sheep's sorrel (*Rumex acetosella* L.) and *Potentilla* sp. would suggest that the sample represents the residue of fine sieving. However, large-seeded plants such as brome grass (*Bromus mollis/secalinus*), black bindweed (*Fallopia convolvulus* Love) and a capsule of wild radish (*Raphanus* cf. *raphanistrum*) are also present.

The presence of by-products from various stages of crop processing suggests that the deposit might represent a mixture of waste from different stages of crop processing. Large seeded weeds tend in fact to appear in association with the final stages of cleaning as their seeds have similar dimensions to those of cereals. Large seeds of weeds are generally removed by hand-picking. Often their presence has been interpreted as evidence that cereals were stored as spikelets rather than cleaned grains (van der Veen 1996). Another possibility is that the two groups of weeds are associated with two different crops, for instance spelt and barley.

The lack of other samples from the same period does not allow a more secure interpretation of this assemblage. The small size of the assemblage does not allow an interpretation of whether the presence of barley and rye grains and rachis internodes is the result of processing of the two cereals or whether they are present only as contaminants of spelt.

Indications that the cereals might have been cultivated on rather poor soils come from the presence of species such as blinks, corn spurrey, sheep's sorrel and *Potentilla* sp.. Interestingly the same group of plants appears in the Iron Age waterlogged sample (see *Waterlogged Seeds*, below) and seems to suggests a similar pattern of land use in the two periods. The presence of several plants associated with damp or wet ground, such as sedges, field wood-rush, common spike-rush, lesser spearwort and blinks, suggests that the fields were probably poorly drained.

Conclusions

The plant remains recovered from the prehistoric and Roman levels at Whitemoor Haye represent a small but significant assemblage. Scanty evidence of agricultural practices was associated with the two Iron Age samples. The presence of false flax (*Camelina sativa* L.) in one of the prehistoric samples is noteworthy. This weed was introduced into Europe as a weed of flax or cereal crops during the Bronze Age and eventually became more common during the Iron Age (Shültze-Motel 1979). The Whitemoor Haye specimen may be the earliest find of false flax in England. The second Iron Age sample has a very characteristic composition and has been interpreted as charred stable manure. Its presence on site suggests that animal pens might have been present in Area A. The evidence from the waterlogged plant and insect remains from the same area is consistent with this interpretation.

The plant assemblage from the Roman sample clearly represents waste from crop processing. The contemporary presence of chaff, small seeded weeds (generally interpreted as by-products of fine sieving) and large seeded weeds (normally associated with the cleaning of the crop just before consumption) suggests that the deposit includes waste from different stages of the cereal cleaning process. The mixing of waste from the processing of different crops may have occurred during the backfilling of the ditch. Roman samples dominated by chaff have already been reported from various sites in the Midlands and they might constitute evidence of the use of crop waste as fuel. Some of the weeds present in the Roman assemblage suggest that cereals were probably cultivated on poor soil. The presence of a large number of species associated with wet and damp places also indicates that the fields were poorly drained.

Table 17: Charred plant remains species list

	Site code		WHS 97	WHS 97	WHS 98	
	Area		A	A	S	
	Feature/Context		F421.04/40 55	F438.01/4062	F505.02/5012	
	Sample vol.		6	10	20	
	Seed/Litre		26.7	1.6	29	
	Type of context		Hut Gully	Hut Gully	Ditch	
	Period/phase		2 (E/MIA)	2 (E/MIA)	3 (mid 2nd AD or later)	
	Cereals					
cereals	Cerealia	gr	5	1	14	
cereals/grasses	Cerealia/Large Poaceae	gr	-	-	10	
wild/cult. barley	*Hordeum sp.*	gr	-	-	1	
barley	*Hordeum vulgare* l.	gr	-	-	6	
oats	*Avena* sp.	gr	-	1		
rye	*Secale cereale* L.	gr	-	-	1	
wheat	*Triticum sp.*	gr	-	2	7	
	Chaff					
cereals	Cerealia	cb	23	-	2	
cereals	Cerealia	cn	107	-	2	
cereals/grasses	Cerealia/large Poaceae	col	14	-	-	
cereals/grasses	Cerealia/large Poaceae	ci	XXX	-	-	
six-row barley	*Hord. vulgare* L. six-row	ci	-	-	2	
rye	*Secale cereale* L.	ci	-	-	2	
rye	*Secale cereale* L.	ri	-	-	2	
spelt	*Triticum spelta* L.	glb/ri	-	-	5	
spelt	*Triticum spelta* L.	glb	-	-	77	
spelt	*Triticum spelta* L.	f	-	-	2	
wheat	*Triticum spelta* L.	ri	1	-	33	
spelt	*Triticum cf. spelta*	glb	-	1	-	
emmer	*Triticum dicoccum* Schübl.	glb	-	1	-	
emmer/spelt	*Triticum dicoccum/spelta*	glb	-	1	174	
emmer/spelt	*Triticum dicoccum/spelta*	f	-	1	-	
wheat	*Triticum sp.*	glb	1	-	-	
wheat	*Triticum sp.*	ri	-	-	50	
	Collected or cultivated					
hazelnut	*Corylus avellana* L.	sh	-	1	-	collected or cultivated
blackthorn, sloe	*Prunus spinosa*	st	1	-	-	collected or cultivated
	Non cultivated plants					
Lesser spearwort	*Ranunculus flammula*	s	-	-	1	damp and wet places
poppy	*Papaver* sp. (immature)	s	-	-	2	
goosefoots	*Chenopodium* sp.	s	-	-	14 modern?	
blinks	*Montia fontana* sbsp. minor	s	1	-	4 modern?	damp places
com.chickweed	*Stellaria media* (L.) Vill.	s	-	1	-	
corn spurrey	*Spergula arvensis* L.	s	-	-	1	sandy cultivated grounds
black bindweed	*Fallopia convolvulus* Love	s	-	-	1	waste and arable grounds
redshank	*Polygonum maculosa/lapathifolia*	s	-	-	2	waste and cultivated grounds
sheep's sorrel	*Rumex acetosella* L.	s	-	-	5	poor sandy soils
	Rumex sp.	s	-	-	5	
false flax	*Camelina sativa* L.	s	-	1	-	weeds of cereals and flax; cultivated
wild radish	*Raphanus raphanistrum* L..	cps	-	-	2	introduced. Waste and arable
cinquefoil	*Potentilla sp.*	s	-	-	3	
	Trif./Medic./Melil.	s	-	-	4	
	Apiaceae	s	-	-	1	
ribwort plantain	*Plantago lanceolata* L.	s	1	-	4	grassl. tramped
	Euphrasia/Odontites	s	-	-	1	

65

nipplewort	*Lapsana communis* L.	s	-	-	1	waste / rough ground; hedgerows
	Compositae *Mayweed* type	s	-	-	4	
annual meadow grass	*Poa annua* L.	s	-	-	2	waste and cultivated land
timothy	*Phleum pratense* L.	s	-	-	1	grassy places and rough grounds
brome	*Bromus mollis/secalinus*	s	-	4	55	weed
	Poaceae small *Poa* type	s	-	-	17	
	Poaceae medium	s	-	-	9	
	Carex sp. (triagonous)	s	1	-	16	wet and damp places
	Carex sp. (flat)	s	-	-	5	wet and damp places
field wood-rush	*Luzula campestris* (L.) DC.	s	-	-	1	grasslands
	Eleocharis cf. *palustris* (L.)	s	-	-	1	wet and damp places
	Cyperaceae	s	-	1	-	wet and damp places
	Other					
	Tuber		-	-	1	
	Bud		-	-	1	
	Indetermined	s	-	-	20	

Key: cb = culm base; ci = culm internode; cn = culm node; col = coleptile; cps = capsule; f = fork; glb = glume bases; gr = grain; ri = rachis internode, s = seed; sh = nutshell; st = stone

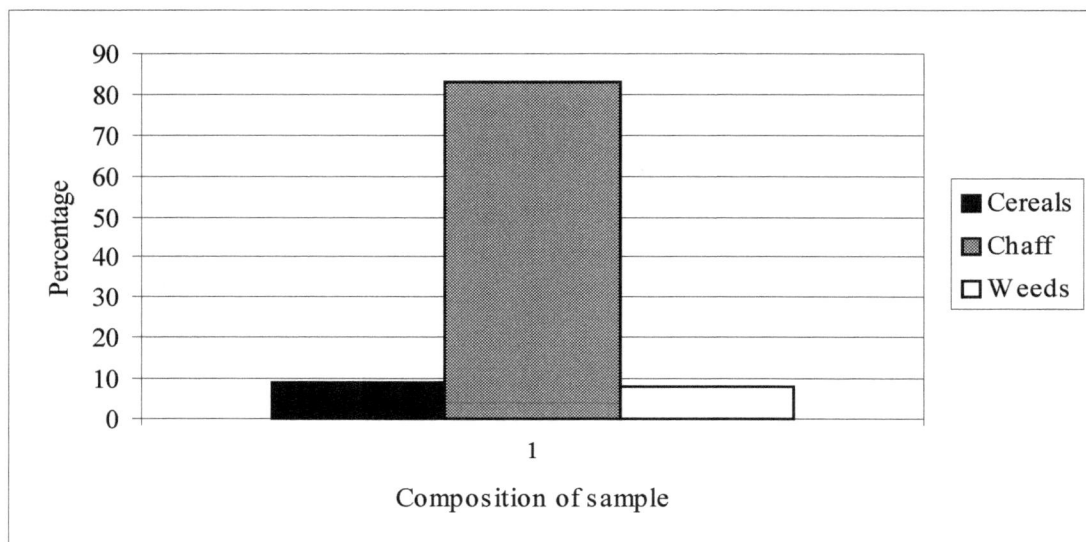

Fig. 42: Percentage of cereals, chaff and wheat from the Roman period (Period 3)

Waterlogged Wood *by Erica Macey*

One item of waterlogged wood was recovered from the bottom fill (4143) of the Iron Age enclosure ditch (F486) in Area A. Steve Allen (pers. comm.) identified this as a small wooden stake.

The item measured 385mm, but the upper end was bent over upon itself - this was probably due to damage during burial rather than during actual use. The maximum width was 53mm, whilst the thickness ranged between 17 and 26mm. Seven tree rings per centimetre were visible, but the item was too small to provide a sample for dendrochronology.

Radially-cleft oak was used to make the stake, which had been worked with a metal axe - this was evident from the sharply cut facets visible on the stake. It was possible to say that the stake had been cut from the heartwood/sapwood boundary of the tree, as some 50% of the item was sapwood, but it was not possible to determine the actual size of the tree.

Allen stated that this type of stake was commonly used in the construction of buildings, fences and revetments. There was no evidence of re-use. From the context, the stake is likely to be of Iron Age date.

Insect Remains *by David Smith*

Introduction

Only one waterlogged deposit with potential for insect analysis was encountered during the excavations at Whitemoor Haye. This material came from the earliest cut (F473) in a sequence of five re-cuts of a bowl shaped pit. This feature has been dated on the basis of the pottery evidence to the Middle Iron Age. The pit itself had been cut into the southern terminal of the Early to Middle Iron Age enclosure ditch F468 in Area A.

It was hoped that an analysis of the insects from this deposit might enable it to be determined whether human settlement was still present at this late stage in the use of the enclosure, and if not how the landscape was being used.

Methods and analyses

The single sample examined from context 4147 weighed 13 kilograms and was 6 litres in volume. The sample was processed using the standard method of paraffin flotation as outlined in Kenward *et al.* (1980) and sorted and identified under a binocular microscope. Where achievable the insect remains present were identified to species by direct comparison to the Gorham and Girling insect collections housed in the Department of Ancient History and Archaeology, University of Birmingham.

The taxa recovered are presented in Table 18. The nomenclature used follows that of Lucht (1987). The majority of the taxa present are beetles (Coleoptera), although large numbers of ants (Formicoidea), bugs (Hemoptera) and earwigs (Dermaptera) are present. The larval resting stages of the water flea (*Daphnia* spp.), and the head capsules and cases of both cased and caseless caddis flies (Tricoptera) are also present. There are small numbers of the head capsules of the larvae of non-biting midges (Chironomidae) as well. In terms of the Coleoptera, 1194 individuals from 176 species were identified.

In order to aid interpretation, where possible the taxa present have been assigned to ecological groupings following the scheme suggested by Robinson (1981, 1983). The affiliation of each species to a particular ecological grouping is coded in the second column of Table 18. The meaning of each ecological code is explained in the key at the base of Table 18. The occurrence of each of the ecological groupings is expressed as a percentage in Table 19 and in Figure 43. The pasture/grassland, dung and woodland/timber species are calculated as percentages of the number of terrestrial species as opposed to the whole fauna. Column four of Table 18 indicates those species of beetle that are associated with specific plants. The ecology for this information was mainly derived from Koch (1989, 1992).

Discussion

Evidence of the presence of human settlement

It is clear from the species list that there are few taxa present that are strictly associated with human settlement. Species such as *Corticaria, Lathridius minutus, Cryptophagus* and *Monotoma brevicollis* are present in human occupation but are also found in nature. The only strong synanthrope (species associated with human settlement) that is present is the spider beetle *Ptinus fur*. However this species will occur away from human settlement if the environment is favourable. This suggests that the pit, and the area surrounding it, were not adjacent to human occupation or settlement. This lack of evidence for settlement is particularly striking since the deposit is only 20 metres from the three Iron Age roundhouses. This probably suggests that the contents of the pit relate to activities which took place after the settlement had been abandoned for some time.

The wider environment

The beetles present provide us with a very clear picture of the environment and landscape that surrounded this feature. There are only minimal numbers of species that are associated with woodland (see Table 19 and Figure 43). Those that are, such as the "woodworm" *Anobium puctatum* and the leaf feeding *Phylobius* species of weevils can be found associated with isolated trees, hedgerows and waterside trees in addition to in dense woodland. This absence of a "forest fauna" clearly indicates that this area of Staffordshire had been cleared by this time. This area also suffers from a paucity of pollen diagrams but the results from the Kings Pool at Stafford (Bartley and Morgan 1990) suggests that partial forest clearance together with pastoral and arable agriculture took place from the Early Neolithic to the Bronze Age onwards. Their results also indicate that large-scale forest clearance occurred mainly between 750-550 BC, with the region probably cleared as a whole by the Early Iron Age.

The immediate surroundings

It is clear from the ecology of the species present that the immediate surroundings of the feature consisted of an area of rough grazed grassland. This is clearly suggested by two aspects of the insect fauna present.

Of the terrestrial taxa present, 11.6% of the fauna consists of species that are indicative of grassland. Particularly suggestive of this are the two chaffer beetles that are present. Both *Hoplia philanthus* and *Phyllopertha horticola* are common inhabitants of old grassland where their larvae feed on the base of the grass. The same is also often true of the species of Elateridae present, and possibly the large weevil *Alophus triguttatus*. Many of the species of phytophage (plant feeding) leaf beetles and weevils also indicate grassland since many of them are associated with plants which are common inhabitants of rough and scuffed pastures. For example the presence of dock is indicated by a number of species (*Gastroidea polygoni, Apion violaceum*) as is clover (*Sitona flavescens, S. hispidulus* and *Hypera murina*). Other species of plants suggested by the insects present are associated with scuffed ground in grasslands. Particularly indicative of this are a number of species that are associated with knotgrass (*Chaetocnema concinna* and the *Phytobius* species). A dominant feature seems to be the presence of both stinging and dead nettles. The former is suggested by a number of plant feeding species such as the *Brachypterus* species, *Apion urticarium, Ceutorhynchus pollinarius* and *Cidnorhinus quadrimaculatus,* and the latter by *Dlochrysa fastuosa.* The insects also suggest that shepherd's purse (often the food plant of *Ceutorhynchus erysimi*), and possibly poppies and bittercress (often the food plants of *Ceutorhynchus contractus* and *C. cochlaeriae* respectively) were present.

Rough open grassy areas are also suggested by many of the ground beetles present. Of particular note are the species typical of open, unvegetated gravely or sandy conditions, such as *Harpalus rubripes, H. tardus, Bradycellus harpalinus, Amara aenea, A. apricaria* and *Syntomus foveatus* (Lindroth 1974). Similar conditions are also suggested by the presence of *Helophorus porculus* (Hansen 1987) and the scarabaedids *Geotrupes vernalis, Onthophagus joannae* and *Heptaulacus testudinrius,* all of which favour dry dung lying in open sandy conditions (Jessop 1986).

Perhaps the clearest evidence for the presence of pasture in the area is the very large numbers of dung beetles and other species associated with decaying, foul matter. These dominate the terrestrial fauna present (see Table 19 and Figure 43). They include a large number of *Apodius* species, *Geotrupes* and *Onthophagus* species. This clearly suggests that large numbers of grazing animals were present in the area around the pit.

Water

The water beetles present clearly suggest that a small, semi-permanent, still and mainly unvegetated body of water existed in this recut of the earlier Iron Age enclosure ditch. Perhaps typical of this situation is the dytiscid *Hydroporus pubescens.* This species favours small rather stagnant bodies of unshaded water (Nilsson and Holmen 1995). The majority of the other dytiscid, hydraenid and hydrophilid water beetles would not be out of place in such a body of water.

There is a suggestion that this pool may have contained a small stand of emergent waterside vegetation. This is indicated by two of the plant feeding weevils present. *Notaris acridulus* and *Limnobaris pilistriata* are associated with stands of sedges, rushes and the reed sweet grass (Koch 1992).

Conclusion

The insect fauna recovered from this feature is the first to be recovered for this period in Staffordshire. The insect fauna from this pit cut into the terminal of an enclosure ditch clearly indicates that it was associated with a small pond set into an area of open pasture. It would appear that an area of scuffed up, sandy ground surrounded the pond and was probably heavily used by stock animals. It would seem likely that the feature represents a small watering pond that was cut into a pre-existing hollow in the landscape. It is noticeable that a similar situation has been suggested by the insect remains from a Roman recut of a similar Iron Age feature at the site of the Covert Farm, Crick, Northants (Smith, forthcoming). At Crick, this occurred once the preceding Iron Age farmstead had been abandoned.

Table 18: Insects from Whitemoor Haye

Species	ecology		Phytophage host plant (data taken from Koch 1989, 1992)
Carabidae			
Nebria salina Fairm. Lab		3	
Notiophilus biguttatus (F.)		3	
Clivina fossor (L.)		2	
Dyschirius globosus (Hbst.)		5	
Trechus quadristriatus (Schrk.)		1	
T. quadristriatus (Schrk.) or *obtusus* Er.		10	
Bembidion lampros (Hbst.)		3	
B. clarki (Daws.)		3	
Bembidion unicolor Chaud.		1	
B. spp.		5	
Harplus ? rufipes (Geer)		1	
H. aeneus (F.)		2	
H. rubripes (Duft.)		1	
H. tardus (Panz.)		4	
Bradycellus harpalinus (Serv.)		3	
Acupalpus exiguous (Dej.)		2	
Athracus consputus (Duft.)		3	
Poecilus versicolor (Sturm)		2	
Pterostichus minor (Gyll.)		6	
P. ?melanarius (Ill.)		1	
Calathus fuscipes (Goeze)		14	
C. melanocephalus (L.)		17	
Agonum nigrum Dej.	ws	1	
A. spp.		1	
Amara plebeja (Gyll.)		1	
A. aenea (Geer)		12	
A. familiaris (Duft.)		4	
A.tibialis (Payk.)		1	
A. bifrons (Gyll.)		1	

A. apricaria (Payk.)		3	
A. spp.		11	
Syntomus foveatus (Fourcr.)		3	
Halipidae			
Halipus spp.	a	1	
Dytiscidae			
Hydroporus palustris (L.)	a	1	
H. erythrocephalus (Marsh.)	a	2	
H. pubescens (Gyll.)	a	15	
H. nigrita (F.)	a	7	
H. spp.	a	6	
Agabus bipustulatus (L.)	a	5	
A. spp.	a	12	
Colymbetes fuscus (L.)	a	1	
Hydreanidae			
Ochthebius bicolon Germ.	a	1	
O. minumus (F.)	a	10	
O. spp.	a	100	
Limnebius spp.	a	30	
Hydrochus carinatus Germ.	a	1	
Helophorus porculus Bedel	a	9	
H. aquaticus (L.)	a	20	
H. ?arvernicus Muls.	a	1	
H. spp.	a	66	
Hydrophilidae			
Sphaeridium scarabaeoides (L.)	d	2	
S. lunatum (F.)	d	7	
Cercyon impressus (Sturm)	df	10	
C. atricaillus (Marsh.)	df	11	
C. tristis (Ill.)	a	5	
C. spp.		30	
Megasternum boletophagum (Marsh.)	df	20	
Cryptopleurum minutum (F.)	df	2	
Hydrobius fuscipes (L.)		13	
Laccobius spp.	a	3	
Chaetarthtria seminulum (Hbst.)	a	1	
Histeridae			
Onthophilus striatus (Forst.)		1	
Acritus nigricornis (Hoffm.)		1	
Saprinus virescens (Payk.)	df	1	
S. aeneus (F.)	df	1	
Kissister minimus (Aubé)	df	4	
Hister cadaverinus Hoffm.	df	2	
H. bissexstriatus F.	df	2	
Atholus duodecimstriatus (Schrk.)	df	2	
Silphidae			
Silpha tristis Ill.		3	
Catopidae			
Choleva spp.		1	
Catops spp.		2	
Ptiliidae			
Ptiliidae Gen. and spp. indet.		8	
Clambidae			
Clambus spp.		1	
Staphylindae			
Micropeplus spp.		1	
Proteinus spp.		5	
Omalium caesum Grav.		2	
O. spp.		5	
Acidota crenata (F.)		1	
Lesteva longelytrata (Goeze)	ws	15	
Trogophloeus bilineatus (Steph.)	ws	3	
T. spp.	ws	4	

Oxytelus rugosus (F.)		2	
O. sculpturatus Grav.		5	
O. nitidulus Grav.		5	
Platystethus arenarius (Fourcr.)	df	2	
P. cornutus (Grav.)	ws	4	
Bledius fracticornis (Payk.)	ws	1	
B. subterraneus Er.	ws	8	
B. spp.	ws	14	
Stenus spp.		6	
Stilicus spp.		1	
Lathrobium spp.		1	
Leptacinus linearis (Grav.)		2	
Gyrohypnus fracticornis (Müll.)		6	
Xantholinus glabratus (Grav.)		2	
Xantholinus linearis (Ol.)		10	
X. spp.		18	
Philonthus spp.		19	
Gabrius spp.		4	
Staphylinus spp.		2	
Quedius spp.		3	
Mycetoporus spp.		2	
Conosoma spp.		2	
Tachyporus ? hypnorum (F.)		2	
T. ?chrysomelinus (L.)		1	
T. spp.		14	
Tachinus rufipes (Geer)		7	
T. spp.		2	
Falagria spp.		2	
Aleocharinae Gen. and spp. indet.		23	
Cantharidae			
Cantharis rustica Fall.		1	
C. spp.		1	
Elateridae			
Agriotes lineatus (L.)	g	11	at roots of various grasses
Adelocera murina (L.)	g	5	at roots of various grasses
Haplotarsus incanus (Gyll.)	g	1	
Dryopidae			
Dryops spp.	a	4	
Oulimnius spp.	a	1	
Limnius volckmari (Panz.)	a	1	
Byrrhidae			
Byrrhus pilula (L.)	g	2	Grass roots and mosses
Simplocaria semistriata (F.)	g	6	
Nitidulidae			
Brachypterus sp.	g	1	Urtica dioica (stinging nettles)
Cucujidae			
Monotoma brevicollis Aubé		1	
M. spp.		2	
Cryptophagidae			
Cryptophagus spp.		2	
Atomaria spp.		2	
Phalacridae			
Phalacrus caricis Sturm.		1	
Lathridiidae			
Enicmus minutus (group)		9	
Corticaria or Corticarina spp.		2	
Coccinellidae			
Coccinella septempunctata L.		1	
Anobiidae			
Anobium punctatum (Geer)	l	10	Decaying timber
Ptinidae			
Ptinus fur (L.)		2	
Scarabaeidae			

Geotrupes stercorarius (L.)	d	1	
G. vernalis (L.)	d	3	
Onthophagus joannae Goljan	d	3	
O. coenobita (Hbst.)	d	1	
Aphodius erraticus (L.)	d	1	
Aphodius luridus (F.)	d	2	
A. zenkeri Germ.	d	1	
A. contaminatus (Hbst.)	d	35	
A. sphacelatus (Panz.)	d	38	
A. prodromus (Brahm)	d	32	
A. prodromus or A. sphacelatus	d	57	
A. fimetarius (L.)	d	61	
A. ater (Geer)	d	1	
A. constans Duft.	d	2	
A. granarius (L.)	d	16	
Heptaulacus testudinrius (F.)		7	
Phyllopertha horticola (L.)	g	5	Old grassland
Hoplia philanthus (Fuessl.)	g	1	grassland
Chrysomelidae			
Dlochrysa fastuosa (Scop.)	g	2	Galeopsis species (dead nettles)
Gastroidea polygoni (L.)	g	5	Rumex species (dock)
Phyllotreta spp.		5	
Chaetocnema concina (Marsh.)		9	Often Polygonaceae (the knotgrasses)
C. spp.		9	
Curculionidae			
Apion violaceum Kirby	g	13	Rumex species (dock)
A. aeneum (F.)	g	3	Malva species (mallows)
A. urticarium (Hbst.)	g	2	Urtica dioica (stinging nettle)
A. spp.		3	
Phylobius spp.	l	7	various trees
Strophosoma faber (Hbst.)	g	3	Adults on Asteracae (daisy) larvae on Hordeum murinum (barley) and grasses
Sitona flavescens (Marsh.)	g	4	Trifolium species often T. pratense (clover)
S. hispidulus (F.)	g	4	Trifolium species often T. pratense (clover)
S. spp.	g	5	
Notaris acridulus (L.)	ws	4	Glyceria species often G. maxima
Tychius spp.		1	
Alophus triguttatus (F.)	g	1	Plantago (Plantain), Symphytum, Eupatorium
Hypera arundinis (Payk.)	g	1	Various Apiaceae (cow parsleys and other umbellifers)
H. murina (F.)	g	1	Mainly on Trifolium species (clover)
Limnobaris pilistriata (Steph.)	ws	1	Juncaceae and Cyperacaea (rushes)
Phytobius spp.	g	5	often on Polygonum (knotgrass)
Ceutorhynchus contractus (Marsh.)	g	1	Brassicacae sometimes Papaveraceae (the poppies)
C. erysimi (F.)	g	8	Brassicacae often Capsella bursa-pastoris (shepard's purse)
C. cochlaeriae (Gyll.)	g	1	Brassicacae often Cardomine pratensis
C. pollinarius (Forst.)	g	2	Urtica dioca (Stinging nettle)
Cidnorhinus quadrimaculatus (L.)	g	4	Urtica dioca (Stinging nettle)
DIPTERA			
Nematocera Family, Genus and spp. indet.		++	
Cyclorrhapha Family Genus and spp. Indet		++	
DERMAPTERA			
Forficula auricularia L.		++	
HYMENOPTERA			
Formicoidea Family Genus and spp. indet.		+++	
Trichoptera			
Trichoptera Genus and spp. indet.		++	

Ecological groupings

a   - aquatic species
ws   - waterside species either from muddy banksides or from waterside vegetation
df   - species associated with dung and foul matter
d   - species associated with dung
g   - species associated with grassland and pasture
t   - species either associated with trees or with woodland in general

For non Coleoptera the numbers present have been estimated using the following scale: +   = >10 individuals   ++ = <10 individuals

Table 19: Ecological groupings of insects

Ecological grouping	Percentage (%)
% aquatic	25
% waterside	5
% dung and foul/terrestrial	33
% grassland and pasture / terrestrial	12
% woodland /terrestrial	2
Total number of species	176
Total number of individuals	1194

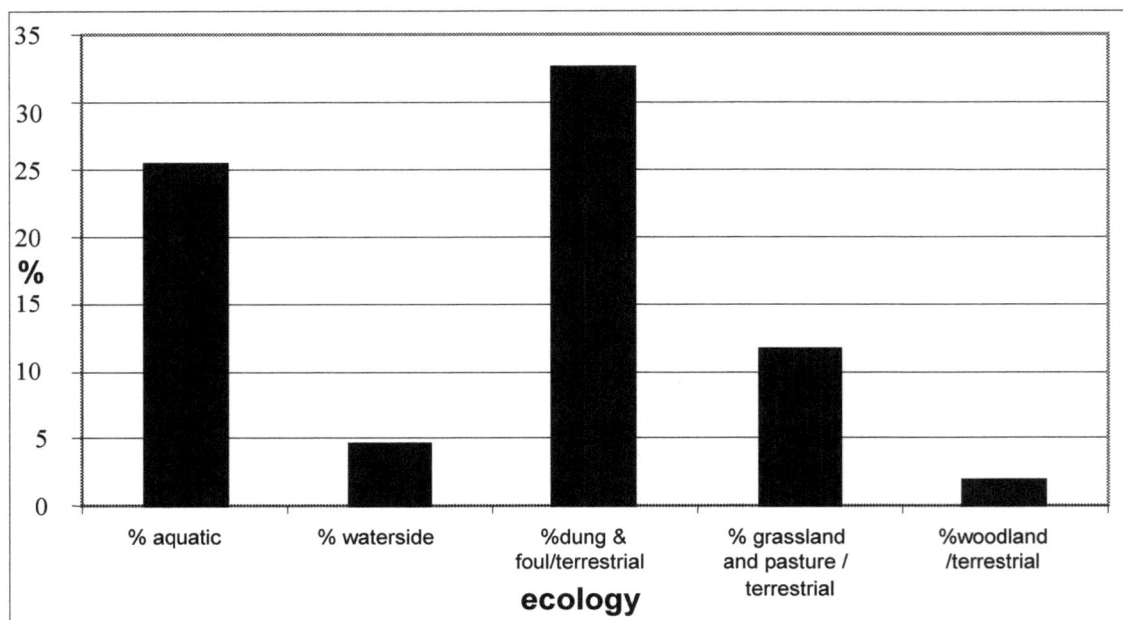

Fig. 43: Histogram of ecological groupings of insects present

Waterlogged Seeds *by James Greig*

Methodology

The waterlogged fill from the earliest cut of pit F473 was sampled for seeds as well insects (see *Insect Remains*, above). This bowl-shaped pit, re-cut five times, had been dug into the southern terminal of the Iron Age enclosure ditch F468. The material was washed over and sieved on a 300-micron mesh by Andy Hammon. Plant remains were very abundant, as identified and listed below by the writer, whose reference collection was used to check the identifications. The numbers given are for seeds in the first small amount examined. Further material was looked through to record some of the many extra taxa, but the huge numbers of commoner seeds were not counted. Records from other Iron Age sites are marked with an asterisk. The results are listed in taxonomic order (Kent 1992, Stace 1997) in Table 20.

Results (Table 20)

The weeds of arable land are the most important habitat indicators, from an archaeological point of view. They are present in small numbers, such as *Spergula arvensis* (corn spurrey), *Fallopia convolvulus* (black bindweed), *Rumex acetosella* (sheep's sorrel), *Aphanes* sp. (parsley piert) and *Hyoscyamus niger* (henbane). These indicate an agricultural landscape on rather light, sandy soils. If pollen analysis had been possible, it would probably have show whether cereals were grown. Charcoal indicates human activity in the vicinity, as might be expected on an archaeological site.

Grasslands are indicated to a slight extent by records of some specific grassland plants such as *Ranunculus* subg *Ranunculus* (buttercup), *Cerastium fontanum* (common mouse-ear chickweed), *Potentilla erecta* (tormentil), *Torilis japonica* (upright hedge parsley) and *Hypochaeris* (cat's ear).

However, most of the plants relate to the deposit itself and its close surroundings, and indicate a range of weedy and overgrown habitats going from dry land through damp ground to wetland and aquatic conditions. Plants such as *Urtica* (nettles) and *Rumex crispus* (curled dock) indicate overgrown land. Damper conditions are shown by *Lycopus europaeus* (gypsywort), the huge numbers of which could perhaps have accumulated by water action, and by various *Persicaria* species (persicarias). Plants such as Lemna (duckweed) and Glyceria (sweetgrass) indicate aquatic conditions. The pit obviously had marsh vegetation growing around it, and floating aquatics such as duckweed floating in it. The archaeological significance of all this is that the pit could easily have been a drinking hole for cattle.

Table 20: Seed list (taxonomic order Kent (1992). * = other Iron Age records (Fisherwick, Tattershall Thorpe, Dragonby)

Ranunculus subg. *Ranunculus*	1	*	buttercup
Urtica dioica L.	24	*	common nettle
Alnus glutinosa (L.) Gaertner	1		alder
Atriplex sp.	4	*	orache
Montia fontana subsp. *minor* Hayw.	+	*	blinks
Stellaria media (L.) Villars	+	*	chickweed
Cerastium fontanum Baumg.	+	*	common mouse-ear
Cerastium sp.	+		mouse-ear chickweed
Spergula arvensis L.	1	*	corn spurrey
Polygonum maculosa Gray	1		persicaria
Polygonum lapathifolia (L.) Gray	+	*	pale persicaria
Polygonum hydropiper L.	+	*	water-pepper
Polygonum aviculare L.	6	*	knotgrass
Fallopia convolvulus (L.) A. Love	+	*	black bindweed
Rumex acetosella L.	1	*	sheep's sorrel
Rumex crispus L.	2	*	curled dock
Rumex sp.	1	*	dock
Rorippa sylvestris (L.) Besser	61	*	creeping yellow-cress
Rubus/Rosa thorn	2		bramble/rose
Rubus sp.	1	*	bramble/raspberry
Potentilla anserina L.	+	*	silverweed
Potentilla erecta L. Räusch	+	*	tormentil
Aphanes sp.	+	*	parsley piert
Prunus/Crataegus thorn	+		sloe/hawthorn
Torilis japonica (Houtt.) DC	+	*	upright hedge parsley
Hyoscyamus niger L.	1	*	henbane
Galeopsis sp.	1	*	hemp-nettle
Lycopus europaeus L.	381	*	gypsywort
Cirsium cf. *palustre* (L.) Scop.	+	*	marsh thistle
Hypochaeris sp.	+	*	cat's ear
Lemna sp.	8	*	duckweed
Juncus sp.	1	*	rush
Isolepis setacea R. Br.	1	*	bristle club-rush
Carex subg *Vignea*	6	?	sedge, biconvex seeds
Poaceae	4		grasses
Glyceria sp.	1		sweet-grass
charcoal	+		

Discussion

A number of other midland Iron Age sites have also produced archaeobotanical results from waterlogged pits and ditches, and these can be compared with those from Whitemoor Haye to give a more regional view of the significance of the results. The nearby site of Fisherwick had waterlogged ditches from which a range of evidence was studied (Smith 1979). In Lincolnshire, waterlogged ditches at Tattershall Thorpe were also studied for plant and insect remains (Chowne *et al* 1986), and very extensive results have recently appeared from Dragonby on waterlogged and charred seeds, beetles and pollen (van der Veen and others, 1996).

The patterns shown by these Iron Age floras are really surprisingly consistent: they are dominated by marshland and wetland plants, as would be expected from such waterlogged deposits. There is also evidence of the surrounding dry land, with various weeds of rather sandy fields present, and of open trampled ground. At some sites either the pollen demonstrated that cereals were grown, or occasional charred cereal remains in the ditches provided this information. There were also some signs of grassland plants indicating meadows and pastures, usually strongly supported by evidence from beetles that live on grassland plants or in dung, showing that stock raising was an important part of the economy. Animal bones at Fisherwick provided evidence of the domestic animals themselves. Some sites provided evidence of thorny scrub or more probably hedge that may have formed field boundaries and stock enclosures, although this aspect is only suggested by a thorn of blackthorn or hawthorn in the small flora from Whitemoor Haye.

To supplement the evidence from particular points in time provided by the results from ditches and pits, there are some longer pollen sequences which show changes in land use over of time. At Dragonby the pollen diagrams show that land was actively being cleared and settled in the Iron Age, possible evidence of a rising population. A pollen diagram from Stafford (Greig, in preparation) shows that the pattern of fairly intensive land occupation at this time may have been repeated in Staffordshire and elsewhere. The surrounding landscape there was substantially cleared of woodland, except alder carr in wetter places, by 1200 cal BC. Land was farmed in the Iron Age, for crops including cereals, and grasslands and heathlands were probably used for stock raising, although the pollen provides no direct evidence for the latter. This evidence probably generally applies to the area that includes Whitemoor Haye and Fisherwick. Such areas of light alluvial soils provided good farmland then as now, which is why they were settled in preference to land on clay and gravel.

Finally, some continuity of this kind of farming economy into the Roman period is shown by the macrofossil and pollen evidence from Dragonby, which spans both periods, and also some change with the introduction of new crops and weeds to the region.

Conclusion

The results from this Iron Age pit show that a mixed farming economy with arable land and grasslands was the local land use. Results from other Iron Age sites support the view that this was a widespread form of land use at this time, which largely continued into the Romano-British period.

Charcoal *by Rowena Gale*

Introduction

Charcoal occurred in Areas A, B, C, F, R and S, and was generally associated with hut gullies, ditches and pits, but also occurred in post-holes and possible hearth features. Twenty-one samples representing contexts from the Neolithic/ Early Bronze Age, Iron Age and Romano-British periods were selected for species identification, including five samples for radiocarbon dating. The identification of the charcoal was undertaken to evaluate the character of local woodland and the use of woodland resources. The study of charcoal from this area of Staffordshire is particularly relevant since current knowledge of the prehistoric landscape in the Tame valley is relatively sparse. The results of the charcoal study are discussed with reference to those from plant macrofossils and insect remains, and the environmental implications are compared with those from other sites in the region.

Methodology

Bulk soil samples were processed in house and the charcoal fragments collected from flots and residues. The charcoal was mostly very poorly preserved, extremely friable and infiltrated with reddish deposits (?iron) which obscured diagnostic cell wall detail. Fragments measuring >2mm in radial cross-section were examined from all samples, except those from context 5045, which was an unusually large sample and from which a 50% subsample was examined.

The fragments from each sample were fractured to expose transverse surfaces and sorted into groups based on the anatomical structure observed with a x20 hand lens. Representative fragments from each group (except hazel (*Corylus*) and alder (*Alnus*), of which every fragment was examined) were selected for detailed examination at high magnification. Transverse, tangential and radial surfaces were prepared and mounted in fine sand. These were examined using a Nikon Labophot incident light microscope at magnifications of up to x400. The anatomical structures were matched to prepared reference slides.

Where possible the maturity (i.e. roundwood, sapwood and heartwood, indicated on Table 21 as r, s and h) and age of the wood were recorded. It should be noted that measurements of stem diameters are from charred material and when living, these may have been as much as 40% wider.

Results

The results of the charcoal analysis are summarised in Table 22, and discussed in detail below. The charcoal was consistent with the taxa or groups of taxa given below (Table 21). The anatomical structure of some related taxa cannot be distinguished with any certainty, for example members of the Pomoideae (*Crataegus, Malus, Pyrus* and *Sorbus*) and Salicaceae (*Salix* and *Populus*). In some samples where the condition of the charcoal was degraded, provisional names have been given. Classification follows that of *Flora Europaea* (Tutin, Heywood *et al* 1964-80).

Table 21: Charcoal: taxa identified

Broadleaf taxa identified
Aceraceae. *Acer* sp., maple
Betulaceae. *Alnus* sp., alder; *Betula* sp., birch
Corylaceae. *Corylus* sp., hazel
cf. Ericaceae. *Calluna vulgaris/ Erica* sp., heathers. These taxa are anatomically similar.
Fagaceae. *Quercus* sp., oak
Oleaceae. *Fraxinus* sp., ash
Rosaceae. Subfamily Pomoideae which includes *Crataegus* sp., hawthorn; *Malus* sp., apple; *Pyrus* sp., pear; *Sorbus* spp., rowan, service tree and whitebeam. These taxa are anatomically indistinguishable. *Prunus spinosa*, blackthorn.
cf. Rhamnaceae. *Frangula alnus,* alder buckthorn
Salicaceae. *Salix* sp., willow and *Populus* sp., poplar. These taxa are anatomically similar.
Coniferous taxa identified
Pinaceae. *Pinus* sp., pine (*sylvestris* group, Scots pine type)

Oak heartwood was common to almost all features. In the following text and Table 22 heartwood is referred to as (h), while roundwood (Ø <20mm) and sapwood (including roundwood Ø >20mm) are designated (r) and (s). Fragmented charcoal of unknown maturity is indicated as (u).

Period 1: Neolithic to Early Bronze Age

Charcoal from the fill of pit F612 (6019), sited roughly in the centre of Area R, included oak (*Quercus*) (s and u), pine (*Pinus*) and hazel (*Corylus*) nutshell. Pottery from the same context suggested an Early Bronze Age date, but radiocarbon dates from the charcoal were consistent with the Early Neolithic (3615 to3595 Cal BC and 3525 to 3100 Cal BC), thereby suggesting that the charcoal was likely to be residual in the feature.

Period 2: Early to Middle Iron Age

Areas A, B and C consisted of rectangular enclosures containing roundhouses or circular structures with hut gullies. Charcoal was examined from features within each area.

Area A
The main features consisted of four round structures in a rectangular enclosure. Evidence from waterlogged and carbonised plant macrofossils (see *Plant Macroremains* and *Waterlogged Seeds*, above), and insect remains (see *Insect Remains*, above) suggests that cattle or other livestock were kept in the enclosure. The roundhouses, however, could have been for either domestic or agricultural use, or for other activities.

Charcoal was examined from contexts associated with three of the four structures, including hut gullies 4035 and 4055 from Structure 3, hut gullies 4061 and 4062 from Structure 4, and posthole 4004 in Structure 1. Oak (*Quercus*) (h and u) was common to all contexts. Other taxa identified included maple (*Acer*), alder (*Alnus*), hazel (*Corylus*), ash (*Fraxinus*), the hawthorn/*Sorbus* group (Pomoideae), blackthorn (*Prunus spinosa*), willow/poplar (*Salix/ Populus*), and probably birch (*Betula*) and heather or ling (*Erica* or *Calluna*) (see Table 22 for distribution). It is probable that the charcoal originated from fuel debris either discarded or washed into these features.

The hut gully F421 around Structure 3 provided evidence of livestock in the form of compacted charred straw (identified by Marina Ciaraldi, this volume), probably from burnt stable

manure. Agricultural origins for the charcoal (4055) residues from the same area could be considered – perhaps from the branches of leaf fodder subsequently burnt with the stable manure, either on a general bonfire or as fuel. Leaf fodder, however, tends to implicate brushwood rather than wide roundwood and the presence of oak heartwood in this context suggests different origins for at least some of the wood. Given the probable paucity of fuel materials (particularly wood), in what was probably an open agricultural landscape, useful combustible materials would probably have been stockpiled for later use. The charred residues (4062) from cereal processing (Marina Ciaraldi, this volume) from the hut gully of Structure 4, F438.01, also suggests that waste materials were used as fuel, kindling or tinder for wood fuel.

The possible site of a hearth or oven was indicated by charcoal-rich silty sand in a shallow sub-circular feature (F433) located in the centre of Structure 3. Charcoal (4051) was abundant and, in contrast to the deposits from the drip gullies, consisted exclusively of oak (*Quercus*) (s and h), possibly implicating a different origin for the charcoal.

Charcoal was sparse in the fills of the enclosure ditch F468. Oak (*Quercus*) (h) and possibly a member of the hawthorn/ *Sorbus* group (Pomoideae) were identified in 4101, and possibly hazel (*Corylus*) in 4191.

Charcoal was examined from three large pits (F456, F445 and F473) located at the corners of the enclosure ditch F486 and associated with the final phases of use of the enclosure. Pit F456 was bowl-shaped and dug into the southwest corner of the enclosure ditch and part of the ditch F457. It was later re-cut. Charcoal from the fill (4124) was very poorly preserved and friable; taxa identified included oak (*Quercus*) (s, u), blackthorn (*Prunus spinosa*), hazel (*Corylus*) and the hawthorn/*Sorbus* group (Pomoideae).

Waterlogged deposits, including insect and plant remains, present in the primary cut of F473 and subsequent later recuts, are indicative of the use this pit as a waterhole for livestock. Charcoal was exceedingly sparse but a few fragments were identified from the primary cut of F473 as birch (*Betula*), and from the latest cut of F445 as hazel (*Corylus*).

Area B

Four circular structures were excavated in Area B. Charcoal (2095) was examined from the hut gully of Structure 3 (F234.01) and identified as ash (*Fraxinus*), blackthorn (*Prunus spinosa*), oak (r and h), narrow hazel (*Corylus*) roundwood (e.g. diameter 3mm, 2 growth rings), alder (*Alnus*), the hawthorn/*Sorbus* group (Pomoideae), and possibly heather or ling (*Erica* or *Calluna*). Some oak wood was extremely slow-grown.

Area C

Charcoal was examined from the hut gullies of both the circular structures in this area. Oak (*Quercus*) heartwood, in 3008, was present in Structure 1, F300.07, whereas in 3031 and 3039, from Structure 2, F304.01 and F306.06, a much wider range of taxa was present including alder (*Alnus*) (r, diameter 15mm), birch (*Betula*), hazel (*Corylus*), ash (*Fraxinus*), blackthorn (*Prunus spinosa*), oak (*Quercus*) (h, u and root), and possibly alder buckthorn (*Frangula alnus*) and heather or ling (*Erica* or *Calluna*). The disparity between these deposits may indicate the use of fuel for different activities.

Area S

A group of post-holes occurred at the northern edge of Area S. The fill (5045) of the deepest of these, F537, included charcoal-flecked brown silt-sand and a large quantity of Iron Age pottery sherds and fired clay. Charcoal was abundant and a 50% subsample was examined and identified as blackthorn (*Prunus spinosa*), the hawthorn/*Sorbus* group (Pomoideae) (roundwood, diameter 12mm), oak (*Quercus*) (h), ash (*Fraxinus*), hazel (*Corylus*), willow/ poplar (*Salix/Populus*) and probably birch (*Betula*).

A double row of circular pits ran in a northwest to southeast alignment. The pits were bowl shaped and many had subsequently been re-cut. Burnt and heat-cracked stones were present in several pits, including pit F526, which also contained charcoal and Iron Age pottery. The charcoal (5058) consisted of alder (*Alnus*), birch (*Betula*), hazel (*Corylus*), the hawthorn/*Sorbus* group (Pomoideae), blackthorn (*Prunus pinosa*) willow/poplar (*Salix/Populus*) and oak (*Quercus*) (r and h).

Probably Period 2

Area F

Charcoal from the fill (8042) of pit F816, a shallow flat-bottomed feature, consisted of oak (*Quercus*) heartwood.

Period 3: Romano-British

Area S

Charcoal was examined from one of several Romano-British ditches. A shallow ditch (F505) re-cut the original ditch (F507) and its fills comprised several of layers of silt-sand, sherds from various types of Roman pottery (2nd century or later), charcoal and crop processing waste (the latter identified by Marina Ciaraldi, this volume). Charcoal from fill 5012 included alder (*Alnus*), oak (*Quercus*) (r and u), hazel (*Corylus*), maple (*Acer*), the hawthorn/ *Sorbus* group (Pomoideae) and probably blackthorn (*Prunus spinosa*).

Undated

Area R

Feature F617 was one of several of doubtful provenance, and although these were located close to a group of pits containing Iron Age artefacts, the function and dating remain obscure. Charcoal from the fill (6026) of ?pit F617 consisted of a quantity of pine (*Pinus*), and although the charcoal was too fragmented to establish the maturity of the wood, it was clear that it was not narrow roundwood. The presence of pine may be significant in the dating of this charcoal, since the only other feature (pit F612) from which pine was recorded was sited in close proximity to this pit. The charcoal from pit F612 was radiocarbon dated to the Early Neolithic (see above).

Discussion

Environmental implications

The site was located on sands and gravels close to the river Tame. Charcoal was studied from Areas A, B, C and F, clustered roughly together, and Areas S and R, which were located to the northeast. Preservation of the charcoal was poor, and red deposits (?iron) had permeated the woody tissues (possibly due to fluctuating water levels). Most of the samples examined related to the Early to Late Iron Age, although the (?early) Neolithic and Romano-British periods were represented.

Despite the paucity of Neolithic charcoal, the single sample from pit F612 included oak (*Quercus*), hazel (*Corylus*) nutshell and pine (*Pinus*). Pine was identified from a closely aligned unphased pit F617, and given the proximity of the two pits and the absence of pine from later contexts, a common origin for the two samples of pine seems likely. Pine was widespread and often dominant in the Britain landscape during the Boreal period but gave way to mixed broadleaf woodland in the Mesolithic (Godwin 1956). By the Early Neolithic pine had declined in the English countryside (except on fenland and in blanket bogs), and its distribution continued to diminish in later periods. Although it is generally accepted that pine had more or less disappeared from England in the ensuing millennium, small local stands appear to have survived in some areas until the Iron Age or later, as, for example, on heathland at Wych Farm Oil Field, near Purbeck in Dorset (Gale 1991). Local evidence from the region around Whitemoor Haye (see below) verifies that pine was present probably at least until the post-boreal period. The occurrence of pine securely dated to the Neolithic period at Whitemoor Haye is therefore of particular interest.

The charcoal residues were more abundant in the post-Neolithic contexts. It is probable that most of the charcoal derived from fuel debris and, as such, is likely to reflect the economic use of woodland resources, rather than proportional distribution of species in the environment. Hence, the dominance of oak throughout the samples can probably be attributed as much to fuel gathering, biased towards high calorie fuels, as to its local status in the woodland community. The absence of pollen data, however, emphasises the potential of the charcoal to provide environmental information. The range of woody taxa identified includes maple (*Acer*), alder (*Alnus*), birch (*Betula*), hazel (*Corylus*), ash (*Fraxinus*), the hawthorn/*Sorbus* group (Pomoideae), blackthorn (*Prunus spinosa*), oak (*Quercus*), willow/poplar (*Salix/ Populus*), and probably heather or ling (*Erica* or *Calluna*) and buckthorn (*Frangula alnus*). There was no apparent differentiation in the selection or use of species in the Iron Age and Romano-British periods, which suggests that woodland composition probably remained relatively stable.

Evidence from insect remains and plant macrofossils in Iron Age deposits (Smith and Greig, see above) suggests that rough pasture and open grassland was dominant in Area A, with some boggy or waterlogged patches. Typical wetland shrubs represented in the charcoal include willow (*Salix*) (and/or poplar, *Populus*), alder (*Alnus*) and alder buckthorn (*Frangula alnus*). If these species were growing on the boggy patches close to the enclosures, they were probably rather sparse, whereas the nearby river banks may have been more densely populated. Species such as birch (*Betula*) and heather or ling (*Erica* or *Calluna*) suggest acidic or impoverished soils in some parts of the site, perhaps rather heath-like. It is probable that small tracts of woodland remained in areas unsuited to cultivation or outside the main agricultural catchment area, which may have included larger woodland trees such as oak (*Quercus*), ash (*Fraxinus*) and maple (*Acer*). Hazel (*Corylus*) and blackthorn (*Prunus spinosa*) were identified from both plant macrofossils (Marina Ciaraldi, this volume) and charcoal deposits, and members of the hawthorn/*Sorbus* group (Pomoideae) were also present. Shrubby taxa such as these grow in open or marginal woodland, and hazel also forms understorey in oak woodland.

When grown as hedging, hawthorn (*Crataegus*) and blackthorn provide stock-proof barriers. The banks of the enclosures would almost certainly have been surmounted by protective hedges (probably of thorn, although other species may also have been incorporated); these would also have provided a useful source of brushwood and roundwood for fuel and other uses.

Comparative evidence from other sites in the region

Taken as whole, the woodland composition of the region is poorly understood, partly due to unfavourable conditions for the preservation of plant material suitable for examination, but mainly because, as yet, few sites have been excavated. From the evidence available (see below) it would appear that by the Iron Age many previously wooded landscapes had been cleared for agriculture. Where woodland persisted on the sandy soils and gravels characteristic of the river terraces, it was more or less similar in composition to that at Whitemoor Haye.

A cluster of sites was excavated on the gravel terraces of the river Tame at Fisherwick, sited just south of Whitemoor Haye. Plant remains were only recorded from the Iron Age site SK187082, where waterlogged wood was recognised. Species identified include alder (*Alnus*), hazel (*Corylus*), hawthorn (*Crateagus*), blackthorn (*Prunus spinosa*), oak (*Quercus*), willow (*Salix*), ash (*Fraxinus*) and elder (*Sambucus*) (Williams 1979). Pollen analysis enlarged the list with lime (*Tilia*), birch (*Betula*), elm (*Ulmus*) and holly (*Ilex*) (Greig 1979). Many of these species were attributed to hedgerows enclosing small fields and meadows.

Other comparable sites in the region include Iron Age deposits at Swarkestone Lowes, Derbyshire, from which the pollen profile suggests arable and pastoral activity in a largely treeless landscape (Hunt 1999). Trees and shrubs included hazel (*Corylus*), oak (*Quercus*), alder (*Alnus*), hornbeam (*Carpinus*), ash (*Fraxinus*) and Rosaceae.

Charcoal from a Middle Iron Age settlement in the Soar valley at Wanlip, Leicestershire (Beamish 1998), included oak (*Quercus*) (predominantly), hazel (*Corylus*), blackthorn (*Prunus spinosa*), ash (*Fraxinus*), the hawthorn group (Pomoideae), maple (*Acer*), willow/ poplar (*Salix/ Populus*), elm (*Ulmus*) and yew (*Taxus*). Plant remains at Wanlip were sparse but included cereal processing waste, arable weeds and grassland plants.

Samples of pollen from sediments underlying a Roman road at Wall, (Godwin and Dickson 1964-5), southwest of Whitemoor Haye, were undated but showed clear evidence of pine (*Pinus*) woodlands in the lower peaty samples. Towards the upper levels pine gave way to predominantly alder (*Alnus*) woodland, which also included elm (*Ulmus*), hazel (*Corylus*), oak (*Quercus*), birch (*Betula*), willow (*Salix*) and heather (*Calluna vulgaris)*. The organic muds were loosely dated to the post-boreal period but the final phases suggested woodland clearance.

Conclusion

Environmental evidence based on the charcoal residues suggests that a relatively wide range of woodland trees and shrubs grew in the vicinity of the settlement at Whitemoor Haye during the Iron Age and Roman-British periods, despite conversion of much of the land to grassland and arable use. Pine (*Pinus*), identified from the Early Neolithic, was not recorded from later phases. A high proportion of the taxa identified (e.g. birch (*Betula*), alder (*Alnus*), hazel (*Corylus*), ash (*Fraxinus*), oak (*Quercus*), willow/poplar (*Salix/Populus*), maple (*Acer*), heather or ling (*Erica* or *Calluna*), blackthorn (*Prunus spinosa*) and hawthorn (*Sorbus* group (Pomoideae)) correspond closely to those identified at other sites in the region on similar soils. The charcoal probably mostly derived from fuel debris, and, as such, it was evident that oak (*Quercus*) was readily available and was probably the preferred fuel throughout these periods.

Table 22: Charcoal from Neolithic to Romano-British deposits. The number of fragments identified is indicated

Cont-ext	Context type	*Acer*	*Alnus*	*Bet-ula*	*Cor-ylus*	*Eric-aceae*	*Fran-gula*	*Frax-inus*	*Pom-oideae*	*Pru-nus*	*Quer-cus*	*Salic-aceae*	*Pinus*
Phase 1: Neolithic – Early Bronze Age													
6019	pit fill	-	-	-	nut	-	-	-	-	-	1s5hu	-	1
Phase 2: Early – Mid Iron Age													
AREA A													
Structure 1													
4004	posthole	-	-	-	2	-	-	2	1	-	1	-	-
Structure 3													
4051	?hearth	-	-	-	-	-	-	-	-	-	98sh	-	-
4035	hut gully	-	?8	-	?9	-	-	-	-	-	21u	-	-
4055	hut gully	-	-	cf1	-	-	-	-	-	-	10hu	cf1	-
Structure 4													
4061	hut gully	3	3	-	-	-	-	-	3	5	2s3h	1	-
4062	hut gully	-	?12	cf3	?12	cf2	-	-	-	-	3r12u	-	-
Ditches													
4101	enclosure ditch	-	-	-	-	-	-	-	?2	-	6h	-	-
4191	ditch	-	-	-	?1	-	-	-	-	-	-	-	-
AREA B													
Structure 3													
2095	hut gully	-	1r	-	20r	?1	-	1	1r	6	3r10h	-	-
AREA C													
Structure 1													
3008	hut gully	-	-	-	-	-	-	-	-	-	20hu	-	-
Structure 2													
3031	hut gully	-	4	3	-	?2	-	-	-	-	3	-	-
3039	hut gully	-	16r	-	1	-	?1r	3	-	1	1h1rt	-	-
AREA S													
Pit arc													
5045	pit fill	-	-	?1	5	-	-	2	36	37	6hu	2	-
Pit alignment													
5058	pit fill	-	15	5	2	-	-	-	9	7	4r8h	2	-
Phase 2B: Middle to Late Iron Age													
AREA A													
4124	pit fill	-	-	-	8	-	-	-	1	1	6su	-	-
4146	pit fill	-	-	2	-	-	-	-	-	-	-	-	-
4082	pit fill	-	-	-	2	-	-	-	-	-	-	-	-
Probably Phase 2													
AREA F													
8042	pit fill	-	-	-	-	-	-	-	-	-	12hu	-	-
Phase 3: Romano-British													
AREA S													
5012	ditch	1	12	-	1	-	-	-	1	?1	3r 10u	-	-
Unphased													
AREA R													
6026	?pit fill	-	-	-	-	-	-	-	-	-	-	-	25

Key.   r = roundwood (diameter <20mm)
s = sapwood (diameter >20mm)
h = heartwood,
u = unknown maturity (oak only)
rt = root

DISCUSSION *by Gary Coates and Ann Woodward*

The Landscape Setting

Whitemoor Haye Quarry is located on a 180 hectare expanse of farmland, a flat open landscape containing gentle undulations varying in height from 51m to 54m A.O.D. The height variation of 3 metres over such a large area may seem insignificant but the difference between a dry and wet location during flooding may have been as little as 1m, as was noted at excavations at the nearby site of Fisherwick (Smith 1979, 1). The eastern half of the site forms the floodplain of the River Tame, with a gentle slope from west to east across the whole site. Within this floodplain there are considerable areas of alluvial deposits, which are interrupted by gravel islands. Over a large part of the site the floodplain has yet to be investigated archaeologically, and the character of land-use in this area is not fully known. The dating of the major alluviations is also not known, although evidence from other river valley systems would suggest that major periods of flooding can be associated with the use of heavy duty ploughs and the expansion of arable farming dating to the late Iron Age/Roman and late Saxon/Early Medieval periods (Lupton 1995, 2.2.6).

Environmental evidence from the excavations does present us with a good picture of the prehistoric and Romano-British landscape at Whitemoor Haye. The earliest evidence comes from the Early Neolithic period, where charcoal samples from two pits contained pine, which had largely disappeared in the countryside by this period and indicates a local pinewood (see *Charcoal*, above). These samples may also relate to woodland clearance taking place then and throughout the following millennia.

The majority of the environmental evidence derives from Iron Age contexts and insects, charred and waterlogged plant remains and charcoal all combine to present a similar image of the surrounding landscape. There was a mixture of grassland and arable land, probably on poorly drained soil. There would also have been areas of marginal woodland, evident from the species present in the charcoal samples. These were dominated by oak, which reflects more on the use of this wood as fuel than its actual domination in the woodland species, although it indicates that oak was readily available (see *Charcoal*, above). The plant macrofossil and insect evidence indicates that there were grazing animals present, at least in the late Iron Age and in the vicinity of Area A (see *Waterlogged Seeds* and *Insect Remains*, above). The land use and environment appears to have remained roughly constant through into the Roman period. The evidence from other excavations at Fisherwick, Wanlip and Willington compares well with that from Whitemoor Haye, and a similar picture of mixed agriculture, marginal woodland and heath-like areas on gravel terraces seems to have been the norm for this period in the Midland river valleys.

All the areas excavated and the majority of the areas covered by the watching brief were outside, or on the edge of, the floodplain, and there was no evidence of deep alluvial deposits within the excavation areas themselves. However, many of the deeper ditches and pits had suffered from repeated silting up and had had to be re-defined on several occasions. This in itself indicates that there were short periods of flooding. Observations during excavation also indicated that in Areas A, B and C there was a particularly high water table, even in dry periods.

Activity post-dating the Roman period was poorly represented in the archaeological record and therefore there is no direct evidence of the environment throughout the Medieval and Post-Medieval periods. However, study of the cartographic and historical sources (Smith 1980) presents us with a picture of continuity from the Roman period with a mixture of arable fields, rough grazing and waste ground. The areas of woodland declined as more land was cleared for agriculture. Ultimately the land became enclosed and hedgerows defining smaller blocks of fields appeared. This pattern continued into the twentieth century until mechanical agricultural techniques opened up larger fields, and improved drainage technology allowed the expansion of arable farming into former areas of grassland.

Neolithic and Early Bronze Age Activity

Structures of Neolithic and Early Bronze Age date investigated by excavation included two ring ditches, one partly investigated in Evaluation Trench B by Tempus Reparatum, and the other ploughed out in Area R. These ring ditches belonged to a scattered group of at least four small circular cropmarks near the northern extremity of the concession. Next to the ring ditch in Trench B was a pit or gully which contained fragments of four Middle Neolithic Peterborough Ware vessels, while possibly cut into the base of the ring ditch in Area R was an oval pit containing a large portion from a Beaker vessel. No human remains were recovered from either site, but it seems likely that the ring ditches were the remains of barrows to which the ceramic deposits were related. A better-preserved barrow was excavated a little further north at Tucklesholme Farm (Hughes 1991). Pits containing Neolithic and Beaker material are commonly found adjacent to and in amongst groups of ring ditches, both in the Midlands, as at Meole Brace, Shropshire (Hughes and Woodward 1995), and in the upper Thames valley, as at Barrow Hills, Radley (Barclay and Halpin 1999) or around the Devil's Quoit henge monument (Barclay *et al* 1995).

A little further north, on the site of the National Arboretum, a second part-Beaker was found deposited in a pit near to a complex circular cropmark. This monument, which shows as three or four concentric crop circles, may have been a large multi-phased round barrow or a mini henge; it is approximately 35m in diameter. This site may be an outlier to the group of henges and cursus monuments know at Catholme, just across the River Trent to the north. The post henge at Catholme (SMR 1397) is 85m in diameter but the circular cropmark with radial lines of pits extending from it

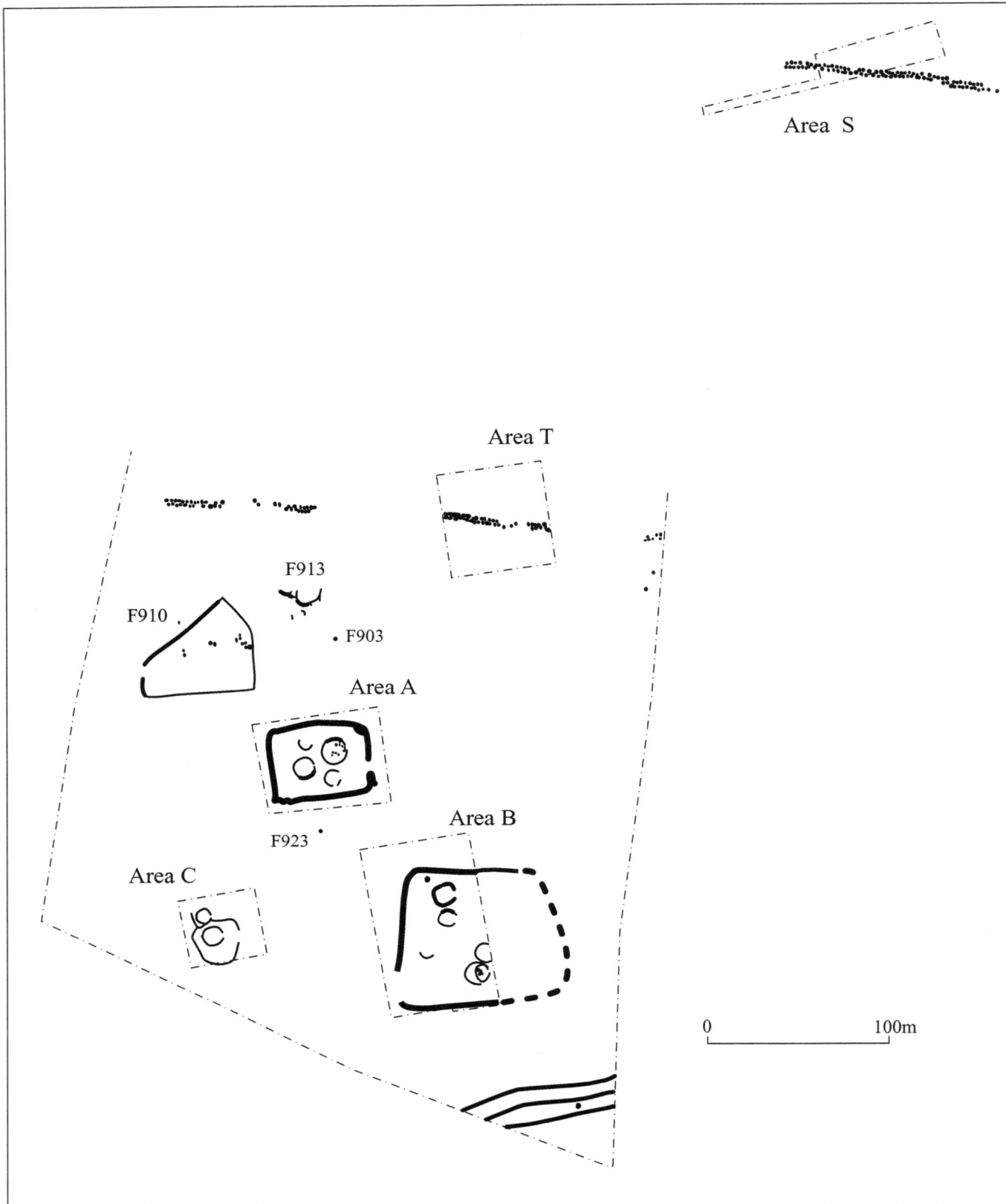

Fig. 44: Composite plan of all Iron Age features (Period 2)

(SMR 0203) is smaller than the monument that lies in the National Arboretum. The Catholme henges are surrounded by more ring ditches and are associated with two possible cursus monuments (SMR 1477 and 0204). Cursus monuments are usually of Middle Neolithic date, although that at Aston on Trent may have been constructed in the Late Neolithic period, and thus have been contemporary with henge monuments elsewhere (Gibson and Loveday 1989).

The complex at Catholme, including the circular monuments at the National Arboretum and at Whitemoor Haye, comprises a remarkable cluster of henges, mini henges, round barrows and cursus monuments, concentrated on the confluence of the Rivers Trent, Tame and Mease. This area shows up as the only marked concentration of round barrows south of the Pennines within the middle Trent basin (Vine 1982, 289). Complexes containing both henge and cursus monuments are in fact rather rare, the best examples being those at Maxey, Cambridgeshire, on a gravel island adjacent to the River Welland (Pryor 1985, fig.15) and at Dorchester-on-Thames, Oxfordshire, lying within the confluence of the Thames and the River Thame (Loveday 1999, fig.5.2). The association of ring ditches, mini henges and cursus monuments is more common. In the Midlands, such complexes are known at Aston on Trent (see above), at Barford, Warwickshire, lying within a loop of the River Avon (Loveday 1989), and on the middle Ouse in Cambridgeshire (Last 1999, fig.8.2). The location of these complexes in close proximity to major watercourses has been the subject of some interesting recent research. This suggests that there was a strong metaphorical link between running water, the routes of procession along cursus monuments, and concepts of purity and basic sustenance (e.g. Barclay and Hey 1999, 73).

The earliest material found in the excavations is the assemblage of charred plant remains from a pit in Area R, which was dated by radiocarbon to the Early Neolithic period. The earliest artefacts are the Middle Neolithic Peterborough Ware vessels from Evaluation Trench B, and another probable piece from Evaluation Trench AE, which lies further south in the gravel zones already examined. Other finds of Peterborough Ware are known from Fisherwick, Fatholme and Lichfield (see *Peterborough Ware*, above). These, like the sherd from Trench AE, may derive from occupation sites. Overall this forms a very marked concentration of Peterborough Ware in this zone of the Trent valley; otherwise Neolithic pottery is mainly known from caves and barrows in the Peak District to the north. In Warwickshire, Ebbsfleet Ware and Peterborough Ware have been found at similar riverine monument complexes around Barford (Oswald 1969) and Wasperton (Woodward in Hughes and Crawford 1995). The groups of large joining sherds from Whitemoor Haye Evaluation Trench B, and from Barford, are likely to have been deliberate ritual deposits.

Beakers have rarely been found in the Trent valley, and the two part-vessels from Whitemoor Haye and the National Arboretum are important finds. Other vessels and fragments are recorded from Aston barrow 1, Derbyshire (Vine 1982, 325, nos. 315-6), Swarkestone barrow 4, Derbyshire (ApSimon

1960) and Lockington, Leicestershire (Woodward in Hughes 2000), and upstream at Stoke-on-Trent and (on the River Dove) at Rocester (Vine 1982, 326, nos. 326-7 respectively). All these date from the Late Neolithic or Early Bronze Age periods. The most significant aspect of these two new Beakers is that careful excavation was able to confirm that both were deposited in a broken condition. It appears that large chunks of each vessel had been deliberately retained for use as heirlooms or as a future source of special grog to be used in the manufacture of new vessels.

The tree species from a pit in Area R, dated to the Early Neolithic, include oak and pine, and hazelnuts were also identified. This evidence indicates that primary forest occurred nearby and that native pine had survived within this Neolithic wildwood (see *Charcoal*, above). However, hazel is found more commonly on the edges of woodland, and it may be that some tree felling had taken place, and that the groups of early monuments thus stood in clearings. The Neolithic Group VI Langdale stone axe found just west of the modern buildings of Whitemoor Haye (SMR 1352) serves to remind us of the felling of trees, as well as hinting at the complex network of forest pathways that would have led to this important place, located where tributary rivers flowed into one of the major water courses of lowland Britain.

Iron Age Boundaries (Fig. 44)

Some of the most dominant features of the cropmark complex and of the areas excavated so far are a series of linear boundaries running roughly east-west, and at right angles to the adjacent stretch of the River Tame. The two more northerly, investigated in Areas S and T, are double pit alignments whilst the two further south are multiple ditches. One of these, comprising three parallel ditches, was examined in Area F. No finds were recovered from the multiple ditches at this location. However it seems likely that this boundary dates from the Iron Age period, defining the southern edge of a block of land containing the Iron Age enclosures occupying excavated Areas A, B and C. There was evidence of a single recut in the central ditch only. The pit alignment in Area T consisted of two rows of circular pits, on average 1.4m in diameter and 0.5 to 0.6m deep. The pits in the two rows were slightly staggered. The pit fillings displayed two episodes of natural silting, but no obvious recuts; no finds were recovered. A wide gap occurred in both rows in the location later occupied by the north-south Romano-British droveway. In Area S the second pit alignment also consisted of two rows of staggered circular pits, but in this case all except three of those excavated had been recut at least once, and one pit had been recut three times. The pits ranged in diameter from 1 to 2.2m and were originally 0.4 to 0.9m deep. Large chunks of Iron Age ceramic jars were found in one original cut, and in one recut; the latter context also produced a fragment from a flint core. Two other recuts contained a small collection of Iron Age sherds, and a single sherd plus a granite rubber, respectively. All these finds came from pits in the northernmost row, and they were evenly spread along the length of alignment investigated. Immediately north of the double alignment was a cluster of pits, one of which contained another substantial deposit of sherds from a single Iron Age jar.

Pit alignments occur extensively in the Midland counties, and a fair number have been excavated. In Northamptonshire most of the pits are rectilinear in shape, as at Briar Hill and Gretton (Jackson 1974) and sub-rectangular pits are also known in the alignment at Barford, Warwickshire (Loveday 1989). However, another pit alignment at Briar Hill was made up of circular and oval pits (Bamford 1985, 49) and at St. Ives, Cambridgeshire alignments of rectangular and circular pits were found next to each other (Pollard 1996, 100-102). Pits in different alignments also vary in size; those at St. Ives are slightly smaller than those at Whitemoor Haye, whilst the rectangular Northamptonshire type, as at Briar Hill, are rather larger and deeper (Jackson 1974). Sometimes, as at St. Ives, it has been possible to detect distinct sets of adjacent pits of similar size and shape, and this has suggested that a system of gang construction was involved. There was no obvious evidence for this at Whitemoor Haye. In some cases, the individual pits were left to silt naturally whilst in others, recuts were detected. This situation applies at Whitemoor Haye where only pits within the northernmost row of the northern double alignment (Area S) showed evidence of recutting. This row also produced the only deposits of finds, which have been summarised above.

Many pit alignments were subsequently recut as linear ditches, or as the sides of Iron Age enclosures, and some are known to have replaced earlier rows of posts set in slighter holes (e.g. Briar Hill, Jackson 1974), or fence and hedge lines (St. Ives, Pollard 1996, 98). None of these actions seem to have occurred at Whitemoor Haye. The existence of two double alignments in close proximity to each other is unusual. Other double sets are known from Tallington, Lincolnshire (French *et al* 1993, figs. 14 and 15), where one row was characterised by squarish pits and the other by pits more circular in shape, and from Barford, Warwickshire (Loveday 1989). Usually it is not possible to demonstrate that both alignments were dug simultaneously, but the staggered layouts of the two examples at Whitemoor Haye might suggest that here this was indeed the case.

Pollard (1996, 111) has drawn attention to the fact that the few finds recovered from pit alignments are unusual, and that they probably represent deliberate structured deposits. Such finds include objects of metal, such as a bronze ring-headed pin and iron currency bars from Gretton, an incised sandstone plaque from Briar Hill (all in Jackson 1974), complete or near complete Late Bronze Age/Early Iron Age pots from Ringstead (Jackson 1978) and Gretton (Jackson 1974), and complete animal bones from some sites in Lincolnshire. The ceramic finds, granite rubber and, possibly, the flint core from Whitemoor Haye fall into this category of special deposits. The radiocarbon dates and pottery from the northernmost row of the northern pit alignment indicate that this row of pits at least was dug in the Middle Iron Age period. Ceramic and metalwork finds from other sites confirms this general dating, as do other radiocarbon dates from Tallington (French *et al.* 1993, 66) and St. Ives (Pollard 1996, 100). However, there are some pit alignments which appear to have been initiated in the late

Neolithic period, notably those in the Milfield Basin, Northumberland (Harding 1981, 115-9 and Miket 1981). It may be that some of the pit rows at Whitemoor Haye were also established long before the Middle Iron Age, and the flint core fragment found in one of the pits in Area S may be evidence, albeit redeposited, for such early activity.

The non-continuous nature of pit alignments has been the subject of much discussion. It is generally agreed that the importance of these monuments lay primarily in the act of their initial construction, and periodic reinforcement through recutting (e.g. Pollard 1996, 110). Thus the alignment served to mark out symbolic boundaries whether they were marked previously by hedges or fences, or by the alignment of a natural feature, such as the river at St. Ives. The Middle Iron Age was a time when settlements in the Midlands were becoming enclosed for the first time, and such enclosures and associated linear ditched boundaries were often connected intimately with the lines of existing pit alignments. The arrangement of pit alignments within prehistoric landscapes is highly variable – they occur in low-lying and upland areas, parallel to streams and rivers in some cases, and perpendicular to rivers in other areas. It is not possible or desirable to seek a general functional explanation for their existence. It seems much more likely that the alignments had different functions and meanings in their various local landscape contexts. At Whitemoor Haye, it is apparent that the two double pit alignments define the boundary area between the complex of Neolithic and Early Bronze Age monuments to the north, and the zone of Iron Age and Romano-British agricultural units that have been investigated to the south. Other alignments occur on similar east-west lines in amongst the henge monuments at Catholme, and defining the northern edge of the extended area of earlier prehistoric sacred landscape. Thus the alignments may have defined the area of early land clearance prior to the development of the extensive farming from the Iron Age onwards, and acted to separate old ancestral monuments from the new-style enclosed farmsteads, and the old pasture clearings from the developing Iron Age agri-scape. But just across the River Tame a different style of landscape apportionment seems to have been in existence. Here there are two cropmark pit alignments running parallel to the river (SMR nos. 1393 and 1382). Sub-circular and rectilinear enclosures lie either side of both, but, in the absence of any excavation, it is not possible to assess the significance of the apparent contrast with the system of landscape organisation elucidated across the river at Whitemoor Haye.

The Iron Age Enclosures (Fig. 44)

Iron Age enclosures investigated during the excavations include two rectangular enclosures in Areas A and B and a curvilinear enclosure in Area C. These enclosures were defined by open ditches, which were probably adjacent to banks or discrete spoil heaps, although there was no evidence for such deposits within the silted up ditches themselves.

The enclosure within Area A defined an area of 50m east-west by 38m north-south, which is larger than Enclosure 1 from Gamston, Nottinghamshire (Knight 1992, 28), but smaller than the enclosures at Willington, Derbyshire (Wheeler 1979, 94). The nearby enclosure at Fisherwick defined an area 52m by 48m, comparable with the Area A enclosure (Smith 1979, 19). The projected Area B enclosure measured over 70m by 70m and is, therefore, considerably larger than the nearby Fisherwick site and Area A. As examples of single ditched enclosures, Area A is of an average size and Area B slightly larger than average size for this area, although the significance of this measurement is difficult to judge as the relationship between size and status or function may not be a simple one. It does, however, illustrate that both of these enclosures define substantial parcels of land, 1900m² and c.5000m², and digging the ditches would not have been a quick and simple task.

The original ditch in Area A was V-shaped, between 1.0m and 1.2m deep and 2.5m to 3.0m wide, which is comparable with Fisherwick in width, but shallower by 0.5m (*ibid.*, 116-7). It had been filled with several episodes of silting, of which the very earliest was a water-logged, organic silt-clay. This type of deposit was also encountered in the enclosure ditches from Fisherwick (SK187082) and was probably the initial silting and slumping of the topsoil or bank deposit. It also suggests that these ditches were filled, at least partially, with water. The re-cut of the Area A ditch was U-shaped and shallower, between 0.4 and 0.8m deep. Enclosures 1 and 2 from Gamston were defined with ditches similar to this re-cut (Knight 1992, 28-33), as was F1 from Willington (Wheeler 1979, 94-7). The Area A re-cut ditch was also filled by several episodes of silting.

The nature of the enclosure ditches in Area A suggests that the original ditch was allowed to silt up over a period of time, which may have included a period of abandonment. This ditch was later re-defined by the shallower recut, which may have coincided with re-occupation of the enclosure or a change in its function. The profile of the ditches may be significant as well. The initial deeper ditch may have been both functional and symbolic: defining an area to confine stock as well as a symbolic living zone for the inhabitants and also creating a drainage system. The later ditch appears to have been much more functional acting purely as a drainage ditch, for something more symbolic or more architectural might have been dug with a more pronounced depth and profile, as was the original ditch. The enclosure at Wanlip, Leicestershire, may have had a similar development, with a more structured and conspicuous ditch in the earliest phase, followed by later shallow redefinition of the ditches for better drainage only (Beamish 1998, 5-13). The scale of all these ditches is matched by many examples in the East Midlands (Knight 1984 I, 191, Table 232, column 17) but those of the Late Iron Age 'defended sites' in Northamptonshire defined by Dix and Jackson (1989, 161) are considerably larger, often more than 2.4m. in depth.

The enclosure ditches in Area B were similar in nature to the re-cut ditch in Area A. They were all U-shaped with a maximum width of 3m and depth of 0.9m, and all had been filled with several episodes of silting. There was no obvious sign that this enclosure had been re-defined at any point. The similarities between the recut in Area A and the Area B enclosure ditches may suggest that the enclosure in Area B was constructed at the same time as the re-definition of the

Area A enclosure. This may lend weight to the argument for an abandonment of the site followed by re-occupation in Area A and a new enclosure in Area B. Unfortunately, the lack of artefactual evidence from these enclosure ditches prevents better definition of the date of construction of the ditches in each area. Although the eastern half of the Area B enclosure was not fully recovered during the watching brief, it seems that the entrance to the Area A enclosure was on the eastern side, whereas the entrance to that of Area B was in the southwest corner. The entrance to the enclosure at Gamston was on the eastern side, as was the enclosure at SK187082, Fisherwick. In the Nene and Great Ouse basins the entrances to enclosures usually faced to the northeast, east or southeast (Knight 1984 I, fig.47), although one at Milton Keynes faced west (*ibid.*) as did that belonging to the enclosure at Wootton Hall Farm (Dix and Jackson 1989, fig. 10.2.5). The easterly orientations, which face the rising sun, are perhaps of cosmological significance.

There was no evidence of complex gate structures, such as those found on a series of Late Iron Age sites in Northamptonshire (Dix and Jackson 1989, fig.10.4), at Whitemoor Haye, although any post-holes may well have been ploughed away, as appears to be the case elsewhere on the site. The entrances were defined by the rounded terminals of the enclosure ditches, and only later were pits cut into the terminals in Area A. The significance of the entrances is difficult to judge, without any stronger evidence, although if the later Romano-British droveway was based on a former, archaeologically invisible, route or boundary, then both the entrances for the enclosures in Areas A and B open out and towards this route. Both enclosures also respect this possible route. The lack of any remains of a gate structure, elaborate or not, may be due to localised erosion or because the entrances were spanned by simple, functional wooden gates. There were certainly no ditch arrangements that would suggest separation of livestock, as has been observed at Wanlip (*op.cit.* 8-12) and in other areas of the country, especially during the previous Bronze Age (Pryor 1999, 100-5).

The Area C enclosure ditch was less substantial than those in Areas A and B and was curvilinear in nature. Although U-shaped, it was only shallow, with a maximum depth of 0.4m. Again, the corroborating artefactual evidence was absent, but stratigraphic relationships suggested that the enclosure ditch was a late addition to the two structures and may have been designed for drainage as much as enclosure. The entrance in this enclosure was on the eastern side and it also appeared that the ring gully associated with Structure 11 had been utilised as an annex to the main enclosure. The only comparative example in the region is the possible curvilinear enclosure ditch, F608/689, at Willington (Wheeler 1979, 96). This was a similar shape and depth to the Area C enclosure ditch, but had been reset eleven times and an insufficient length had been exposed in plan to determine whether this was really a curvilinear enclosure or the curving corner of a rectangular enclosure, as observed in Areas A and B.

There is insufficient dating evidence to allow the chronological relationships of the Iron Age enclosures at Whitemoor Haye to be closely defined. There seems to be some correlation between the re-cut enclosure ditch of Area A and the Area B enclosure on morphological grounds, and it is tempting to separate the Area C enclosure as an earlier or later style. However the differences could be more functional than chronological. The actual function of the ditches could be varied. The evidence suggests that they were not defensive and served as means of demarking an area, probably for stock control and human occupation. They almost certainly served as water management systems, whether deliberate or not, and the re-definition of the Area A enclosure ditch may be evidence of the maintenance of this enclosure ditch to provide effective drainage. Research has shown that these type of ditches take a number of years to silt up naturally, and even over decades would remain effective as both a barrier and drainage system (Beamish 1998, 39). Localised conditions may prevail, but the degree of suggested maintenance evident at Gamston (Knight 1992, 28) may not have been required elsewhere, as at Whitemoor Haye, for the ditches to remain efficient as boundaries and for drainage. It has also been suggested by Reynolds that prehistoric ditches may have been deliberately dug in the knowledge that they could both erode and silt up over a long period of time and still remain effective with very little maintenance (Reynolds 1996, 227).

The Iron Age Structures (Fig. 44)

Within the enclosures in Areas A, B and C were a number of ring gullies and associated post-holes, which appear to be the remains of eaves-drip ditches associated with round houses. Four structures were recorded in Area A, six from Area B and two in Area C. There were also a number of isolated pits, including four large pits cut into the enclosure ditch in Area A. The examination of the nature of these structures and the pits may elucidate the nature of occupation of these enclosures and their function.

Table 23: Dimensions (m) of Structures from Whitemoor Haye

Structure (Area)	Max. Internal /External Diameter	Average Ditch Width	Average Ditch Depth	Width of Entrance
1 (A)	13/15	1	0.35	3.6
2 (A)	6/7	0.4	0.15	N/A
3 (A)	11/12	0.6	0.3	4
4 (A)	9/10	0.5	0.25	4.4
5 (B)	11/13	1	0.7	3.6
6 (B)	8/9.5	0.7	0.3	3.6
7 (B)	10.5/11.5	0.5	0.25	N/A
8 (B)	11.5/13	0.8	0.4	2.6
9 (B)	6/7	0.4	0.3	4
10 (B)	NA/8.5	0.6	0.25	N/A
11 (C)	8/9	0.4	0.4	2.2
12 (C)	10/12	1	0.5	2.6
Average	9.4/10.6	0.66	0.35	3.4

Table 23 compares the different hut circles encountered at Whitemoor Haye, including the partially surviving hut circle from Area B (Structure 10). All the hut circles had common features: for instance the entrances were all on the eastern side. They were all single ditch structures with no evidence of surviving post-holes from possible hut walls. The largest, in terms of external diameter, was Structure 1 from Area A and the smallest Structures 2 and 9. The difference between

these two extremes is highlighted by the fact that Structure 1 is more than twice as large as Structures 2 and 9, with a cluster of structures grouped with external diameters between 10 and 13m. The difference in size between Structures 1 and 2 or 9 is particularly evident if we compare the area enclosed by the ring gullies; Structure 1 enclosed an area of 132.7m², whereas structures 2 and 9 enclosed areas of only 28.3m².

In terms of average ditch widths and depths, there is a general correlation between the larger ring gullies and wider and deeper ditches, although this is not exact, as illustrated by Structure 1, which had one of the widest ditches but not the deepest. One has to be particularly wary when comparing widths and depths of ditches, as there have been varying degrees of truncation across the site, which is likely to have been the most influential factor in the degree of preservation of the different ring gullies. However, Structures 5 and 12 appear to have had reasonably wide and deep ditches and, as they were located next to other structures (6 and 11, respectively), one can assume that they were subject to similar levels of truncation and that there is some relevance in the differences in ditch widths and depths.

The ditches of Structures 5 and 12 had been redefined, twice in the case of the latter. Of the remainder of the structures on the site only Structures 4 and 11 showed signs of redefinition. At Structure 4 there were indications of an earlier ditch in two excavated sections, and the original ring ditch defining Structure 11 had been re-cut with two later ditches. If the evidence for re-cuts has not been lost due to truncation in the other ring ditches, then it seems plausible that most of the structures were used only once and possibly for a relatively short period of time, i.e. decades rather than centuries. Those structures that showed signs of re-definition of ditches may have been subject to repair and/or re-occupation over a longer period of time.

Where the width of the entrances was discernible, there appeared to be three distinct groups; Structures 8, 11 and 12 with entrances measuring between 2.2m and 2.6m. Structures 1, 5 and 6 all had entrances measuring 3.6m wide and Structures 3, 4 and 9 had entrances measuring between 4m and 4.4m wide. There was also evidence for entrance structures, possibly gates or doors, from Structures 1, 3, 6 and 11. The significance of the groupings is difficult to decipher; one may be looking at specific periods of construction associated with different sized entrances. Equally, there may have been different functions associated with those hut circles with smaller or larger entrances. The orientation of entrances towards the east, as in the case of the enclosure entrances discussed above, is matched in the East Midlands area (Knight 1984 I, 145, fig.38).

The ring gullies observed at Whitemoor Haye can be classified as Group 3b ground plans after Knight 1984 (137 ff.). These are penannular gullies with little or no sign of interior palisade trenches (Group 2) or a ring of post-holes, without the drainage ditch (Group 1). Examples of Group 3 type of structures are widespread throughout the country, but more locally the Iron Age structures observed are of a slightly different type. At Fisherwick (SK 187082) the excavated structure appeared to be of a Group 2 type, with an inner palisade trench, although the lack of stratigraphic relationships, as at Whitemoor Haye, may suggest there were two Group 3 structures of slightly different periods (Banks in Smith 1979, 27-33). Hut circles excavated at Willington, Derbyshire, were of Group 3 type, with both annular and penannular ring gullies, although they were not located neatly within their own enclosures, but were instead closely associated with the ditch systems (Wheeler 1979, 103ff.). They were also smaller than those at Whitemoor Haye, with the largest at Willington under 7m in diameter (*ibid.*, 104). The post ring structure excavated at Swarkestone Lowes (Elliot and Knight 1999) is rather earlier than the main occupations at Whitemoor Haye. The size range of ring gullies is similar to that recorded for the East Midlands sites by Knight (Knight 1984 I, 141, Table 14, column 4: internal diameters for his Group 3 structures).

The ring gullies themselves were almost certainly drainage ditches, for the run off from the eaves of the hut roof. There was no sign of any post-holes or trenches at the base of any of the gullies, although it remains possible this type of evidence may have been lost when or if posts had been removed (Knight 1984, 137). Structures 1, 3, 4, 5 and 6 had evidence of a central post, which implies that the structures were likely to have been traditional round houses, although with a lack of interior palisade trenches or ring of post-holes there remains a possibility that some of the structures may simply have been stockades for animals. The evidence of domestic activity from these structures is very slight. There were the remains of possible hearths or ovens associated with Structures 1 (F402), 3 (F433) and 5 (F78). Iron Age pottery was also recovered from several of the structures or their associated features. However, it appears that some of this pottery may well have been deposited at the time of abandonment of the relevant structures (see *Prehistoric Pottery*, above). Evidence for the presence of livestock was recovered from the ring gully of Structure 3, in the form of compacted charred straws probably from burnt stable manure (see *Charcoal*, above). There was also evidence of crop processing on the site from the ring gully defining Structure 3 (see *Plant Macroremains*, above). The evidence of discarded fuel debris can also be associated with structures from both Area A and Area B. This points, not surprisingly, to human occupation engaged in agricultural activity.

The enclosures seem to have defined small farmsteads, which probably contained pairs of structures. Structures 2 and 3 could have been a pair, replaced by Structures 1 and 4, which may also have coincided with the re-definition of the enclosure ditch in Area A. Structures 5 and 6, as well as Structures 7 and 8/9, in Area B could also have been pairs. Stratigraphic evidence also suggested that Structures 11 and 12 existed at a similar period. It is tempting to suggest that each pair included a living hut and an ancillary structure used for stock, crafts or storage, but there is no definite evidence from Whitemoor Haye to substantiate this theory.

The evidence also suggests that by the Late Iron Age these farmsteads were no longer occupied. Areas B and C may well have been abandoned completely, but in Area A there is evidence that the nature of the occupation changed. Four large pits were excavated into the silted up enclosure ditch, of which stretches may have remained open. F445 was the final of four re-cuts of a pit at the southern terminal of the

entrance to the Area A enclosure and F456 had been re-cut twice. The insect and plant macrofossil remains (see *Insect Remains* and *Waterlogged Seeds*, above) indicated that the original south terminal pit was probably a watering hole for cattle, but that there was no evidence of human activity in the immediate vicinity of the pit. This type of waterlogged feature was also present at nearby Fisherwick (Smith 1979, 94ff.) and pits cut into the silted up ditches and hut circles were observed at Willington (Wheeler 1979, 94). The fact that the pits were redefined several times is indicative of human presence although probably not in the enclosures identified. It also remains likely that these watering holes continued to be used and maintained into the Romano-British period.

The Romano-British Enclosures and Droveway
(Fig.45)

The Romano-British activity at Whitemoor Haye was characterised by the extensive droveway that crossed the quarry concession area from north to south, and by enclosures in Areas A and S. There were also a number of ditches that appeared to form land divisions (see Fig. 45).

The droveway was recorded and sample excavated at various points along its route over two seasons of excavation and during the watching brief. The westernmost ditch varied in depth and width and had both U- and V-shaped profiles. In Areas B and T this ditch appeared to have been re-defined with a later ditch. The eastern side of the droveway was defined with a single ditch in some places and a double ditch in others. Again these ditches varied in size and profile. This variance can be explained by the degree of truncation that the ditches have been subjected to over the centuries and, over such long lengths, there were probably different periods of construction and repair, illustrated by the different profiles observed. The cropmark plot shows the droveway continuing southwards until it meets the River Tame and northwards until it disappears in the vicinity of the modern A513 road. In Area B, it also followed the same alignment as the western side of the Iron Age enclosure ditch. It is also evident that the Iron Age enclosures in Areas A, B and C respected the route of the droveway as did the pit alignment in Area T, but not in Area S. This would suggest that this route had existed in some form prior to the digging of the ditches, and certainly there may have been banks and hedges as there probably were in the Romano-British period.

In the area where the droveway meets the pit alignment in Area T there were a number of features that may have supported a form of gateway between fields or other land divisions. There was very little in the way of artefactual evidence over the whole length, which may be indicative of the extent to which the droveway was used. The pottery dated to the mid-2nd to late-3rd century AD., which suggests that the droveway ditches were dug in the 1st or early 2nd centuries. If these had been associated with banks and hedges then it is likely that the droveway remained defined beyond the Romano-British period into the Medieval period. A similar droveway was sample excavated at Fisherwick, SK184103, with western and eastern ditches,

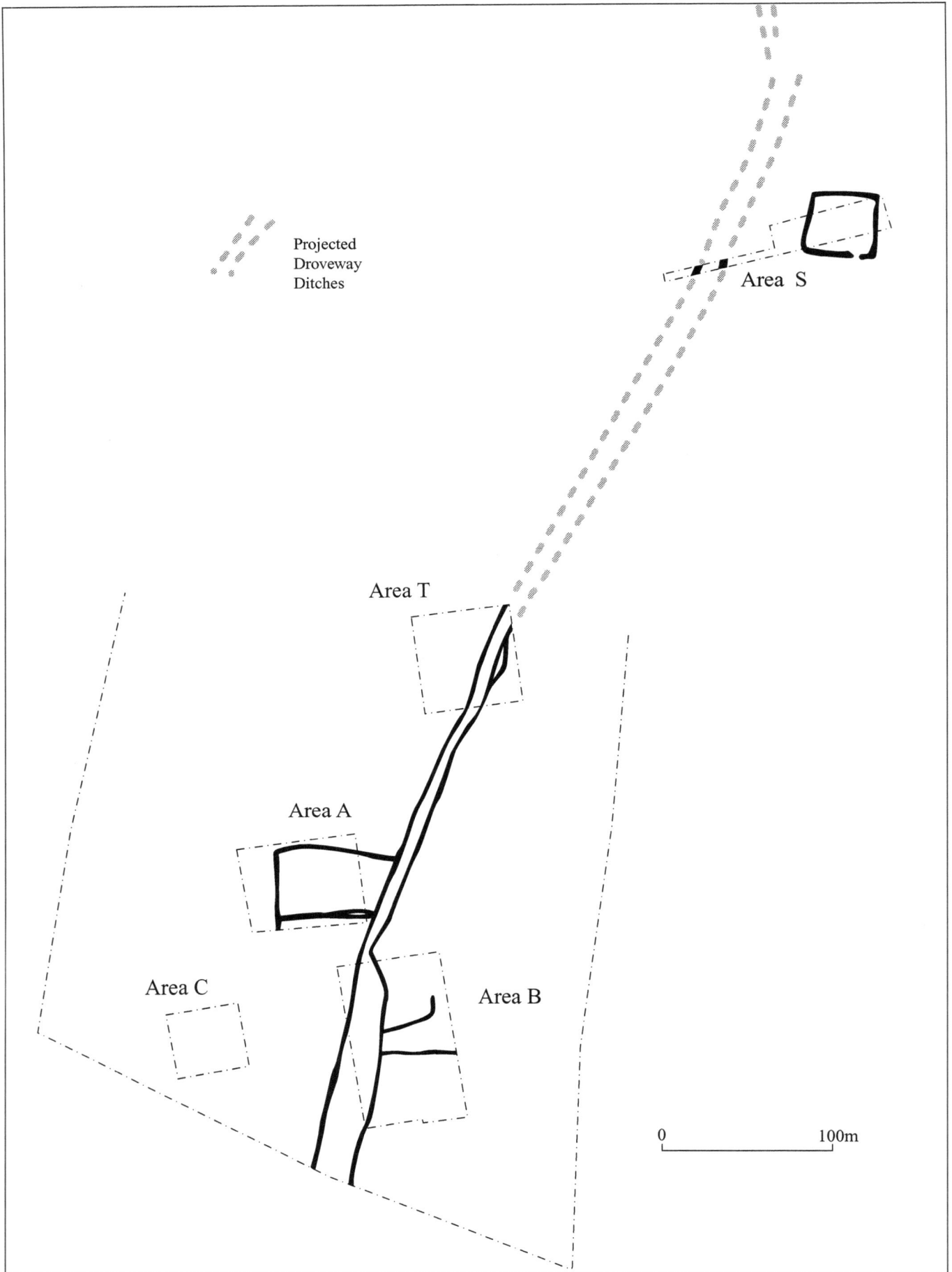

Fig. 45: Composite plan of all Romano-British features (Period 3)

and the construction dated to the early 2nd century AD. (Miles 1969, 7ff.). It seems that the whole area along the Tame valley was subjected to the construction of substantial boundaries, which were possibly associated with allocation of land to Roman army veterans from nearby Wall.

The enclosure in Area S probably had an agricultural function; it may have been some form of animal enclosure for stock management. There was no evidence of internal structures or substantial domestic activity. Pottery and artefacts recovered from the ditches can be associated with cooking activity and food storage, which indicates some level of human presence within or near the enclosure. This was likely to have been in the form of temporary buildings, perhaps like shepherds' bothies, with residency on a daily basis or at certain times of the year when the animals needed particular attention. It remains possible that the enclosure was also an area for processing crops; one of the enclosure ditches produced evidence of spelt and the waste from cereal crop processing (see *Plant Macroremains*, above).

The enclosure in Area A probably fulfilled the same function as that from Area S. The enclosure was not as well defined as the one discussed above, in the sense that there was a series of new ditches excavated to join with the Iron Age enclosure ditches, some of which probably remained open into this period. This enclosure joined directly with the droveway and may have had a specific function associated with it. It certainly seems likely that this enclosure was for corralling animals as there were a number of drinking holes identified in the Iron Age, and these probably continued in use during this period.

Similar enclosures have been excavated at Fisherwick, to the south, in association with a droveway (Miles 1969, 7-13). Here, they also seem to have been for stock control and rearing of either cattle or horses, which were usually grazing freely in open forest conditions (*ibid.*, 11). This seems a plausible explanation for the activity at either of the enclosures at Whitemoor Haye too. Enclosure ditches have also been identified at Rocester, Staffordshire, where a lack of structural evidence from the interior suggested that they were probably used for corralling stock (Ferris *et al.* 2000, 73-4), although this was in close association with a vicus settlement.

The evidence of Romano-British activity across the whole site follows a similar pattern to the previous Iron Age activity. There were enclosures principally designed for the management of stock and some crop processing from both periods. The droveway possibly existed in the earlier period and was developed into a more visible feature in the landscape by the Romano-British period. The hut circles were more substantial evidence of human occupation in the Iron Age, although the pottery assemblage from the later period attests that there was human activity associated with these enclosures, although the structures may have been insubstantial and, therefore, lost to the archaeological record. The evidence does strongly suggest that the nature of activity on the site continued to be the same as in the Iron Age, carried out by the same native population, who adopted some aspects of romanised culture. Samian pottery was reaching the site in small amounts over a long period of time, but overall the pottery assemblage included few fine wares (see *Production: Artefacts*, below).

Production: Artefacts

The archaeology of production involves the modification of raw materials and the making of things by human agency. For the Neolithic period at Whitemoor Haye it seems that most surviving artefacts were made on or near to the site. The main categories are the Peterborough pottery, which, like that from neighbouring Fisherwick, was made from local clay and rock (see *Prehistoric Pottery*, above), and flint flakes and tools manufactured on pebbles from suitable local gravel deposits (see *Worked Flint*, above). In the Iron Age a similar picture emerges, but rather more detail can be discerned. No tools or ornaments of metal or bone were recovered, although undoubtedly they were used on the site. Indirect evidence for the use of a metal axe is provided by the toolmarks on the oak stake from Area A, but evidence for any metalworking on the site was absent. Nor were any tools associated with textile production recovered, although the flint scraper may have been used in the treatment of animal skins. This resource would have provided fur and leather for clothing, and sinews for sewing and binding.

Timber probably would have been used for the production of artefacts such as spoons and bowls as well as for components, notably handles for tools, and was certainly used widely in structural construction. The oak stake and charcoal samples show that the main wood used for huts and fence posts was oak, whilst hazel and willow would have been used for hurdles, wattling and basketry. Fragments of daub probably derived from hut walling; some pieces may have been part of clay ovens or hearth lining, but no diagnostic fragments were identified. Most of the Iron Age pottery contained inclusions which suggest the use of local clays (see *Prehistoric Pottery, Late Bronze Age/ Iron Age Fabric*, above). Potting could therefore have taken place on site, although no direct evidence for the craft was found. This was in direct contrast to the situation in the Romano-British period, when it is extremely unlikely that any pottery was made in the vicinity of the site, and wares were being imported from production sites both within and beyond the Midlands (see *Roman Pottery*, above and see below).

The production of food would have involved the major tasks of grinding, cutting and cooking. Quern stones are the most common class of small finds from the Iron Age period, and one fragment was found in one of the Romano-British droveway ditches. These pieces of equipment were a crucial element for domestic life and may have been found in every household. Their importance is reflected by the practice of depositing complete stones or broken fragments in pits or ditches, often at the time of settlement abandonment (see below). Food was cooked on fires. There were central hearths or ovens in Structures 1 and 3 in Area A and also in Structure 5 in Area B, while several features contained deposits of burnt and fire-cracked stones. Analysis of the charcoal samples (see *Charcoal*, above) has shown that the main fuel was oak, which was very slow-burning, but timber from other trees, heather and stable manure were also employed, and the residues from plant processing were used as tinder. This pattern applies in both the Iron Age and Romano-British periods (see *Plant Macroremains*, above). A similar system of fuel consumption was discerned at Fisherwick and Wanlip, but, interestingly, some other settlements, such as Swarkestone Lowes, were set in a treeless landscape. Here wood must have been brought in from a distance, or perhaps there was more dependence on dung, manure and cereal waste. The Iron Age pottery from Whitemoor Haye mainly comprised medium and large jars which would have been used for storage and cooking, although no direct evidence for this survived. However, in the Romano-British period, 18% of the pottery was sooted, mostly on the exterior surfaces. These vessels were mainly Derbyshire lid-seated bell-mouthed jars and Black Burnished cooking pots, which had been placed on fires to facilitate the heating of water and the cooking of stews, broths and gruel. Some burnt fragments of animal bone may indicate that some meat was roasted over the fire, or that bone was used as yet another source of fuel.

Production: Farming

In both the Iron Age and Romano-British period the principal activity at Whitemoor Haye was agricultural. The landscape included areas of woodland and open grazing, along with some marshy areas towards the River Tame. This type of terrain provided the raw materials to support a broad range of agricultural activity, and this was reflected in the archaeological record during excavation.

The survival of animal bone was poor throughout the different periods and there is little direct evidence for the presence of animals on site. This also means that there is no detailed evidence for the breed of animals, animal husbandry and butchery techniques. There is, however, corroborating evidence for a pastoral farming regime from the Iron Age onwards. The enclosures from Areas A, B and C are best interpreted as farmsteads of some description, with the enclosure ditches acting as barriers to contain animals. The actual size and nature of the ditches suggest that they could have been constructed to contain cattle or horses, as simple hurdling would have been sufficient to corral sheep. Animal bones were also poorly preserved at other sites in the Trent valley, such as Swarkestone Lowes, but for Iron Age sites in the East Midlands, Knight deduced that sheep were the most common domestic stock, followed by cattle and pig (according to minimum numbers of individuals statistics) (Knight 1984, 256), while the finds of fish and fowl bones from Cat's Water (Peterborough) hint at the other animal resources that might have been exploited in the riverine environment around Whitemoor Haye. Plant macro remains from the ring gully of Structure 3 have been interpreted as burnt stable manure (see *Plant Macroremains*, above), which lends strength to the evidence for the presence of animals within the enclosure from the Middle Iron Age onwards. At the same time there was evidence of some crop processing being carried out on site in the form of chaff and weed seeds, in particular a seed of false flax, which had only previously been recorded in Roman and Saxon deposits (*ibid.*). The watering holes recorded from the later Iron Age, and possibly beyond, in Area A, attest the presence of animals, both by their nature and from the insect remains (see *Insect Remains*,

above). This evidence strongly supports the hypothesis that there was a mixed farming regime during the Iron Age on this site, of which it is impossible to judge whether the crops or animals played a greater part. The lack of evidence for grain storage, i.e. four post structures, indicates that the farming regime was likely to have been largely one of subsistence, supported by hunting of wild animals and undoubtedly fishing in the River Tame.

The farming regime does not appear to have changed substantially during the Romano-British period. The enhancement of the droveway seems to suggest that there was movement of animals of some description. The enclosure in Area S seemed to have had the same function as the enclosure in Area A, to contain animals. Indeed, the Area A enclosure was adapted from an earlier enclosure and was connected directly to the droveway during this period. Changed socio-economic conditions during the Roman period would have certainly provided a ready market for crops, cattle and horses both for civilian and military consumption. The lack of domestic evidence could suggest a more intensive agricultural use of the Whitemoor Haye landscape designed to produce surplus for a market economy, unlike the subsistence farming that appeared to have dominated during the Iron Age phases. The assemblage of animal bones from the Roman fort at Rocester was dominated by the remains of cattle, both in the military and civilian deposits (Levitan in Esmonde Cleary and Ferris 1996). These animals may have been an important source of hides as well as of beef (Esmonde Cleary and Ferris 1996, 221). Plant remains from Area S indicated a typical assemblage of Roman crops present: spelt, barley and rye, which is comparable with the cereals found in deposits from Orton's Pasture, Rocester (Ferris *et al.* 2000, 68). There was also evidence for different stages of crop processing (see *Plant Macroremains*, above). Again, there was no extensive evidence to further examine the extent of crop processing or livestock management, only to suggest that it was present.

The ditches such as those excavated in Areas A, C and S, taken together with the adjoining cropmark evidence, indicate that the droveway and rectangular enclosures were linked in to an extensive system of large fields. The land boundaries generally conform to NNE-SSW or WNW-ESE alignments, thus implying the former existence of a formal grid layout of fields. Similar systems are also apparent in the cropmarks further south, around Hurst Farm, as well as within the Fisherwick loop of the River Tame (see Map 4 in Smith 1980). As Smith pointed out, the pattern of droveways within all these systems links to Ryknield Street to the west and, to the east, with the sites of ancient fords on the line of the river (Smith 1980, 10).

Exchange and Status

For the Neolithic period, evidence for long-distance exchange is provided by the polished axes from Alrewas parish – two from the Langdale factories and one of flint (Gunstone 1964, 14). These form part of a concentration of Neolithic axes in the immediate area and this is probably related to the presence of the complex of ritual monuments focussed on the confluence of the Trent and Tame rivers. In the Iron Age evidence of regional exchange networks is provided by the quern stones, briquetage and some of the pottery, while in the Romano-British period the pottery is representative of marketing at both regional and long-distance scales.

The querns include three items from sources in the Peak District, one from the Mountsorrel area in Leicestershire, one from the more local New Red Sandstone and one formed from an igneous erratic, originally derived from northern England or southern Scotland (see *Worked Stone*, above). Similar selections of stones, mainly from the Peak District, are known from other rural sites in the Midlands, including Fisherwick, Gamston (Wright and Firman in Knight 1992, 70-74), and Wanlip (Marsden in Beamish 1998, 62-63). Groups of fragments from a minimum of three salt containers (briquetage) came from the Cheshire salt production centre. Such material is known from Anglesey to the Trent and Soar valleys and represents 'an energetic exchange system' (see *Briquetage*, above).

In the Iron Age period, pottery finds from Whitemoor Haye were relatively rare and mainly came from the enclosure in Area A and the pit alignment in Area S. However, the assemblage did include a sherd with granodiorite inclusions. The vessel from which this sherd derived came from south Leicestershire, but not from Mountsorrel, which was the source of one of the querns from Whitemoor Haye, and of the igneous pottery fabrics described for sites further east such as Wanlip, Gamston or Swarkestone Lowes (see *Prehistoric Pottery, Late Bronze Age/ Iron Age Fabric*, above). In the Romano-British period, most of the pottery was made up of locally-traded wares such as the Derbyshire products, along with the regionally marketed Severn Valley wares and Black Burnished wares, from Dorset. The mortaria were from local production centres, and the only imports were the fragments of amphora and samian, which occurred at only the 3% level, by count (see *Roman Pottery*, above).

The sizes of the huts, shape and areas of the enclosures, and the scale of the ditches indicates that the Iron Age farming communities at Whitemoor Haye were typical rural homesteads of relatively low status. The absence of bronze and iron tools or ornaments is not particularly significant, as items of value are likely to have been removed from the site at the time of abandonment. However, the number and variety of quern stones suggests that there was active contact with other communities and the contemporary exchange network. The occurrence of salt containers is also significant in this respect; salt would have been a very valuable commodity, important for food preservation as well, probably, as a highly desirable table condiment. On the other hand, in both the Iron Age and Romano-British periods, the composition of the ceramic assemblages suggests that the establishments were of low status. There are no cups and few bowls in the Iron Age groups, and the Romano-British assemblage is similarly dominated by utilitarian coarsewares, which would have been employed mainly in food preparation and storage. There was a very low percentage of fine table wares (see *Roman Pottery*, above). The samian included a relatively high frequency of decorated pieces but this may

not be indicative of high site status. However, small amounts of this valued fine ware were reaching Whitemoor Haye over a long period of time (see *Samian*, above).

It has been argued above that the Neolithic and Early Bronze Age finds were located on the southern edge of a major complex of ritual sites, which was centred on the cursus and henge monuments at Catholme. The two half Beakers are examples of deliberately deposited heirlooms. For the Iron Age and later periods no possible ritual focus had yet been identified, but there is ample evidence for ritual activity that was embedded in the processes of everyday life. This evidence mainly takes the form of special deposits which had been laid down in a fashion which was both deliberate and structured. Instances of this kind of deposition include the Neolithic/Early Bronze Age flint scraper found with fragments from a set of pots in Early Iron Age pit F903 (Watching Brief area), possibly the flint core fragment in pit F536 belonging to the pit alignment in Area S, the quern and stone rubber fragments from a pit in Structure 1 and the enclosure ditch F471.2 in Area A, and the rubber from pit F519 of the pit alignment. Amongst the pottery, there were several sets of vessels, represented by large chunks, placed in different features of the pit alignment, and there were also the near complete bases of jars from features belonging to Structures 3 and 4 in Area A. The latter deposits, and the querns from Area A, were probably closing deposits, laid down at the time of the abandonment of this settlement enclosure.

Chronology and Population

The level of human activity at Whitemoor Haye appears to be disproportionally represented in the archaeological record. The periods represented most strongly are the Iron Age and Romano-British, although the evidence of some level of activity exists from the Late Neolithic to the Post-Medieval. To some extent, this is a crude representation of the population dynamic of the site.

The Late Neolithic/ Early Bronze Age activity is confined to the north of the site and appears to be ritual in nature. This may mark the southern extent of a sacred landscape centred on the confluence of the Rivers Tame and Trent. Environmental evidence points to some episodes of clearance during the Neolithic period on the site. Any other evidence of activity on the site from this period and the Bronze Age is negligible. Either it has been lost or did not exist in the first place.

The first substantial block of evidence dates from the Iron Age and comprises the pit alignments and enclosures. The boundary features appear to be dividing the agricultural landscape from the previous ritual landscape. The construction of the pit alignments and the enclosures would have required considerable effort; whether this was done *en masse* or over a longer period by a smaller group is difficult to judge. The domestic occupation remains are of such a low level to suggest that there was never a large population living on the site at any one point. In fact the three enclosures may have housed as few as three families, who may have remained here over several generations.

The Iron Age people lived and worked on the land at Whitemoor Haye. In contrast, the principal habitations of the Romano-British population do not seem to have been on the site, at least in the area excavated so far. There was a presence, perhaps in times when animals needed particular attention or labour intensive periods during the crop growing season, e.g. ploughing, planting and harvesting. The permanent residence of the farming population at Whitemoor Haye must have been elsewhere and may be revealed during further excavations within the quarry concession. The formalising of the droveway perhaps highlights the importance of the seasonal movement of animals and their movement to market. This may also be true for the movement of surplus grain. One should not forget that both the Rivers Tame and Trent, along with Ryknield Street (the modern A38 road) would have widened the distribution network for any goods from this site, as well as items imported.

In terms of agricultural use, Whitemoor Haye may have not returned to its maximum potential until the Post-Medieval period. The excavations certainly revealed little evidence of post-Roman and Medieval activity on the site. Again, the population was working the land but living elsewhere, probably in the village of Alrewas.

Conclusion

The 1997 and 1998 excavation seasons at Whitemoor Haye, along with the watching brief up until 1999, have provided an insight into the development and use of the landscape in this area of Staffordshire over four millennia.

The first major impact made by man would have been during the forest clearances of the Neolithic period. Previously the site would have been dominated by woodland and marginal areas close to the River Tame. The clearances do not seem to have been extensive as wooded areas survived right up until the Post-Medieval period. The creation of a ritual landscape accompanied these clearances, with the appearance of barrows containing burials. These were confined to the north of the site and may have been associated with other barrows further north. The Rivers Tame and Trent would have been ideal liminal places and may also have served as territorial boundaries in this region.

Further land divisions appeared by the Iron Age and we may well be in an area that divides a northern and southern territory.

Certainly there was no evidence of widescale Iron Age activity in the area associated with the Neolithic/Bronze Age barrows. Are we looking at two separate tribal areas or is it one territory within which the ancestral monuments were respected? The pit alignments defined some form of land division, even if it was within the territory of one community. Further land clearances continued during the Iron Age as the landscape became dominated by the farmsteads and associated agricultural land. The farming would not have been extensive, but characterised by small family groups working with small fields of crops and a few animals. The land itself would have carried a mixture of woodland, pasture and marshes over a largely flat expanse, probably divided by the long droveway. There would have been periods of inundation, but the farmsteads were located beyond the regular floodplain.

As we move into the Romano-British period it would appear that the landscape became more stabilised. Dominated by agriculture, there may have been more clearances but in general there were wooded areas right up until the nineteenth and twentieth centuries. One might have seen more in the form of flocks of sheep and herds of cattle as well as more fields of spelt, barley and rye reflecting the more intensive farming of this period. The droveway would have dominated the landscape and one can imagine the movement of flocks or herds at certain times of the year and even the odd cart full of grain trundling up and down.

In the post-Roman centuries, with the collapse of the distribution network of the Roman period, there was probably a return to a largely subsistence farming regime, with little evidence of this finding its way into the archaeological record. The Medieval period saw more extensive enclosure of land and the creation of fields, but was probably still dominated by pastoral farming rather than arable.

The biggest change the landscape has experienced since the Neolithic clearances has been in the last fifty years with the introduction of intensive farming techniques. Hedges have been removed to create an open, sometimes bleak landscape. Marshy areas have been reclaimed with the introduction of vast drainage systems. The cattle and sheep have gone, to be replaced by fields of crop. This process has culminated in the establishment of the quarry itself, a major change which has precipitated these excavations. When the quarrying is completed, Whitemoor Haye will be re-instated to agricultural land and the traditions of the previous millennia will continue through the twenty-first century and beyond.

CALIBRATION OF RADIOCARBON AGE TO CALENDAR YEARS

(Variables: C13/C12=-25.3:lab. mult=1)

Laboratory number:	Beta-135226
Conventional radiocarbon age:	2290±50 BP
2 Sigma calibrated results: (95% probability)	Cal BC 410 to 340 (Cal BP 2360 to 2290) and Cal BC 320 to 205 (Cal BP 2270 to 2155)

Intercept data

Intercept of radiocarbon age with calibration curve:	Cal BC 385 (Cal BP 2335)
1 Sigma calibrated result: (68% probability)	Cal BC 395 to 365 (Cal BP 2345 to 2315)

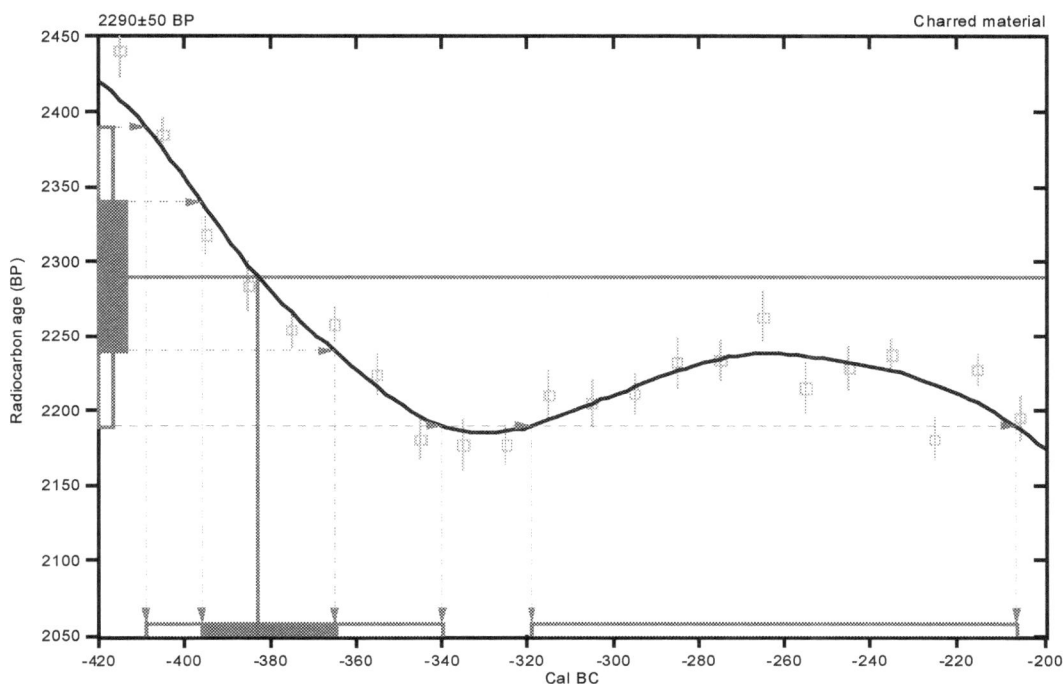

References:
  Database used
    INTCAL98
  Calibration Database
  Editorial Comment
    Stuiver, M., van der Plicht, H., 1998, Radiocarbon 40(3), pxii-xiii
  INTCAL98 Radiocarbon Age Calibration
    Stuiver, M., et. al., 1998, Radiocarbon 40(3), p1041-1083
  Mathematics
  A Simplified Approach to Calibrating C14 Dates
    Talma, A. S., Vogel, J. C., 1993, Radiocarbon 35(2), p317-322

Beta Analytic Radiocarbon Dating Laboratory

4985 S.W. 74th Court, Miami, Florida 33155 • Tel: (305)667-5167 • Fax: (305)663-0964 • E-mail: beta@radiocarbon.com

CALIBRATION OF RADIOCARBON AGE TO CALENDAR YEARS

(Variables: C13/C12=-25.4:lab. mult=1)

Laboratory number: **Beta-135227**

Conventional radiocarbon age: **2230±60 BP**

2 Sigma calibrated result: **Cal BC 400 to 155 (Cal BP 2350 to 2105)**
(95% probability)

Intercept data

Intercepts of radiocarbon age
with calibration curve:
Cal BC 360 (Cal BP 2310) and
Cal BC 280 (Cal BP 2230) and
Cal BC 240 (Cal BP 2190)

1 Sigma calibrated result: Cal BC 385 to 195 (Cal BP 2335 to 2145)
(68% probability)

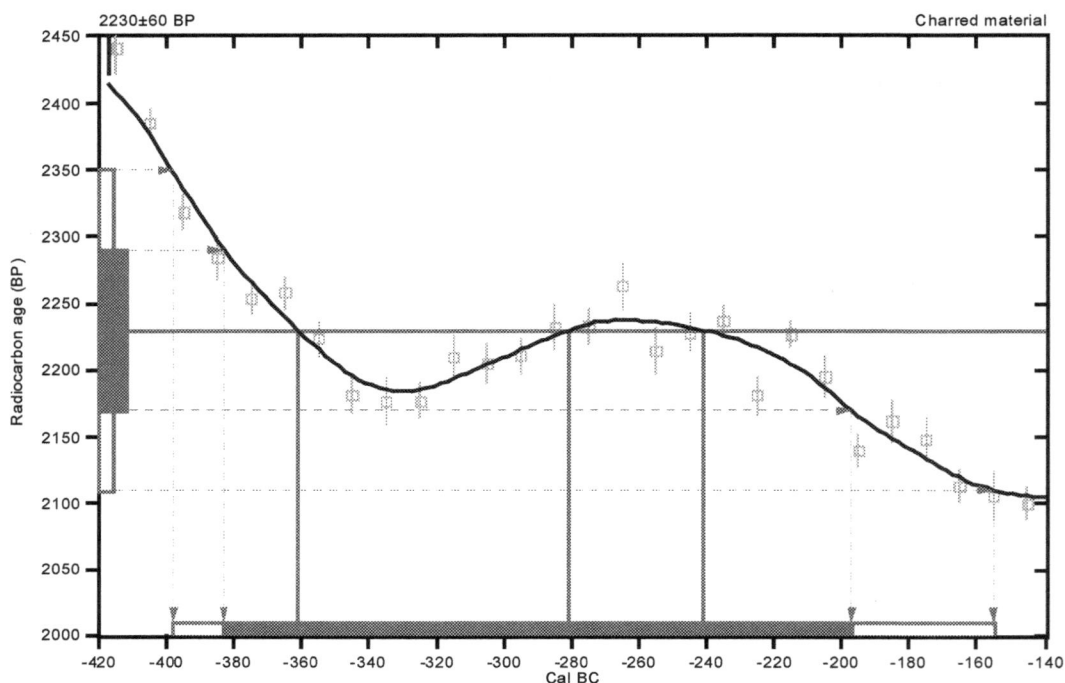

References:
  Database used
    INTCAL98
  Calibration Database
  Editorial Comment
    Stuiver, M., van der Plicht, H., 1998, Radiocarbon 40(3), pxii-xiii
  INTCAL98 Radiocarbon Age Calibration
    Stuiver, M., et. al., 1998, Radiocarbon 40(3), p1041-1083
  Mathematics
  A Simplified Approach to Calibrating C14 Dates
    Talma, A. S., Vogel, J. C., 1993, Radiocarbon 35(2), p317-322

Beta Analytic Radiocarbon Dating Laboratory

4985 S.W. 74th Court, Miami, Florida 33155 • Tel: (305)667-5167 • Fax: (305)663-0964 • E-mail: beta@radiocarbon.com

CALIBRATION OF RADIOCARBON AGE TO CALENDAR YEARS

(Variables: C13/C12=-25.1:lab. mult=1)

Laboratory number:	**Beta-135228**
Conventional radiocarbon age:	**4600±70 BP**
2 Sigma calibrated results:	**Cal BC 3615 to 3595 (Cal BP 5565 to 5545) and**
(95% probability)	**Cal BC 3525 to 3100 (Cal BP 5475 to 5050)**

Intercept data

Intercept of radiocarbon age with calibration curve:	Cal BC 3360 (Cal BP 5310)
1 Sigma calibrated results:	Cal BC 3500 to 3445 (Cal BP 5450 to 5395) and
(68% probability)	Cal BC 3380 to 3340 (Cal BP 5330 to 5290)

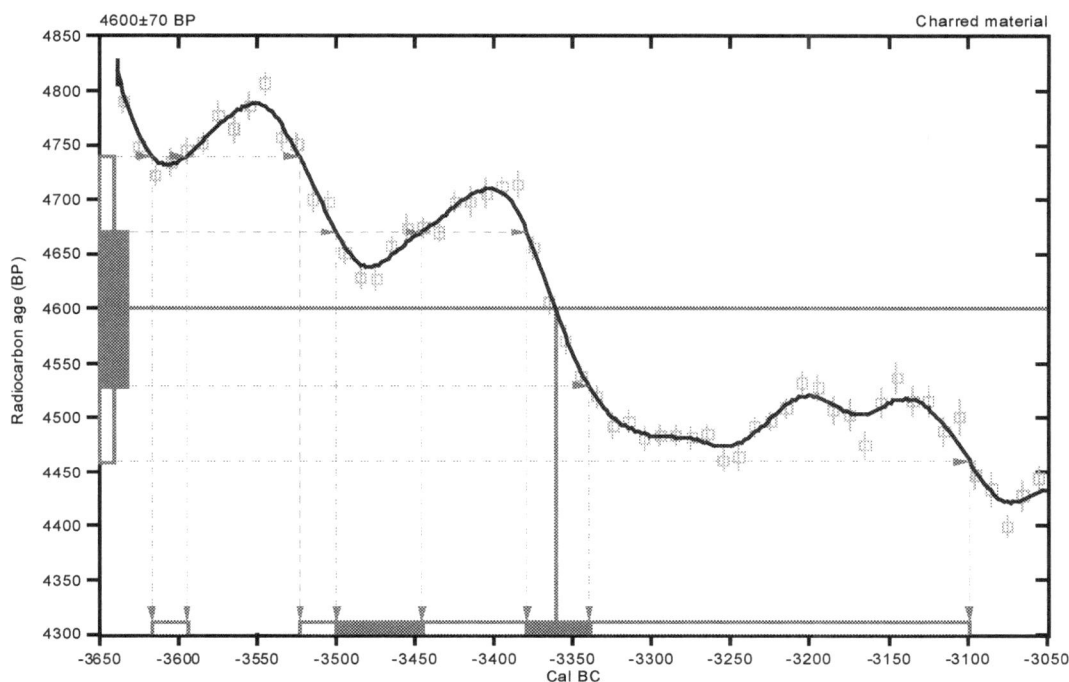

4600±70 BP — Charred material

References:
    Database used
        INTCAL98
    Calibration Database
    Editorial Comment
        Stuiver, M., van der Plicht, H., 1998, Radiocarbon 40(3), pxii-xiii
    INTCAL98 Radiocarbon Age Calibration
        Stuiver, M., et. al., 1998, Radiocarbon 40(3), p1041-1083
    Mathematics
    A Simplified Approach to Calibrating C14 Dates
        Talma, A. S., Vogel, J. C., 1993, Radiocarbon 35(2), p317-322

Beta Analytic Radiocarbon Dating Laboratory

4985 S.W. 74th Court, Miami, Florida 33155 • Tel: (305)667-5167 • Fax: (305)663-0964 • E-mail: beta@radiocarbon.com

APPENDIX 2

Petrographic Descriptions *by Rob Ixer*

Methodology

Each sherd was sliced and a standard thin section made. The sherd, sliced surface and thin section were investigated using a x10 lens. The thin section was petrographically described using standard transmitted light microscopy methods.

Descriptions

Pottery

Sample fabric 11: STALWH 95/3 TR31102 Tr. B 60. A siliceous rock-tempered pot. Peterborough Ware.

Sherd
A coarsely made, sparsely tempered pot with evenly distributed, angular, white vein quartz and quartzite clasts, 2-3mm in diameter but up to 8mm in length. A 9mm thick, (dark grey, N3 on the GSA rock-colour chart) core is overlain by a 5mm thick, brown-red (light brown 5YR 6/4) rim.

Thin section
A 6mm wide, dark yellowish-orange (10 YR 6/6 on the GSA rock-colour chart) rim overlies a 9mm thick, black (N1) core. Angular, pale-coloured and cloudy quartz-rich clasts, up to 5mm in length, rounded black clasts up to 1mm and a siltstone clast up to 2mm in length, are present within a clean clay.

Petrographically the clay carries very minor to trace amounts of microcline, plagioclase feldspar, brown and green tourmaline and zircon, together with small muscovite laths that locally are common and are aligned subparallel to the well-developed fabric. The rock clasts are silicic; the smaller, rarer clasts include micaceous, feldspathic siltstone, quartzite and stretched quartz, whereas the larger clasts comprise a silicified mudstone/micaceous chert cut by later quartz veins and a silicified, acidic rock with potassium feldspar phenocrysts. Rounded grog/mudstone pellets are common and range in composition from a clean clay to clay with scarce fine white mica ± rounded quartz. Although some have fired to a paler colour, most have a darker colour than the main clay. Locally shale/mudstone pellets have pronounced bedding laminae and so are natural and may derive from the local Permo-Triassic mudstones.

The pot has suffered extensive post-burial alteration with the development of neomorphic gypsum infilling void spaces. Euhedral, hexagonal and tabular, authigenic gypsum crystals, many of which show a combination of planar and rounded faces, are abundant. They carry fluid inclusions and irregular void spaces, often infilled with the clay matrix. Rare, polycrystalline gypsum aggregates also show complex intergrowths with the clay. The gypsum has grown from local groundwaters that in the Permo-Triassic area around Burton-on-Trent is calcium sulphate-rich.

Sample fabric 9: WHS 98, Area R, 6019, F612. A grog-tempered, thin-walled pot. Beaker.

Sherd
A uniform dark grey (N3 on the GSA rock-color chart) clay has fired to a less than 1mm thick greyish-orange (10YR 7/4) outer surface. Clasts are not visible on the surfaces.

Thin Section
A dark clay carries small, angular quartz grains and rare muscovite flakes. Although rock clasts are rare grog, up to 1mm in diameter, is present.

Petrographically, the clay carries many angular quartz crystals. Larger, single quartz grains show strained extinction and are accompanied by rounded to lath-shaped potassium feldspar and trace amounts of plagioclase, white mica, tourmaline and rounded opaques. Rare rock clasts include polycrystalline quartz/metamorphic quartzite, quartz-white mica rock and a rhyolite with quartz phenocrysts. Grog is abundant and represents the main temper and its presence can be seen to disturb the flow of the main fabric. The grog clasts show a range of sizes, firing colours and internal alignments and the densities of their non-plastic components also differ; they are all, however, angular in shape and not too dissimilar to the main pot fabric. Some grog clasts have grog within them. Later limonitic staining is concentrated along the main fabric. The pot is either intentionally grog-tempered in a quartz-bearing clay or is grog and quartz tempered in a cleaned clay, perhaps the former. The clay and quartz clasts are probably local in origin.

Sample fabric 6: Area A, 4119, F454. A poorly made, granodiorite-tempered, thick pot.

<u>Sherd</u>
The interior colour of the sherd varies but much is a dusky yellowish brown (10 YR 2/2 on the GSA rock-color chart) it has fired to a pale yellow-brown (10YR 6/2) on one surface. The inner surface is medium grey (N5) and rough to the touch, with abundant <1 to 2mm diameter, pink-white rock clasts. Clasts are evenly distributed in the body of the pot and comprise feldspathic rocks and rare, black clasts up to 5mm in diameter. Void spaces are rare and there is a poorly-defined fabric.

<u>Thin Section</u>
The pot has a uniform, brownish black colour (5YR 2/1) with 2–3mm diameter, angular rock fragments.

Petrographically, the pot has a brown-black, clean clay with rare, scattered, fine-grained quartz and traces of lath-shaped white mica. The temper comprises a medium to fine-grained quartz-altered plagioclase-amphibole rock, a granodiorite. Individual clasts, all of which are very feldspathic, range from altered feldspar-quartz to altered feldspar-amphibole-quartz in composition. Within the granodiorite, cores to zoned plagioclase have altered to epidote enclosed within unaltered, or locally, potassium feldspar, rims. Pale brown-green, weakly pleochroic and rare purple amphibole are twinned. Abundant, simply twinned feldspar laths may include potassium feldspars. Trace amounts of apatite, calcite and a brown, unidentified, alteration product are present. Biotite is absent. Other, non-igneous, rock clasts are very rare but include metaquartzite and sandstone. Much of the pot is heavily limonitically-stained but these areas do not look like clasts. The pot has been intentionally tempered with angular granodiorite. The mineralogy of this rock differs in a number of significant ways from the Mountsorrel granodiorite, notably in the absence of biotite and untwinned potassium feldspar.

Sample fabric 1: Area S, 5058, F526. A quartz-feldspar sand-tempered pot.

<u>Sherd</u>
A medium grey (N5 on the GSA rock-color chart) clay has a dark grey surface (N3). The outer surface is smooth but the inner is rough to the touch. White to liver-coloured quartz clasts, up to 8mm in diameter, are present and there are a few void spaces.

<u>Thin Section</u>
The core is an olive-black (5YR 2/1) with a 1mm light brown (5YR 5/6) rim. Quartz clasts, up to 1mm in diameter and 1–2mm diameter, dark brown, iron oxides including magnetite are common.

Petrographically, a dark brown clay has densely packed, small, angular quartz and very rare white mica laths. Large, single quartz grains with fluid inclusions and strained extinction show authigenic overgrowths; rounded potassium feldspar, including perthite and microcline also shows overgrowths. Trace amounts of plagioclase occur as do a number of rock clasts, including polycrystalline metamorphic quartz, stretched quartz, metasandstone/siltstones, cherts and quartz-white mica metamorphics. Rounded, grog-like limonitic areas are common. They differ from the main clay in their firing colours and in their non-plastic to clay ratios but not in the composition of the non-plastic components. Mudstone with clean, very red clay, carries a sparse temper whereas darker areas carry a very minor non-plastic component. Other, more grog-like, areas have quartz, potassium feldspar and white mica inclusions within them. Limonite areas show concentric textures and include magnetite-rich clasts but limonite is also concentrated along the main fabric and so at least some is post-burial in origin as are minor amounts of gypsum infilling void spaces. The clay and non-plastic components are probably Permo-Triassic or Pleistocene-Recent in origin suggesting a local manufacture.

Sample fabric 1: Area S, 5045, F537. A quartz-feldspar sand-tempered pot.

<u>Sherd</u>
A roughly made, thick pot. The core colour is dark yellow-brown (10 YR 4/2 on the GSA rock-color chart) firing to a dusky yellowish-brown (10 YR 2/2) surface. Quartz and limonitic, rounded areas, up to 5mm across, are present.

<u>Thin Section</u>
The thin section shows a greyish-brown core (5YR 3/2) firing to light brown (5YR 5/6), 1mm thick rim. Single mineral grains and large, rounded limonite clasts are present.

Petrographically, a clean clay carries a little quartz but no mica. Large, rounded, strained quartz and rounded potassium feldspar are accompanied by trace amounts of plagioclase and rock fragments, including polycrystalline, metamorphic quartz and stretched quartz and a single clast of a fine-grained, acid lava. Red and brown grog-like, limonitic areas are present; they are darker than the main matrix and display concentric textures. Some are inclusion-free but other areas carry polycrystalline quartz or single quartz grains but the density of the non-plastic grains is less than within the main matrix. The clay and clasts could have come from local sources within the Pleistocene-Recent or Permo-Triassic sediments suggesting a local manufacture.

Sample fabric 3: Watching Brief, 9005, F903. A quartz-bearing pot with limonitic areas.

Sherd
A mottled outer surface is pale yellowish brown (10YR 6/2 on the GSA rock-color chart) and is rough to the touch with limonitic concretions up to 5mm across, some of which have a magnetite core. The core is mid-grey (N5) but is overlain by a moderate orange-pink (5YR 8/4) outer surface. Rounded limonitic concretions to 5mm are present. Some linear void spaces lie along a poorly defined fabric. A 2mm long ?animal bone fragment lies on the surface.

Thin Section
A dusky brown (5YR 2/2) core has fired to a light brown (5YR 6/2), 2mm thick, surface; limonitic areas are abundant and are rounded and up to 5mm in diameter.

Petrographically, a brown, clean clay has sparse, fine-grained, angular quartz within a restricted size range; white mica is not present. The grain size of the sparse non-plastics is fine. Large, rounded quartz, perthite and microcline clasts are accompanied by minor amounts of rhyolite, chert, stretched quartz, sandstone and metaquartzite. Rounded, limonite-rich areas and euhedral, cubic, opaque clasts are widespread; some of the latter are oxidised magnetite. Other limonitic clasts have minor amounts of quartz scattered throughout them or concentrated at their outer margins, or have organic matter in them, or show concentric/collomorphic textures. A little post-burial gypsum is present.

Sample fabric 10: WMH 92, Evaluation Trench AE, F086. A quartz-tempered pot.

Sherd
A light brownish grey (5YR 6/1 on the GSA rock-color chart) inner half passes out to a medium grey (N5) outer area with a very thin <1mm pale reddish brown (10YR 5/4) surface. The pot is well-made with few void spaces and 1–3mm, rounded to angular, white quartz clasts.

Thin Section
The thin section shows a brownish black (5YR 2/1) inner half overlain by a mid yellowish-brown (10YR 5/4) outer half. Small, white quartzite clasts are present but are sparsely distributed. The pot is monolithic and the temper has a restricted size range.

Petrographically, the pot has a brown clay with abundant, small, angular quartz with a restricted size range and trace amounts of white mica. Large, angular to rounded mono or polycrystalline quartz clasts are present and the quartz shows fluid inclusions and strained extinction. Other clasts include rounded potassium feldspar and plagioclase and trace amounts of tourmaline. Rock clasts are present in very minor amounts but include fine-grained sandstone and chert. Rare, limonite-rich areas comprise densely packed quartz in a dark matrix and limonitic staining is also very minor. A little post-burial gypsum is present.

Sample fabric 7: WHS 97, Area A, 4082, F445.01. This is a quartz- feldspar sand-tempered pot.

Sherd
The smooth exterior surface of the pot is interrupted by black iron-rich concretions. The body of the sherd is medium grey (N5 on the GSA rock-color chart) but fires to a 1mm thick, light brown (5YR 6/4) outer and inner rim. Small, 1mm diameter, white quartz and 2–3mm diameter black clasts, are present. Some of these black clasts are magnetite. Small void spaces represent ?burned-out, oxidised and weathered iron-rich clasts.

Thin Section
A brownish black (5YR 2/1) core with 1mm thick, light brown (5YR 5/6) outer and inner rims. Opaques, up to 2mm and white quartz, up to 1mm in diameter, are present and void spaces, up to 5mm, some of which are cubic in shape, represent oxidised or plucked opaque material, perhaps magnetite.

Petrographically, the pot comprises a dark brown clay with abundant, fine-grained quartz grains and very rare muscovite flakes. There is a poorly defined fabric and limonite lies along fractures in this fabric. The non-plastics are evenly distributed. The main non-plastic components are rounded to subangular, single grains of quartz or alkali feldspar and siliceous rock fragments. Opaque or limonitic areas are common and some are oxidised magnetite clasts. Discrete, rounded quartz grains with abundant fluid inclusions, showing strained extinction, are common and have euhedral, authigenic overgrowths. Rounded to lath-shaped potassium feldspars, including perthite crystals altering to white mica are also common, some within unaltered, authigenic overgrowths. Microcline, zoned and altered plagioclase, epidote and tourmaline are rare. Minor amounts of rock clasts include polycrystalline, metamorphic quartz, stretched quartz, fine-grained sandstone/siltstones, chert and quartz-feldspar rocks plus very rare, fine-grained, acid lavas. Limonite-rich areas/clasts are common; some are oxidised magnetite and so show concentric textures and others enclose sparse, angular quartz and potassium feldspar grains. These areas are neither grog nor mud clasts but may be post-burial in origin due to the action of iron-bearing groundwaters. The clay and non-plastics within the pot could have come from the local Pleistocene-Recent or underlying Permo-Triassic sediments suggesting the pot is of local manufacture.

Worked stone

Sample: Area A, Structure 1, F441, post-hole. A medium-grained granite-granodiorite rubber.

<u>Thin section</u>
A rubber comprising major plagioclase-potassium feldspars-quartz-brown-green amphibole-biotite. Trace amounts of apatite and zircon and secondary epidote, chlorite, white mica and deep green amphibole are present. Graphic intergrowths between perthite and quartz are noticeable. Biotite, which is more abundant than amphibole, carries small apatite crystals. Potassium feldspar includes perthite and microcline. Zoned plagioclase is altered to white mica and epidote and displays altered cores enclosed within fresh margins or within orthoclase. Amphibole alters to epidote and chlorite and biotite to chlorite and secondary biotite. The rock shows fracturing with strained quartz and alteration along the fractures.

<u>Provenance</u>
The petrography is consistent with Mountsorrel.

Sample: WHS 99, watching brief, F923, 9039. A quartz arenite quern.

<u>Thin section</u>
A very clean, white sandstone (quartz arenite) comprising quartz and trace amounts of perthite, microcline, zircon and white mica. Few heavy mineral grains are present. The sandstone is matrix supported but there is much void space. Angular to rounded quartz grains display serrated contacts where they touch and these are accompanied by some grain size reduction. Elsewhere, thin, authigenic quartz overgrowths form euhedral terminations into void spaces. Trace amounts of perthite and microcline are fresh, although other potassium feldspar grains are altered, white mica flakes, opaque minerals, chert, fine-grained sandstone and polycrystalline, metamorphic quartz are all very rare. Some fine-grained white mica/clay minerals lie about quartz grains.

<u>Provenance</u>
The purity of the sandstone and pale colour suggest that the quern was made from Coal Measures, rather than the local Permo-Triassic, sandstone.

APPENDIX 3

Roman Pottery Fabric Descriptions *by Annette Hancocks*

Amphorae (Fabric Group A)

Baetican fabrics
A02   Baetican (Late) amphorae 2 (BAT AM 2); Tomber and Dore 1998, 85

Burnished reduced wares (Fabric Group B)

B02   (Southeast) Dorset Black-Burnished ware 1 (DOR BB 1); Tomber and Dore 1998, 127
B03   (Southwest) Dorset Black-Burnished ware 1 (SOW BB1); Tomber and Dore 1998, 129

Colour-coated wares (Fabric Group C)

C02   Lower Nene Valley ware, white (LNV CC)
Wheelmade, LNVCC (grey); Tomber and Dore 1998, 118

Grog tempered wares (Fabric Group F)

F02   Grog and shell
Wheelmade, soft to hard. Colour varies; may be brownish yellow (10YR 6/6) throughout or have a reduced yellowish brown core (10YR 6/4) and oxidised reddish yellow (7.5YR 6/6) surfaces. Inclusions: varying proportions of illsorted angular grog and calcareous inclusions, the latter including plate-like shell and more angular fragments. May be other sparse inclusions, including black streaks of carbonised organic material, and iron rich inclusions. Reacts with hydrochloric acid.

F03   Grog
Wheelmade, reduced bluish grey (Gley 5/1) core with oxidised reddish yellow (5YR 6/6) margins and surfaces. Dense, poorly sorted angular grey grog (0.03mm)

F09   Grog and quartz
Wheelmade, very pale brown (10YR 8/4) surfaces and grey (10YR 6/1) margins and core. Common grog (2mm) and sparse quartz (1mm)

Reduced wares (Fabric Group G)

G02   Lower Nene Valley grey ware (pipeclay fabric)
Tomber and Dore 1999 LNV CC, 117-8, plate 91. Our type sherds have a distinctive white fabric (2.5Y 8/1) with a dark grey slip (2.5Y 4/1 to GLEY 1 44/N), and the fabric includes the black grains noted by L Rollo.

G04   Reduced Severn Valley Ware, grey plain; Tomber and Dore 1998, 149

G06.4   Derbyshire Coarseware (DER CO); Tomber and Dore 1998, 125

G07.3   Variant with calcareous and quartz inclusions. Wheel-made, bluish grey (Gley 6/1) core with mid-grey (Gley 5/1) margins and brown (7.5YR 3/4) surfaces. Sparse, poorly sorted, angular calcareous inclusions (0.02mm) and well-sorted, rounded, common fine micaceous quartz (0.01mm). Sandwich effect.

G08   Fumed grey wares

G08.1   Fine sandy grey ware with blackened surface
Wheelmade, hard. May have an oxidised strong brown core (7.5YR 5/6) or have oxidised margins and a reduced grey core (5Y 5/1). The internal surface is greyish brown (2.5Y 5/2), while the external surface varies from greyish brown to black (2.5Y 2.5/1). Common fine inclusions of illsorted white and clear sand with red and black grains. May be occasional burnt out organic inclusions.

G09 <u>Self coloured grey wares</u>

G09.2 Very fine sandy grey ware
Wheelmade, soft to hard. Reduced throughout though may be slight variations between the core and margins, colour generally grey ranging from 5Y 5/1 to GLEY 1 5/N. Few inclusions visible by eye. Abundant silt-sized sand, sparse to common larger grains of white/clear sand (the latter only just visible by eye).

G09.3 Very fine calcareous grey ware
Wheelmade, soft. Reduced throughout greyish brown 2.5Y 5/2, though one sherd has very pronounced light brownish grey margins and surfaces (2.5Y 6/2). Sparse fine calcareous inclusions (not visible macroscopically, but reacts with hydrochloric acid) and sparse inclusions of white/clear quartz together with red and black grains.

G09.4 Sandy grey ware
Wheelmade, soft to hard. Often has a very marked distinction between the margins and the core. Sometimes the sherd is reduced throughout but the margins are lighter than the core, or vice versa. Sometimes the margins are partially oxidised to brown (7.5YR 5/3). Colour range includes grey (GLEY 1 6/N and 5/N) and very dark grey (GLEY 1 3/N), and surfaces can be a light brownish grey (2.5Y 6/2). Common inclusions of fine white sand (< 0.1mm); sparse black grains and calcareous inclusions.

G09.6 Sandy ware
Wheel-made, reduced dark bluish grey (Gley 4/1) core, external and internal surfaces with light brown (7.5YR 6/3) margins. Well-sorted, very micaceous rounded quartz (0.02mm). Sandwich effect. R11

G09.7 Sandy greyware with black mica
Wheelmade, very hard. Reduced grey (2.5YR 5/1) surfaces, reddish brown (5YR 4/4) margins and grey (Gley 5/N) core. Common, poorly sorted black mica (1-3mm) and rare, well-sorted quartz (0.5-1mm). Local product to Whitemoor Haye?

Calcite-gritted wares (Fabric Group J)

J03 Whitemoor Haye Calcite gritted ware (CGW WH)
Wheelmade, soft to hard. Oxidised reddish/yellow (7.5YR 8/6) throughout. Common, well-sorted angular calcite (2-3mm). Local product to Whitemoor Haye

Mortaria (Fabric Group M) *by Kay Hartley*

(Fabric examined with hand lens at X20 magnification. Fabric descriptions are standardised, but care is taken to point out any unusual feature of the fabrics of any sherds under examination. v = variant)

M02a Mancetter-Hartshill. Tomber and Dore MAH WH (1998, 188-189)
A usually fine-textured, cream fabric, varying from softish to very hard, sometimes with pink core. Inclusions usually moderate, smallish, transparent and pinkish quartz with sparse opaque orange-brown fragments and sometimes-white clay pellets (or re-fired pottery). The range in fabric is, in fact, quite wide, from that with scarcely any inclusions to fabrics with a fair quantity and fabrics with hard, ill-sorted black inclusions. The trituration grit after the mid-second century consisted of hard red-brown and/or hard blackish, re-fired pottery fragments (Drs D.P.S. Peacock and D.F. Williams *pers. comm.*) with only very rare quartz fragments. Earlier mortaria usually have a mixed trituration grit in which quartz and sandstone are normal components and some early second-century mortaria appear to have entirely quartz trituration grit.

M02b Mancetter-Hartshill. MAH H Tomber and Dore (1998, 188-189)
A hard, buff fabric with largish random black inclusions together with some white and rare orange-brown and quartz inclusions; buff slip. There is abundant, vesicular blackish trituration grit. This is a variant of M02a, produced in the Mancetter-Hartshill potteries; it has been noted especially in mortaria made in the mid to late Antonine period.

M08 Southwest White-Slipped/Caerleon mortaria. Tomber and Dore (1998, 206)
A soft, fine-textured, micaceous, red-brown fabric with few random, ill-sorted quartz inclusions and a thick cream slip. The fabric points to manufacture either in southwest England (second century), or south Wales (Caerleon in the first rather than the second century; the use of white slip was fairly common at Caerleon in the first century, but rare in the second). I would personally expect it to be first-century and, if it is a mortarium, to be from Caerleon, but this cannot be regarded as certain (see Marvell and Owen-John 1997 (Loughor), fig. 114, nos.37, 39 for fairly similar mortaria and fabric).

M09   Little Chester LCH

Hard, fine-textured, cream fabric with a slight greyishness in the core; moderate to fairly frequent, ill-sorted inclusions, mostly transparent pink quartz and rare orange-brown and black material. No slip is discernible because all surfaces are weathered to the same colour, although brown-buff slip survives on some sherds. Three trituration grits survive: quartz, quartz sandstone and black material.

Oxidised wares (Fabric Group O)

O02.1   Severn Valley Oxidised ware 2, (SVW OX 2); Tomber and Dore 1998, 148

O03.1   Severn Valley ware, organic, (SVW OX ORG1); Tomber and Dore 1998, 148-149

Wheelmade, soft to hard. Yellowish/brown margins and core (10YR 5/4) and dark grey surfaces (2.5YR 4/1). Common, ill-sorted, angular grog (2mm), rare, well sorted and rounded quartz (1mm) and common, poorly sorted organics.

O06.2   Sandy oxidised ware

Wheelmade, hard, red 2.5YR 5/6, external and internal margins and surfaces with dark bluish grey Gley 2 4/1 reduced core. Common quartz inclusions white/clear quartz. Occasional iron rich inclusions and grog pellets.

O06.8   Sandy oxidised ware with fine shell (SOW OXSH)

Wheelmade, very hard. Light red (2.5 YR 6/8) throughout. Abundant, well rounded quartz (1-2mm) with rare, well-sorted calcite (2-3mm). Local source to Whitemoor Haye?

Parchment/pipeclay, pale fabrics (Fabric Group P)

P04 Fine white wares

P04.1 (3) Very fine white ware

Wheelmade, hard fabric. Colour varies from very pale brown (10YR 8/2) to pink (5YR 8/4), and the surfaces can be mottled. Few visible inclusions; occasional red iron rich inclusions and white pellets.

Samian (Fabric Group S)

S01   South Gaulish (mostly La Graufesenque) LGFSA
S02   Central Gaul (Les Martres-de-Veyre) LMVSA
S03   Central Gaul (Lezoux) LEZSA2
S04R   Eastern Gaul (Rheinzabern) RHZSA

White slip wares/whitewares (Fabric Group W)

W06   Lower Nene Valley White ware (LNV WH); Tomber and Dore 1998, 119

APPENDIX 4

List Of Roman Vessel Classes Represented

Code	Description
BC	Curving-sided bowl
BI	Drag 37
B/DA	Drag 18/31
B/DB	Drag 31
DA	Straight-sided dish
J	Jar type
JE	Necked jar
JJ	Lid-seated (Bell-mouthed) jar
JK	Cooking pot
JN	Narrow-mouthed jar
JW	Wide-mouthed jar
LA	Flat, conical, domed lid
MA	Bead and flange mortarium
MG	Reeded-flange mortarium
NA	Tankard

BIBLIOGRAPHY

ApSimon, A M 1960 'The pottery and flints', in Greenfield, E The excavation of barrow 4 at Swarkestone, Derbyshire. *Journal of the Derbyshire Archaeological and Natural History Society* **80**, 19-39

Bamford, H M 1985 *Briar Hill: excavations 1974-1978.* Northampton Development Corporation, Northampton

Banks, P J and Morris, E L 1979 'Iron Age pottery and briquetage' in Smith, C A 1979a, 45-57

Barclay, A and Halpin, C 1999 *Excavations at Barrow Hills, Radley, Oxfordshire. Volume I: The Neolithic and Bronze Age Monument Complex.* Oxford Archaeological Unit, Thames Valley Landscapes Volume 11, Oxford

Barclay, A and Harding, J (eds), 1999 *Pathways and Ceremonies. The cursus monuments of Britain and Ireland.* Neolithic Studies Group Seminar Papers 4, Oxbow Books, Oxford

Barclay, A and Hey, G 1999 'Cattle, cursus monuments and the river: the development of ritual and domestic landscapes in the Upper Thames Valley', in Barclay, A and Harding, J (eds), 67-76

Barclay, A, Gray, M and Lambrick, G 1995 *Excavations at the Devil's Quoits, Stanton Harcourt, Oxfordshire 1972-3 and 1988.* Oxford Archaeological Unit, Thames Valley Landscapes: the Windrush Valley, Volume 3, Oxford

Barfield, L 1982 Neolithic material in excavations south of Lichfield Cathedral, 1976-77 (MOH Carver). *Transactions of the South Staffordshire Archaeological and Historical Society* **22**, 35-69

Barnatt, J 1994 Excavations of a Bronze Age unenclosed cemetery, cairns, and field boundaries at Eagleston Flat, Curbar, Derbyshire 1984, 1989-90. *Proceedings of the Prehistoric Society* **60**, 287-370

Barrow, G, Gibson, W, Cantrill, T C, Dixon, E E L and Cunnington, C H 1919 *The geology of the country around Lichfield.* Memoirs of the Geological Survey of England and Wales

Bartley, D D and Morgan, A V 1990 The palynological record of the King's Pool, Stafford, England. *New Phytologist* **74**, 375-381

Beamish, M 1998 A Middle Iron Age site at Wanlip, Leicestershire. *Transactions of the Leicestershire Archaeological and Historical Society* **72**, 1-91

Birmingham University Field Archaeology Unit 1992 *An Archaeological Evaluation at Whitemoor Haye, Alrewas, Staffordshire 1992.* Birmingham University Field Archaeology Unit Report No. 231

Birmingham University Field Archaeology Unit 1998 *On-site Guide to Environmental Sampling and Processing*

Bradley, R 1992 'The gravels and British prehistory from the Neolithic to the Early Iron Age' in Fulford, M and Nichols, E (eds) *Developing Landscapes of Lowland Britain. The Archaeology of the British Gravels: A Review.* Society of Antiquaries Occasional Papers. **14**. London, 15-22

Brassington, M 1971 A Trajanic kiln complex near Little Chester, Derby, 1968 in *Derbyshire Archaeological Journal* **51**, 36-69

Brassington, M 1980 Derby Racecourse kiln excavations 1972-3. *Antiquaries Journal* **60**, 8-47

Brown, L 1984 'Objects of stone' in Cunliffe, B *An Iron Age Hillfort in Hampshire. Volume II The Excavations 1969-1978: the Finds.* Council for British Archaeology Research Report 52, 412-418

Buckley, D 1979 'The stone' in Wainwright, G J *Gussage All Saints: An Iron Age Settlement in Dorset.* Department of the Environment Archaeological Report No. 10, 89-97

Buckley, D 1991 Querns in ritual contexts. *Quern Study Group Newsletter* **2**, 1-4

Cane, J and Cane, C K B 1986 The excavation of a Mesolithic cave site near Rugeley, Staffordshire. *Staffordshire Archaeological Studies* **3**

Case, H J 1977 'The Beaker culture in Britain and Ireland' in Mercer, R J (ed.) *Beakers in Britain and Europe.* British Archaeological Reports, International Series **26**. Oxford, 71-101

Case, H J 1993 Beakers: deconstruction and after. *Proceedings of the Prehistoric Society* **59**, 241-268

Case, H J 1995 'Beakers: loosening a stereotype' in Kinnes, I and Varndell, G (eds) *Unbaked Urns of Rudely Shape,* Oxbow Monograph 55. Oxford, 55-68

Chapman, J 2000 *Fragmentation in Archaeology.* Routledge

Charles, M 1998 Fodder from dung: the recognition and interpretation of dung-derived plant material from archaeological sites. *Environmental Archaeology* **1**, 111-122

Chowne, P 1986 Excavations at an Iron Age defended enclosure at Tattershall Thorpe, Lincolnshire. *Proceedings of the Prehistoric Society* **52**, 159-188

Clarke, D L 1970 *Beaker Pottery of Great Britain and Ireland.* Cambridge University Press

Clay, P 1981 *Two multi-phase barrow sites at Sproxton and Eaton, Leicestershire.* Leicestershire Museums, Art Galleries and Records Service Archaeological Report No.2

Clay, P 1992 An Iron Age harmstead at Grove Farm, Enderby, Leicestershire. *Transactions of the Leicestershire Archaeological and Historical Society* **66**, 38-52

Coates, G 1998 *Archaeological excavations at Whitemoor Haye, Alrewas, Staffordshire; an interim report.* Birmingham University Field Archaeology Unit Unpublished Report

Coates, G 1999 *Excavations at Whitemoor Haye Quarry, Alrewas, Staffordshire 1997-1998. A Post-Excavation Assessment and Updated Project Design.* Birmingham University Field Archaeology Unit Report No.495

Cooper, L and Humphrey, J 1998 'The lithics' in Beamish, M A Middle Iron Age Site at Wanlip, Leicestershire. *Transactions of the Leicestershire Archaeological and Historical Society* **72**, 63-74

Crickmore, J 1984 *Romano-British Urban Settlements in the West Midlands.* British Archaeological Reports, British Series 127. Oxford

Dix, B and Jackson, D 1989 'Some Late Iron Age defended enclosures in Northamptonshire' in A Gibson (ed), *Midlands Prehistory.* British Archaeological Reports, British Series 204. Oxford

Dunning, G C 1977 'Salmonsbury, Bourton-on-the-Water, Gloucestershire' in Harding, D W (ed.) *Hillforts. Later Prehistoric Earthworks in Britain and Ireland,* 75-118

Elliott, L and Knight, D 1999 An Early Mesolithic site and first millennium BC settlement and pit alignments at Swarkestone Lowes, Derbyshire. *The Derbyshire Archaeological Journal* **119**, 79-152.

Elsdon, S M 1991 'The Iron Age and Anglo-Saxon pottery' in Sharman, J and Clay, P Leicester Lane, Enderby: An Archaeological Evaluation. *Transactions of the Leicestershire Archaeological and Historical Society* **65**, 10-11

Elsdon, S M 1992 'The Iron Age pottery', in Clay, P An Iron Age Farmstead at Grove Farm, Enderby, Leicestershire. *Transactions of the Leicestershire Archaeological and Historical Society* **66**, 38-52

Elsdon, S M 1994 'The Iron Age pottery', in Clay, P An Iron Age and Romano-British Enclosure System at Normanton-le-Heath, Leicestershire. *Transactions of the Leicestershire Archaeological and Historical Society* **68**, 35-45

English Heritage 1991 *Exploring Our Past: Strategies for the Archaeology of England.* London

English Heritage 1992 *Environmental Archaeology in Middle England - Research Directions for Projects Funded by English Heritage.* Unpublished Discussion Document

Ferris, I 1992 *An Archaeological Evaluation at Echills Farm, Kings Bromley, Staffordshire.* Birmingham University Field Archaeology Unit Report No. 214

Ferris, I M and Smith, J 1996 Discovered under other skies: prehistoric stone tools in Romano-British and Gallo-Roman ritual and religious contexts. *Journal of Theoretical Archaeology* **5/6**. Cruithne Press, Glasgow, 175-186

Ferris, I M, Bevan, L and Cuttler, R 2000 *The Excavation of a Romano-British Shrine at Orton's Pasture, Rocester, Staffordshire.* British Archaeological Reports, British Series 314

Ford, S, Bradley, R, Hawkes, J, and Fisher, P 1984 Flint-working in the Metal Age. *Oxford Journal of Archaeology* **3**, No.2, 157-173

French, C A I, Gurney, D A, Pryor, F M M and Simpson, W G, 1993 'A double pit alignment and other features at Field OS 29, Tallington, Lincolnshire' in Simpson, W G, Gurney, D A, Neve, J and Pryor, F M M *The Fenland Project, Number 7: Excavations in Peterborough and the Lower Welland Valley 1960-1969.* East Anglian Archaeology 61

Fulford, M 1992 'Iron Age to Roman: a period of radical change on the gravels' in Fulford, M and Nichols, E (eds) *Developing Landscapes of Lowland Britain. The Archaeology of the British Gravels: A Review.* Society of Antiquaries Occasional Papers 14. London, 23-38

Gale, R 1991 'Charcoal identification', in Cox, P W and Hearne, C M *Redeemed from the heath: the archaeology of the Wych Farm Oil Field (1987-90).* Dorset Natural History and Archaeological Society Monograph Series No. 9, 201-203

Gelling, M 1992 *The West Midlands in the Early Middle Ages.* Leicester

Gibson, A (ed) 1989 *Midlands Prehistory.* British Archaelogical Reports, British Series 204, Oxford

Gibson, A and Loveday, R 1989 'Excavations at the cursus monument of Aston on Trent, Derbyshire', in A Gibson, A (ed) 1989, 27-50

Gibson, A and Kinnes, I 1997 On the rrns of a dilemma: radiocarbon and the Peterborough problem. *Oxford Journal of Archaeology* **16**, 15-72

Gifford and Partners Ltd. 1995 *Report on an Archaeological Evaluation at Tucklesholme Farm, Barton under Needwood, Staffordshire.* Unpublished Report

Gillam, J P 1939 Romano-British Derbyshire ware. *Antiquaries Journal* **19**, 429-37

Godwin, H 1956 *The History of the British Flora*. Cambridge

Godwin, H and Dickson, J H 1964-5 'Report on plant remains in organic deposits below Roman road (Watling Street) at Wall, monolith cut and examined', in Gould, J Excavations in advance of road construction at Shenstone and Wall (Staffordshire). *Lichfield and South Staffordshire Archaeological and Historical Society* **6**, 17-78

Greig, J R A 1979 'Seeds and pollen from site SK187082' in Smith, C A (ed.) 1979a, 71-77

Greig, J in prep. *Stafford, Lammascote Road pollen diagram*

Grimes, W F 1960 *Excavations on defence sites, 1939-1945, 1: mainly Neolithic-Bronze Age*. Ministry of Works Archaeological Report 3. HMSO, London

Gunstone, A J H 1964 An archaeological gazetteer of Staffordshire. Part I. Chance finds and sites, excluding barrows and their contents. *North Staffordshire Journal of Field Studies* **4**, 11-45

Gunstone, A J H 1965 An archaeological gazetteer of Staffordshire II. the barrows. *North Staffordshire Journal of Field Stud*ies **5**, 20-63

Hansen M 1987 The Hydrophiloidea (Coleoptera) of Fennoscandia and Denmark. *Fauna Entomologica Scandinavica* **18**. Leiden and Copenhagen: Scandinavian Science Press

Harding, A F, 1981 Excavations in the prehistoric ritual complex near Milfield, Northumberland. *Proceedings of the Prehistoric Society* **47**, 87-136

Hermet, F 1934 *La Graufesenque (Condatomago)*. Librairie Ernest Leroux, Paris

Hill, J D 1993 Can we recognise a different European past? A contrastive archaeology of later prehistoric settlements in southern England. *Journal of European Archaeology* **1**, 57-75

Hillman, G *et al.* 1996 Identification of archaeological remains of wheat: the 1992 London workshop. *Circaea* **12 (2)**, 195-20

Hilton, C 1979 Bower Farm near Rugeley. *West Midlands Archaeological Newsletter* **22**, 7

Hingley, R 1984 'Towards social analysis in archaeology: Celtic society in the Iron Age of the Upper Thames Valley' in Cunliffe, B and Miles, D (eds) *Aspects of the Iron Age in Central Southern Britain*. Oxford University Committee for Archaeology Monograph 2, 72-88

Hodder, M A 1982 The prehistory of the Lichfield Area. *Transactions of the South Staffordshire Archaeological and Historical Society* **12**., 13-23

Hughes, E G 1991 *The Excavation of a Ring Ditch at Tucklesholme Farm, Barton-under-Needwood, Staffordshire, 1990-1991*. Birmingham University Field Archaeology Unit Report No.163

Hughes, G and Crawford, G 1995 Excavations at Wasperton, Warwickshire, 1980-1985. Introduction and Part 1: the Neolithic and Early Bronze Age. *Transactions of the Birmingham and Warwickshire Archaeological Society* **99**, 9-45

Hughes, G and Woodward, A, 1995 Excavations at Meole Brace 1990 and at Bromfield 1981-1991. Part 1: A ring ditch and Neolithic pit complex at Meole Brace, Shrewsbury. *Transactions of the Shropshire Archaeological and Historical Society* **70**, 4-21

Hughes, E G 1999 The excavation of an Iron Age cropmarked site at Foxcovert Farm, Aston-on-Trent 1994. *Derbyshire Archaeological Journal* **119**, 176-188

Hughes, E G 2000 *The Lockington Gold Hoard: an Early Bronze Age Barrow Cemetery at Lockington, Leicestershire* Oxbow, Oxford

Hughes, E G forthcoming *Excavations at Willington, Derbyshire*

Hunt, C O 1999 'Palynology', in Elliott, L and Knight, D An early Mesolithic site and first millennium BC settlement and pit alignments at Swarkestone Lowes, Derbyshire. *Derbyshire Archaeological Journal* **119**, 139-143

Jackson, D A 1974 Two new pit alignments and a hoard of currency bars from Northamptonshire. *Northamptonshire Archaeology* **9**, 13-45

Jackson, D A 1978 A Late Bronze-Early Iron Age vessel from a pit alignment at Ringstead, Northants.. *Northamptonshire Archaeology* **13**, 168-9

Jacomet, S 1987 *Prehistoric cereal finds: a guide to the identification of prehistoric barley and wheat finds*. A translation by James Greig of Prähistorische Getreidefunde: Eine Anleitung sur Bestimmung prähistorischer Gersten- und Weizwn Funde

Jessop, L 1986 Dung Beetles and Chafers. Coleoptera: Scarabaeoidea. *Handbooks for the Identification of British Insects*. V. part 11. Royal Entomological Society of London, London

Jones, R J A 1979 'Soils and cropmarks' in Smith, C A 1979a, 103-9

Jones, G 1982 *Plant remains from the Roman Villa at Norfolk Street, Leicester.* AML Report, Old Series 4973

Jones, A 1992 *Catholme, Staffordshire: An Archaeological Evaluation.* Birmingham University Field Archaeology Unit Report No. 209

Jones, A 1998 Excavations at Wall (Staffordshire) by E. Greenfield in 1962 and 1964 (Wall Excavation Report no.15). *Staffordshire Archaeological and Historical Society Transactions 1995-96* **37**

Jones, G D B and Webster, P V 1969 Derbyshire ware: a reappraisal. *Derbyshire Archaeological Journal* **89**, 19-24

Jones, G E M, Straker, V and Davis, A 1991 'Early medieval plant use and ecology in London' in Vince, A (ed) Aspects of Saxo-Norman London: II finds and environmental evidence. *Transactions of the London and Middlesex Archaeological Society Special Paper 12. [Watling Court]*, 347-85

Kay, S O 1962 Romano-British pottery kilns at Hazelwood and Holbrook, Derbyshire. *Derbyshire Archaeological Journal* **82**, 21-42

Kent, D H 1992 *List of vascular plants of the British Isles.* Botanical Society of the British Isles. London

Kenward, H K, Hall, A R and Jones, A K G 1980 A tested set of techniques for the extraction of plant and animal macrofossils from waterlogged archaeological deposits. *Scientific Archaeology* **22**, 3-15

Kenward, H and Hall, A 1997 Enhancing bioarchaeological interpretation using indicator groups: stable manure as a paradigm. *Journal of Archaeological Science* **24**, 663-673

Kenward, H and Hall, A 1998 Disentangling the dung: stable manure. *Environmental Archaeology* **1**, 123-126

Knight, D 1984 *Late Bronze Age and Iron Age Settlement in the Nene and Great Ouse Basins.* British Archaeological Reports, British Series 130. Oxford

Knight, D 1992 Excavations of an Iron Age settlement at Gamston, Nottinghamshire. *Transactions of the Thoroton Society* **96**, 16-90

Knight, D 1998 *Guidelines For The Recording of Later Prehistoric Pottery From the East Midlands.* Unpublished Trent and Peak Archaeological Trust Guidelines

Knight, D 1999a 'Late Bronze Age and Iron Age pottery' in Elliot, L and Knight, D 1999 An Early Mesolithic site and first millennium BC settlement and pit alignments at Swarkestone Lowes, Derbyshire. *Derbyshire Archaeological Journal* **119**, 125-136

Knight, D 1999b 'Iron Age briquetage and miscellaneous fired clay' in Elliot, L and Knight, D 1999 An Early Mesolithic site and first millennium BC settlement and pit alignments at Swarkestone Lowes, Derbyshire. *Derbyshire Archaeological Journal* **119**, 137

Koch, K 1989 *Die Kafer Mitteleuropas.* Okologie. Band 2. Krefeld: Goecke and Evers

Koch, K 1992 *Die Kafer Mitteleuropas.* Okologie. Band 3. Krefeld: Goecke and Evers

Latalowa, M 1998 Botanical analysis of a bundle of flax (*Linum usitatissimum* L.) from an early medieval site in Northern Poland, a contribution to the history of flax cultivation and its field weeds. *Vegetation History and Archaeobotany* **7**, 97-107

Last, J, 1999 'Out of line: cursuses and monument typology in eastern England', in Barclay, A and Harding, J (eds), 86-97

Leary, R S 1996 'Roman coarse pottery' in Esmonde Cleary, A S and Ferris, I M *Excavations at the New Cemetery, Rocester, Staffordshire, 1985-1987,* Trans. Staffs Historical and Arch. Soc., **35**, 40-59

Leeds, E T 1940 New discoveries of Neolithic pottery in Oxfordshire. *Oxoniensia* **5**, 1-12

Lindroth, C H 1974 Coleoptera: Carabidae. *Handbooks for the Identification of British Insects.* IV. part 2. Royal Entomological Society of London

Longworth, I H 1984 *Collared Urns of the Bronze Age in Great Britain and Ireland.* Cambridge University Press

Losco-Bradley, S 1984 *Fatholme, Excavations 1983-84.* Unpublished Interim Report

Losco-Bradley, S and Wheeler, H M 1984 'Anglo-Saxon settlement in the Trent Valley: some aspects'' in Faull, M L (ed) *Studies in Late Anglo-Saxon Settlement,* Oxford, 101-114

Loveday, R, 1989 'The Barford ritual complex: further excavations (1972) and a regional perspective', in A Gibson (ed) 1989, 51-84

Loveday, R, 1999 'Dorchester-on-Thames – ritual complex or ritual landscape?' in Barclay, A and Harding, J (eds), 49-63

Lucht, W H 1987 *Die Käfer Mitteleuropas.* Katalog. Krefeld: Goecke and Evers

Lupton, A 1995 *Whitemoor Haye, Alrewas, Staffordshire. Archaeological Evaluation Report* Unpublished Tempus Reparatum Report TR31102DFA

Manby, T C 1975 Neolithic occupation sites on the Yorkshire Wolds *Yorkshire Archaeol. J.* **47**, 23-60

Manby, T C 1995 'Neolithic and Bronze Age pottery – implications' in *The excavation of seven Bronze Age barrows on the moorlands of northeast Yorkshire.* Yorkshire Archaeological Series Reports No. 1. Yorkshire Archaeological Society. Leeds

Marsden, P 1998 'The Querns' in Beamish, M 1998 A Middle Iron Age site at Wanlip, Leicestershire. *Transactions of the Leicestershire Archaeological and Historical Society* **72**, 62-63

Marvell, A G and Owen-John, H S 1997 *Leucarum: excavations at the Roman auxiliary fort at Loughor, West Glamorgan 1982-84 and 1987-88.* Britannia Monograph Series No. 12. Society for the Promotion of Roman Studies

May, J 1970 An Iron Age square enclosure at Aston-upon-Trent, Derbyshire. *Derbyshire Archaeological Journal* **90**, 10-21

May, J 1976 *Prehistoric Lincolnshire*

Meeson, R 1991 *Archaeological Evaluation, Moat Field, Hamstall Ridware, March 1991*, Staffordshire County Council. Unpublished Report.

Miket, R 1981 Pit alignments in the Milfield Basin, and the excavation of Ewart 1. *Proceedings of the Prehistoric Society* **47**, 137-46

Miles, H 1969 Excavations at Fisherwick, Staffs., 1968 - a Romano-British farmstead and a Neolithic occupation site. *Transactions of the South Staffordshire Archaeological and Historical Society* **10**, 1-22

Miller, N 1984 Intentional burning of dung as fuel: a mechanism for the incorporation of charred seeds into the archaeological record. *Journal of Ethnobiology* **4(1)**, 15-28

Moffett, L 1986 *Crops and crop processing in a Romano-British village at Tiddington: the evidence from the plant remains.* AML report, New Series 15/86

Moffett, L 1992 'Charred plants remains' in Knight, D Excavation of an Iron Age settlement at Gamston, Nottinghamshire. *Transactions Thoroton Society of Nottinghamshire* **96**, 79-83

Moffet, L 1999 'Charred plants remains' in Coates, G *Excavations at Whitemoor Haye Quarry, Alrewas, Staffordshire 1997-1998. A Post-Excavation Assessment and Updated Project Design.* Birmingham University Field Archaeology Unit Report No.495, 38-39

Moffet, L and Ciaraldi, M forthcoming 'Plants and economy at Salford Priory', in Palmer, S (ed.) Excavations at Salford Priors 1995. *Transactions of the Birmingham and Warwickshire Archaeological Society*

Morris, E L 1985 Prehistoric salt distributions: two case studies from western Britain. *Bulletin of the Board of Celtic Studies* **32**, 336-379

Morris, E L 1994 Production and distribution of pottery and salt in Iron Age Britain: a Review. *Proceedings of the Prehistoric Society* **60**, 371-393

Morris, E L 1999 'Other ceramic materials', in Hughes, E G The Excavation of an Iron Age cropmarked site at Foxcovert Farm, Aston-on-Trent 1994. *Derbyshire Archaeological Journal* **119**, 183-185

Murphy, P 1992 'Concretions and coprolites' in Crummy, P *Excavation at Culver Street, the Gilbert School and Other Sites in Colchester 1971-1985.* Colchester Archaeological Report 6. Colchester, 275-276

Nilsson, A N and Holmen, M 1995 The aquatic Adephaga (Coleoptera) of Fennoscandia and Denmark II. Dytiscidae. *Fauna Entomologica Scandinavica* **32**. Leiden and Copenhagen: Scandinavian Science Press

Oswald, F 1936-7 *Index of Figure-Types on Terra Sigillata ('Samian Ware')*, University Press of Liverpool

Oswald, A 1969 Excavations for the Avon/Severn Research Committee at Barford, Warwickshire. *Transactions of the Birmingham and Warwickshire Archaeological Society* **83**, 1-64

Palmer, R 1976 Interrupted ditched enclosures in Britain: the use of aerial photography for comparative studies. *Proceedings of the Prehistoric Society* **42**, 161-86

Palmer, R 1992 *Alrewas, Staffordshire: Aerial Photographic Assessment.* Air Photo Services.

Philips, J T 1950 'A survey of the distribution of querns of Hunsbury or allied types' in Kenyon, K Excavations at Breedon-on-the-Hill, Leicestershire 1946. *Transactions of the Leicestershire Archaeological Society* **26**, 17-82

Piggott, S 1962 *The West Kennet long barrow, excavations 1955-56*, Ministry of Works Archaeological Report **4**. HMSO, London

Pollard, J 1996 Iron Age riverside pit alignments at St Ives, Cambridgeshire. *Proceedings of the Prehistoric Society* **62**, 93-115

Pryor, F 1985 'Chapter 2: Excavations at Maxey, 1979-81. Introduction', in Pryor, F, French, C, Crowther, D, Gurney, D, Simpson, G and Taylor, M *The Fenland Project, No.1: Archaeology and Environment in the Lower Welland Valley Volume 1.* East Anglian Archaeology 27, 24-9

Pryor, F 1999 *Farmers in Prehistoric Britain.* Tempus

Reynolds, P J 1996 'Experimental domestic octagonal earthworks' in Bell, M, Fowler, P J and Hillson, S W (eds) *The Experimental Earthwork Project 1960-1992*. Council for British Archaeology Research Report 100

Rich, T C G 1991 *Crucifers of Great Britain and Ireland*. BSBI Handbook No. 6. London

Richards, C and Thomas, J 1984 'Ritual activity and structured deposition in later Neolithic Wessex' in Bradley, R and Gardiner, J (eds.) *Neolithic Studies: a Review of Some Current Research*. British Archaeological Reports, British Series 133. Oxford, 189-218

Richmond, A 1997 *Specifications for Post-Evaluative Archaeological Investigation. Whitemoor Haye, Alrewas, Staffordshire*. Doc. P/104/B

Robinson, M A 1981 'Appendix 1. The use of Ecological Groupings for Coleoptera for Comparing Sites' in Jones, M and Dimbleby, G *The Environment of Man: The Iron Age to the Anglo-Saxon Period*. British Archaeological Reports, British Series 87. Oxford

Robinson, M A 1983 'Arable/pastoral ratios from insects?' in Jones, M *Integrating the Subsistence Economy*. British Archaeological Reports, International Series 181, Oxford

Rogers, G B 1974 *Poteries Sigillées de la Gaule Centrale*, 28th supplement to *Gallia*, Paris

Samuels, J 1979 'Stone artifacts' in Smith, C A 1979a, 65-66 and 69

Schültze-Motel, J 1979 Die Anbaugeschichte des Leindotters: *Camelina sativa* (L.) Crantz.. *Archaeo-Physika* **8**, 267-281

Seager Smith, R and Davis, S M 1993 *Black Burnished Ware Type Series: The Roman Pottery from Excavations at Greyhound Yard, Dorchester, Dorset*

Shotton, F W 1973 Two Lower Palaeolithic implements from South East Staffordshire. *Transactions of the South Staffordshire Archaeological and Historical Society* **14**, 1-14

Smith, C A 1976 Second report of excavations at Fisherwick, Staffs. 1973. Ice wedge casts and a Middle Bronze Age settlement. *Transactions of the South Staffordshire Archaeological and Historical Society* **16**, 1-17

Smith, C A 1979a *Fisherwick: The Reconstruction of an Iron Age Landscape*, British Archaeological Reports, British Series 61. Oxford

Smith, C A 1979b 'Flint artifacts' in Smith, CA 1979a, 67-69

Smith, C A 1980 The historic development of the landscape in the parishes of Alrewas, Fisherwick and Whittington; a retrogressive analysis. *Transactions of the South Staffordshire Archaeological and Historical Society* **20**, 1-14

Smith, D N 1998 'An assessment of the insect remains from Whitemoor Haye, Alrewas, Staffordshire' in Coates, G *Archaeological excavations at Whitemoor Haye, Alrewas, Staffordshire; an interim report*. Birmingham University Field Archaeology Unit. Unpublished Report.

Smith, D N forthcoming *The Insect Remains from Covert Farm (DIRFT East), Crick, Northamptonshire*. Report to Birmingham University Field Archaeology Unit

Smith, I F 1968 Report on late Neolithic pits at Cam, Glos. *Transactions of the Bristol and Gloucestershire Archaeological Society* **87**, 14-28

Smith, I F 1965 *Windmill Hill and Avebury*. Clarendon Press, Oxford

Smith, W 1999 'Assessment of the charred plant remains from Whitemoor Haye, Alrewas, Staffordshire' in Coates, G 1999 *Excavations at Whitemoor Haye Quarry, Alrewas, Staffordshire 1997-1998. A Post-Excavation Assessment and Updated Project Design*. Birmingham University Field Archaeology Unit Report No.495

Stace, C 1997 *New Flora of the British Isles*, second edition. Cambridge University Press, Cambridge

Staffordshire County Council 1991 *Willowbrook Farm, Alrewas*. Unpublished Report.

Stanfield, J A and Simpson, G 1958 *Central Gaulish Potters*. Oxford University Press, London

Tempus Reparatum Archaeological and Historical Associates 1995 *Whitemoor Haye, Alrewas, Staffordshire. An Archaeological Evaluation*. Doc.TR 31102DFA. Unpublished Report.

Terrisse, J-R 1968 *Les Céramiques Sigillées Gallo-Romaines des Martres-de-Veyre (Puy-de-Dôme)*. 19th supplement to *Gallia*. Paris

Thorpe, R and Sharman, J 1994 An Iron Age and Romano-British enclosure system at Normanton le Heath, Leicestershire *Transactions of the Leicestershire Archaeological and Historical Society* **68**, 1-63

Todd, M 1991 *The Coritani*. London

Tomber, R and Dore, J 1998 *The National Roman Fabric Reference Collection. A handbook*. MOLAS Monograph 2. MOLAS/English Heritage

Tomlinson, P and Hall, A 1996 A review of the archaeological evidence for food plants from the British Isles: an example of the use of the Archaeobotanical Computer Database (ABCD). Internet Archaeology 1 (http://intarch.ac.uk/journal/issue1/tomlinson_index.html).

Trent and Peak Archaeological Trust 1985 *Fatholme, Barton-under-Needwood, Staffs*. Archive Report.

Tutin, T G, Heywood, V H *et al.* 1964-80 *Flora Europaea* **1-5**. Cambridge

Tyers, I 1988 'Environmental evidence from Southwark and Lambeth' in Hinton, P (ed) Excavations in Southwark and Lambeth 1973-76. *London and Middlesex Archaeological Society and Surrey Archaeological Society Joint Publication* **3**, 443-77

van der Veen, M 1996 'The plant macrofossil from Dragonby' in May, J *Dragonby 1: Report on excavations at an Iron Age and Romano-British settlement in north Lincolnshire* Oxbow Monograph **61**, Oxford,197-210

Vine, P M 1982 *The Neolithic and Bronze Age Cultures of the Middle and Upper Trent Basin*. British Archaeological Reports, British Series 105. Oxford

Webster, G 1975 *The Cornovii*. London

Webster, P V 1976 Severn Valley Ware: A preliminary study. *Transactions of the Bristol and Gloucestershire Archaeological Society* **94**, 18-46

Wheeler, H 1979 The excavation at Willington, Derbyshire, 1970-1972. *Derbyshire Archaeological Journal* **99**, 58-220

Whimster, R 1989 *The Emerging Past. Air Photography and the Buried Landscape*. London

Williams, P 1979 'Waterlogged wood remains', in Smith, C A 1979a, 71-77

Willis, S H 1997 'Samian: beyond dating' in Meadows, K I, Leek, C R and Heron, J (eds) *TRAC96: Proceedings of the 6th Theoretical Roman Archaeology Conference, Sheffield 1996*. Oxbow, Oxford, 38-54

Wilson, D G 1979 'Horse dung from Roman Lancaster: a botanical report' in Körber-Ghrone, U (ed) Festschrift Maria Hopf. *Archaeo-Physika* **8**, 331-350

Zohary, D and Hopf, M 1994 *Domestication of Plants in the Old World,* second edition. Claredon Press, Oxford.

Plate 1: 1995 Cropmark Photograph, (c) Crown Copyright. RCHME, produced courtesy of Royal Commission on the Historical Monuments of England.

Plate 2: General view of Areas A and T, taken from the south. (G.Coates)

Plate 3: Late Neolithic Beaker Vessel, *in situ*, in F612 (Area R). (E.Ramsey)

Plate 4: Pit Alignment, Area S, viewed eastwards. (G.Coates)

Plate 5: Pit F526, Area S, viewed from the east. (G.Bellavia)

Plate 6: Post-hole cluster from Area S, viewed from the south. (G.Coates)

Plate 7: Post-hole F537 in Area S. (E.Ramsey)

Plate 8: Area T Pit Alignment, viewed from the west. (G.Coates)

Plate 9: Area A general view, taken from the south-east. (G.Coates)

Plate 10: Area B general view, taken from the north. (G.Coates)

Plate 11: Area B, Structure 5, viewed from the east. (G.Coates)

Plate 12: Area B, Structure 6, viewed from the east. (G.Coates)

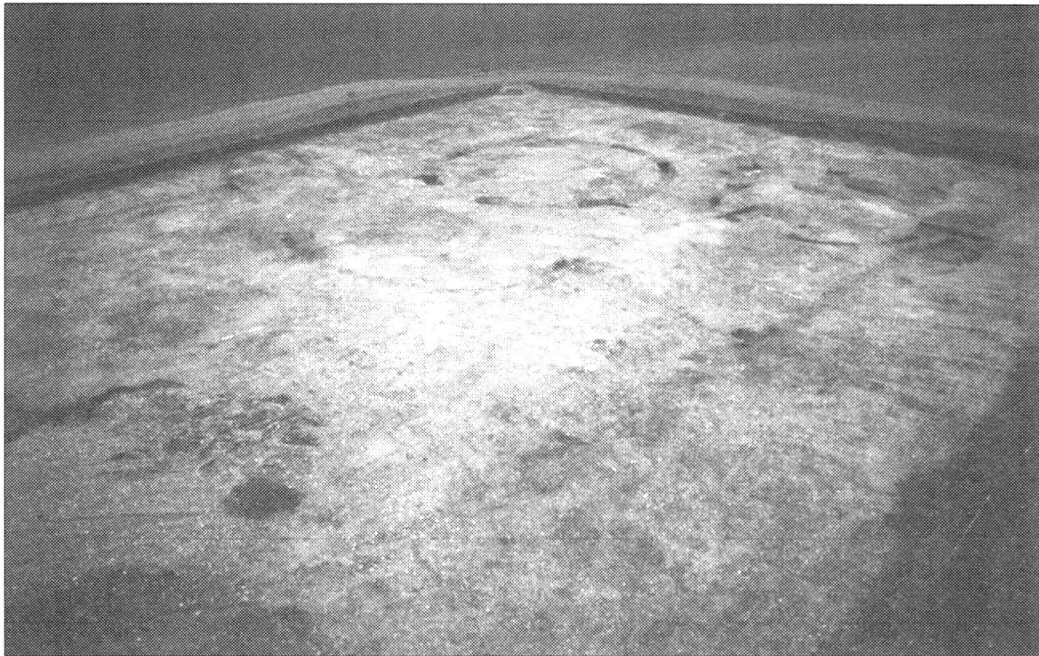

Plate 13: Area C, viewed from the north-east. (G.Coates)

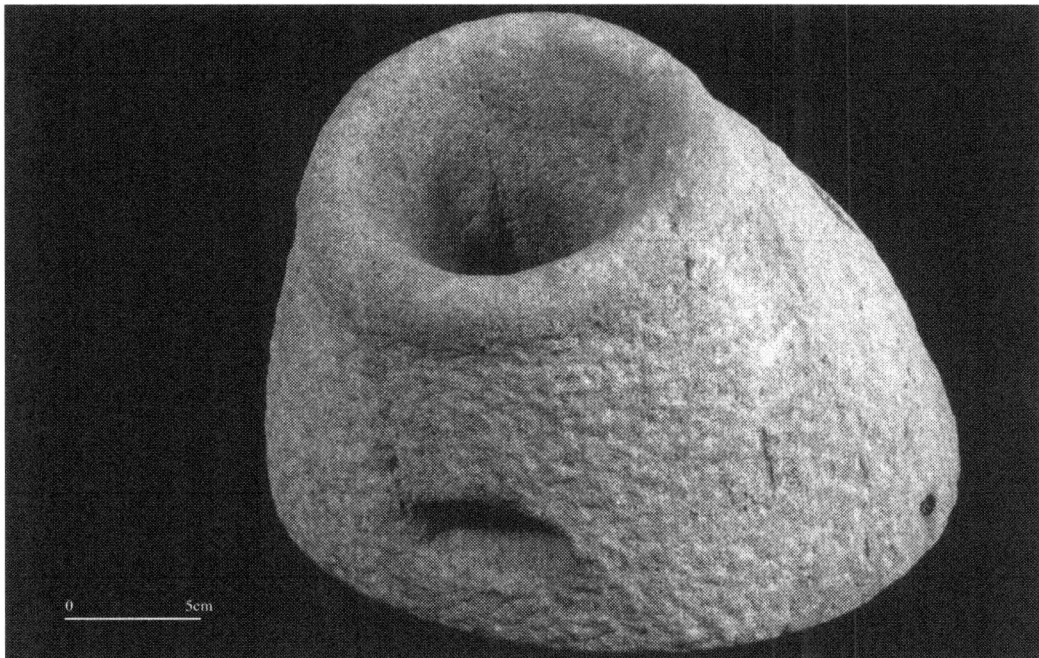

Plate 14: Beehive rotary quern from the watching brief. (G.Norrie)

www.ingramcontent.com/pod-product-compliance
Lightning Source LLC
Chambersburg PA
CBHW061002030426
42334CB00033B/3325